The Insider's Guide To
THE BEST SKIING IN
NEW ENGLAND

The Insider's Guide To THE BEST SKIING IN NEW ENGLAND

By Peter Oliver

MENASHA RIDGE PRESS

Printed in the United States of America
Published by Menasha Ridge Press
Second edition, first printing

ISBN 0-89732-154-5

Printed in Arkansas City, Kansas
by Gilliland Printing.
Designed by Lito Tejada-Flores
Cover photo: Former free-style champion
Scott Brooksbank tears up the powder at
Sunday River. Photo courtesy of Sharon
McNeill/Sunday River.

Special Thanks to all the ski areas covered
in this guidebook for permission to use
their trail maps

Special Note: Outdoor activities are
assumed risk sports. While every effort has
been made to insure the accuracy of this
book, conditions change. This guide cannot
take the place of wisdom and experience
necessary for a safe trip.

Menash Ridge Press
3169 Cahaba Heights Road
Birmingham, Alabama 35243

CONTENTS

Chapter 1
Getting to Know
New England Skiing

FOLLOW ME BACK to a day in March, many years ago. The names of people, the exact date, even the year have long since washed from my conscious recollection. What I can still dredge from memory is that the day was warm, that the place was Mad River Glen in central Vermont, that I had hooked up with three hot-skiing Mad Riverites, and that we were skiing Fall Line, a steep and serpentine quirk of a trail.

Fall Line is New England skiing at its finest and its meanest, a combination of narrow trail skiing and tree skiing through changing pitches and fall lines, over a surface mix of snow, ice, roots, and rock. It can alternately exhilarate the senses and lay to waste one's skis, body, and ego.

My skiing partners of the moment knew things I didn't: the precise location of rocks and frozen rivulets, the best lines through mogul fields, preferred traverses, and so on. As I followed in their tracks, they reinvented the trail for me. Their route selection down Fall Line was one of rhythm and relative ease. It had nothing to do with the rock-bashing, side-slipping battle against the trail's demons that would have been my own, unescorted method. For that brief moment, I had become one of the anointed—a skier blessed with the insider's edge.

Perhaps your own skiing memories include similar chance encounters on the slopes; you hooked up with someone—a local skier, most likely—who showed you how to bring out the best in a trail or mountain. If so, you are intimately aware of how insider info—knowing what those in the know know—can be a passport of sorts, an entry into a land of privilege. It's like getting a box seat for the price of general admission; it's valet parking, gratis; it is like being whisked to the best table in the house.

It's also more than knowing the right line down a trail like Fall Line, although that's a large part of it. It's knowing where to park the car, where and when to avoid lift lines, which trails have the best skiing depending on the weather and time of year, knowing where to get a decent meal without getting ripped off, and so on. It prescribes fun, but it goes beyond that. With the arriving specter of the $40 lift ticket, it promises a better return on your investment in a sport that even people in the business of skiing—people who set ticket prices—concede is getting painfully expensive. They have said so to me.

I'm into my fourth decade of New England skiing, qualifying me as a New England insider in a backwards way: I have many years of experience in doing pretty much everything wrong that can possibly be done wrong. I've dressed wrong, skied the wrong areas at the wrong time, had the wrong equipment, and so on. I'm very familiar with the misery that New England skiing can be: the cold toes and fingers, the slow stampede of holiday lift lines, snow with less edge grip than the windshield of my Honda. There have been moments when New England skiing has utterly defeated me, literally bringing me to tears.

The pay-off, though, is that I'm now a lot more savvy about doing things right. And I've come through whatever misery I've experienced with an enduring, even feisty, appreciation for all that New England skiing is. I feel my skin warm with combativeness when I hear skiers disparage New England alongside the great mountains and snows found in other parts of the world. I defy them. I know that New England skiing can, in its unique way, stand alongside skiing anywhere else in the world in quality, challenge, and natural beauty. Yes—I'm saying that New England can march in the same band as the Alps, the Rockies, and the Sierras. If you say no way, I say: Read on.

WHY NEW ENGLAND? When people think New England, they often think small-mountain skiing. Obviously the mountains of New England lack the elevation or bulk of the Rockies or the Alps. But let's compare ski areas, not just mountains. Compare ski-area vertical rises: Vermont, New Hampshire, and Maine have 14 areas with more than 2,000 feet of vertical rise, the same number (and in closer proximity to one another) as in Colorado, and six more than in Utah.

I've used 2,000 feet as a figure only to make a point; realistically, that's more mountain than most skiers want anyway. Whether in New England, Europe, or the U.S. West, skiers rarely use up more than 1,800 vertical feet in a single run. New England differs from other regions not so much in the length but in the character of its runs. Trail skiing is New England's forte, meaning that the experience of skiing New England is principally one of skiing along corridors cut from trees.

That's a far cry, to be sure, from skiing the more open terrain of the Rockies, Sierras, and Alps. I've certainly put in enough time skiing the bowls, chutes, and slopes of the big-mountain regions to know how pleasurable that experience can be. So I'm not suggesting New England trail skiing is any better than all that. But if you enjoy, as I do, the combination of physical challenge and mind game that trail skiing presents, New England is the place you should be.

"Trail skiing," of course, can mean a lot of things. It used to mean navigating your way down ultra-narrow squiggles on the mountainside. The first trails of more than 50 years ago had to be hand-cut, and producing a trail much wider than the average New England back road called for undue grunt labor.

More recently, however, New England ski areas have expanded the scope of what can be considered trail skiing. A few of the old-style squiggles still exist, but the powerful tree-slashing machinery of recent years has literally cleared the way for wider, straighter, more cruisable swaths, cut more flushly to the fall line.

To be honest, I lean toward old times: I remain a fan of the narrow, twisting oldies, even if they are hard to groom, are hard to make snow on, and are ill-suited for skiing in long, aerobic stints. It's stop-and-start skiing in which I must think my way through a run as I ski it, and I like that. But, except for a very few cases of overzealous deforestation by modern trail cutters, I'm not knocking the newer, wider cruisers—they are fun to ski and fun to ski fast, and the fact that their width makes them groomable on a daily (nightly) basis almost assures snow quality of a high order.

That leads to the most significant changes that the 80's brought to New England skiing: Snowmaking and grooming. While ski areas in other parts of the world use manufactured snow mainly to patch up high-traffic spots, New England areas now rely on it as their main skiing surface. Typically, major ski areas in New England have snowmaking on 60 percent or more of their terrain, and several claim more than 90-percent coverage. And New England snowmaking is not just a matter of quantity. What fires forth from the snow-gun artilleries at major New England resorts now is pretty fair match for the real thing. I can say that with some authority, having been deceived more than a few times in recent years into thinking I was skiing natural snow when I wasn't.

Now as a rule I prefer skiing on natural snow, and in general I feel pretty confident in distinguishing real snow from the manufactured stuff. But the weather gods in New England, as elsewhere, aren't always obliging. What the widespread capacity for making snow has enabled New England to do is guarantee quality skiing, regardless of weather, as no other region of the world can.

Making snow, however, is only half the story. The parallel advances in grooming technology have been equally revolutionary. Suffice it to say that the water content and crystal formation of manufactured snow is not the same as natural snow. Manufactured snow must be worked over and fluffed up regularly in order to produce the best possible skiing surface.

I recommend you stop some day after skiing at the snow-maintenance garages at a place like Killington, Okemo, or Sunday River. You're in for a bedazzling array of vehicular technology—fleets of grooming machines that can climb 30-degree slopes and till the snow surface to peach-fuzz smoothness with the precision of an electric razor. Most impressive is what the machines can do in restoring a good skiing surface to a slope that has iced up or been skied off. On a ski trip not long ago, I experienced excellent skiing on a cold day after a two-inch rainfall— something unimaginable a decade ago.

Every skier survey I've seen tells the same story: Long lift lines are the number-one nuisance in skiing. Ski-area operators, of course, have seen those surveys, too, and in the last decade or so have gone after Nuisance Number One with money-letting vengeance. New England areas up- graded lift systems to the point now where an area like Killington can now boast of being able to put more than 30,000 skiers an hour up the mountain. If you crunch a few numbers, you'll discover that most major New England areas have at least twice the hourly lift capacity as the average number of skiers on a busy Saturday. That might not eliminate lift lines entirely, but even at the busiest of times, the 15-minute lift line has become a rarity.

Actually, I think some New England areas have gone overboard trying to meet skiers' demands for shorter lift lines. Resorts that have made recent high-speed installations—Killington, Waterville Valley, Sunday River, for example—have been forced to over-widen trails to accommo- date the higher skier volume. And that extra volume, with traveling at varying speeds and varying states of control, can at times be nothing less than scary. I'm willing to wait a few extra minutes in line if it means preserving a bit of old-fashioned, on-slope serenity.

But I know not all skiers agree. On busy weekends at Sugarbush, for example, complaints about the long line at the slow, widely spaced Castle Rock double chair reverberate around the area. Yet the chair's low capacity effectively reduces skier traffic to a trickle on Castle Rock's marvelously intricate and narrow trail network. The integrity of that private, in-the-woods character—part of the essence of New England skiing—remains unviolated. Apparently, a lot of skiers appreciate that; if they didn't, there wouldn't be a line.

New England areas might not have matched Colorado's pace of high-speed lift installation, but I'd rate New England lift-system layouts among the most efficient in the world. With all that can be said for skiing in Europe, it has a major drawback: a lot of time can be spent on lifts that only lead to other lifts, a succession of T-bars and pomas that seem to go nowhere. There's not much of that in New England, where, despite relatively small mountains, lifts rising 2,000 vertical feet or more aren't uncommon. Of the 19 areas I have written up in this book, 15 have base-to-summit lifts. In New England, you ride lifts to ski.

You also ride lifts, in New England as anywhere, to take in the views. Youthful familiarity once made me blase about New England summit views; I figured I was just looking at a bunch of runt mountains and lots of trees. But having traveled in the Rockies, the Alps, the Sierras, and other ranges, I've come back to New England with a clearer perspective, a more discerning eye. Lift-top views in the Rockies and Alps tend to be on a vertical plane—high peaks around you, valleys below you. New England views, by comparison, tend to be more horizontal; at New England ski-area summits, you tend to be above the landscape, rather than surrounded by it, with the world rolling away below you like an ocean of forest and farmland. You might not be 10,000 feet above sea level, but on a clear day you feel as if you're standing on top of the world.

Let's turn for a moment to the matter of tradition; nowhere in America do skiing's roots run deeper than they do in New England. This is where lift-serviced skiing in the U.S. began, with the instillation of a rope tow near Woodstock, Vermont in 1934. Many of the best New England ski areas—Cannon, Mad River Glen, Stowe, Sugarloaf, and Wildcat, to name a few—are saturated in skiing tradition: famous trails, famous skiers, famous events. They readily evoke an era of lace boots, long-thongs, bear-trap bindings, and bamboo poles with 10-inch, leather-strapped baskets.

It is interesting, too, to see the ways in which history bonds with the future, how new traditions rise amidst old ones in New England. New England—Stratton to be specific—is where Jake Burton first tried out a newfangled contraption that would birth the revolution that has redefined skiing: the snowboard. Yes, snowboarding was born in time-honored, tradition-bound New England. The past percolates into the present of New England skiing in a way I find wholly satisfying.

Of course, long before skiing established its own tradition, New England could claim plenty of tradition in general. New England today nestles into the national consciousness as a metaphor bordering on cliche—a symbol of old-fashioned values and time-tested ways, of things fundamentally, traditionally, American.

Sure—a lot of New England tradition has disappeared. It has been encroached upon or smothered by change and development, or been commercially reconstituted for the sake of tourism. But you still come across many New Englanders who pride themselves mightily and genuinely in going about their business as generations have before them. Resistance to change burrowed itself long ago into New England's soul, which is probably why you can still find New England ski areas in religious defiance of change. Mad River Glen, for example, continues to run its 45-year-old single chair as its main lift.

This is not to say that New England ski areas have barred the door to modern development and amenities. Far from it at places like Killington, Stratton, and Sunday River, which evolved rapidly through the 80's as full-service resorts. But the development, by and large, hasn't spread much further than the ski-area basins. Most of those postcard New England towns—with notable exceptions like North Conway, New Hampshire—have remained largely unaffected.

In short, you can still find old-country authenticity if you want it. And if you want modern, slopeside convenience or nightlife, you can find those things, too. New England has a little bit of everything.

AVOIDING THE PITFALLS. A little bit of everything includes some negatives, but these can be avoided—at least minimized—if you prepare for them.

New England's most notorious negative is cold: New England winters might not be colder than winters in the west or Europe, but the dampness of the air at lower elevations makes them seem so. Winters don't seem to me to be getting much warmer, despite all that's said about global warming. What has changed is skiwear, which now gives New England skiers a fighting chance against the cold. I consider my most valuable gear for New England skiing to be a good, top-to-bottom long-underwear outfit, well-insulated mittens, and warm socks. I always bring several clothing layers, since layering allows me to adapt to varying temperatures, and I prize maximum insulation from minimum bulk. If I'm bulky,

I can't move, and if I can't move, I can't stay warm.

Snowmaking might have enabled New England ski areas to guarantee quality skiing, but it hasn't done away with the obvious fact that New England receives a relatively small amount of natural snow. I say "relatively" because although the annual snowfall averages of the areas covered in this book—ranging from 150 to 280 inches—might be substantial, they fall well short of the 300- to 500-inch averages reported in Utah and Colorado. You do come across powder days in New England, but variable snow conditions are obviously more the norm. Ice, powder, wind-packed crud, groomed corduroy: I've often encountered all of them in a single run. And I won't leave out roots, rocks, stumps, and other "unmarked obstacles" (as ski areas like calling them) despite the fact that many areas have invested considerable summer time and money to ridding their slopes of that stuff. New England's mountains can still be like some of the old-timers that live among them: gnarled, sinewy, and unyielding.

Now, variation of snow conditions happens to be something I like about New England, although I know that many skiers don't share my sentiments. It demands good balance and good turning fundamentals; skiing variable snow well means skiing at your technical best. Whether you like that sort of skiing or you don't, however, you're in for hard times without a well-tuned pair of skis. Skiers in the West have told me they've gone a whole season without tuning their skis. Eastern skiing won't let you get away with that. So keep your edges in shape—even if it's just a two-minute matter of a nightly emery-cloth rub-down to remove burrs.

One final negative—not unique to New England, of course—is price. Grooming, snowmaking, and better lifts may have done wonders to improve the skiing, but along with inflation, insurance, general development, etc. they've wreaked havoc on lift-ticket prices. $40 daily lift tickets are a reality.

Full daily ticket prices, however, are somewhat like full-coach airline fares: If you plan ahead, you can find substantial discounts. Bargains and packages abound, especially in January, when business tends to be slow. I can't tell you which deals are best, since packages and discounts are constantly being restructured. All I can recommend is that you call for package information from ski areas before booking your vacation. Savings can be substantial. Ski-club membership or discount ski cards are other avenues to explore to keep this painfully expensive sport from bursting your budget.

USING THIS BOOK. Saving you money is only part of what this book is all about. I haven't filled pages with tear-out discount coupons, as one enterprising skier whom I met in my travels suggested I do. The purpose of this book is to help you get the most from your New England skiing regardless of what you pay. If you insist on a quantitative pay-off, I'm willing to bet that the information in this book will bring you at least an extra run or two a day and will reduce to near zero the number of runs capable of producing quit-the-sport distress.

First, I've divided chapters by region. One of the great things about New England skiing is the proximity of ski areas to one another, and with a minimal amount of driving, it's easy to take in more than one area on a multi-day trip. So I've grouped in each chapter ski areas that can most easily be skied in combination.

Geography, of course, doesn't always compartmentalize itself neatly. If you're interested in skiing a certain region of New England, look through the chapters before and after the chapter on your target region. The ski areas of northern and central Vermont, for example, aren't far from one another; Sugarbush, Bolton Valley, and Stowe combine well in a multi-day itinerary. Similarly, the ski areas of western New Hampshire and southern Maine are close enough to be included in the same ski trip—Sunday River is within an hour's drive of North Conway.

Each ski area description begins with a character study, a summary of the area's assets and shortcomings. Fast-paced or low-key? Old-fashioned or modern? Gentle cruising or precipitous steeps? Over-crowded on holidays or undercrowded on weekdays? Best for early-season, mid-winter, or spring skiing? These descriptions should provide a basis for choosing areas that best match your abilities and interests.

The bulk of the inside stuff follows—essentially a dress rehearsal, in words, for your ski day at a given area. I have begun with a "starter's kit" to get you oriented, ticketed, geared up, and out on the slopes with minimum of hassles. After that, the information about the skiing itself is based not only on my own experiences and impressions but also on those of ski patrollers, instructors, ski-shop employees, and other local habitues. If what I've given you here isn't enough, I encourage you to seek out the guidance of these same people. Any ski area can ski differently from day to day, storm to storm, month to month, season to season. That variability—that unpredictability—is, after all, one of the reasons this sport enchants us and hooks us.

I've also included a brief section on snowboaring within each ski area description. In most cases, snowboarders should be able to use the terrain descriptions in this book just as readily as skiers in finding the best trails with the best snow. However—although I'm not a snowboarder myself—I've spent enough time skiing with snowboarders to appreciate that certain terrain and snow conditions that are problematic for skiers can be nirvana for snowboarders.

Finally, I've included bits and pieces about where to eat and where to stay, singling out places that are exemplary for no other reason than the fact that they suit my own tastes. I've also included mention of known "locals" spots, where the most current insider info can fly fast and furious after the day's skiing. In the main, however, this is principally a book about skiing, rather than dining and lodging. If you want detailed descriptions of where to stay and eat in New England, there is no shortage of other guide books on the subject.

AND A FINAL WORD. I first skied New England in the winter of 1963, so New England skiing and I have grown up and changed together. New England skiing is a long plank on my bridge from youth to adulthood; it is something close to my heart. This book is an expression of that closeness, and it isn't without bias: I'm fond of old-fashioned New England skiing in the way that I look back fondly on youth. That's one of the reasons I have enlisted the help and opinions of other New England insiders—to entwine my own opinions with those of others, giving you a well-rounded perspective of the nuance, complexity, and allure of New England skiing. To enable you to ski New England at its best— that's what this book is all about. Because at its best, New England skiing can be as good as it gets.

Inside Story
Getting Started: Sorting Out Snow Reports

It's Tuesday, and you're psyched for a weekend ski trip. You want to go where there's good snow, but the snowless landscape outside your window doesn't reveal much about the conditions a few hundred miles away in ski country. So you scrounge around for the newspaper, flip to the ski report, and come across lines like this:

SITZMARK VALLEY—pp, lsgr, frgr, 12-60 base, 34 trails, 3 lifts, sm, 35 km x-c.

Such cat-scratch might as well be navigational coordinates for interstellar travel for all the help it renders the average skier. So let me suggest a few tricks for deciphering New England ski reports.
A little background first: Today's reporting is actually an improvement over yesteryear's methodology. It used to be ski areas gave you a subjective rating of conditions, ranging from poor to excellent. Great idea—except that it didn't take ski-area operators long to realize that, no matter how truly terrible the skiing was, reporting "poor" conditions was dumb marketing. Pretty soon, no one was reporting anything much worse than good-to-excellent skiing. So the subjective ratings were scrapped, leading to the current, "objective," ski reports.
Here's how I go about interpreting what I read in the paper:
I start by trying to get a sense of the natural snowpack—first, because I like skiing natural snow; second, because the weather conditions that make for natural snowfall also tend to be good for snowmaking. So I check the conditions at areas I know have minimal snowmaking. Best for this is Vermont's Mad River Glen, with almost no snowmaking at all. Mad River's reported base tells me a lot about the natural snowpack at other areas in the region.
In New Hampshire, I check the base at Cannon Mountain for the same reason (although Cannon's snowmaking capacity exceeds Mad River's). And in Maine I look up the number of trails open at Saddleback. If Saddleback reports more than 30 open trails, I know there is enough natural snow to open its non-snowmaking trails. Mad River, Cannon, Saddleback—those are my natural-snow yardsticks.

Next, I look at the low figure in an area's reported snow depths. An area's high base figure is generally meaningless, often representing the snow depth on the one or two trails absolutely blasted with man-made snow. Any time the low figure is under 20 inches, I know bare spots are likely, especially on steeper trails.

The open-trail statistics in the reports are pretty worthless, and many ski-area operators say so. When I diplomatically suggested to one ski-area executive that trail-counting was inexact, he responded with surprising candor. "It's not just an inexact science," he said, "it's downright dishonest." That's because a "trail" can be anything from a 100-yard cat track to a 3-mile top-to-bottom cruisers. Open acreage or trail mileage would be much more helpful.

I do check on the number of open lifts if I know an area's total lift count. When Sugarloaf, for example, reports at least 10 lifts operating, and I know that that's from a total of 13 lifts, I know most of the mountain's best terrain is open. But without being familiar with an area's lift layout, this can mislead, too. Sugarloaf's lift count is inflated by a couple of lifts used for little more than village access. Just because Sugarloaf reports 6 (of 13) lifts operating, that doesn't necessarily mean half the mountain is skiable.

As for the snow-surface reports, I'm leery of anything other than new (for new snow), p (for powder), and pp (for packed powder). Frgr stands for frozen granular, a ski-talk euphemism for ice. Lgr is loose granular, which might be corn in the spring, but loose granular in my experience usually ends up being more like frozen granular, and we all know what that is. Loose granular that's skiable is usually reported as packed powder or, in the case of corn, spring conditions.

Finally, I check the reports of several areas in the same region for abberations. If snow depths or reported surfaces differ significantly between two areas within a few miles of one another, I get very suspicious. My rule: Measure the skiing according to the area reporting the worst conditions.

Maine (800-533-9595) and New Hampshire (800-258-3608) have toll-free ski-report numbers; in Vermont, the ski-report number is 802-229-0531. Remember, though, these are services geared to promote skiing. Ski areas have snow-report numbers, too—generally of a promotional nature as well. I figure my phone energy and money is better spent calling a ski shop (or other business) in the region, where I can usually get a first-hand, skier's assessment from the shop manager or salesperson.

PART I
VERMONT SKIING

Chapter 2
Southern Vermont

SOUTHERN VERMONT, along with southern Vermont skiing, is schizo-phrenic in regard to time, leaping toward the future while keeping its feet cemented in the past. Southern Vermont can be as old-New-England as northern New England gets, its history of human settlement reaching well back before the Revolutionary era. Yet it has seen the future, and the future is tourism, which is slowly reworking the regional landscape and way of life.

Nowhere is this time schizophrenia more apparent than in Manchester, which is not one but—count 'em—three towns in one. First is Manches-ter Village, which, thanks to strict zoning and preservation-minded locals, is so meticulously maintained in its centuries-old state that you'd think it was make-believe. Then there is Manchester Center, which jumped on the tourism bandwagon in the 80's when factory-outlet commerce started popping up all over town. Manchester Depot followed suit, though, its development was slowed to some degree by a backlash of local sentiment against the boutiquing of Manchester Center.

Southern-Vermont skiing has similarly reached its tentacles into both the future and the past. Bromley, more than a half-century old, remains almost as it has been for 25 years. Its steadfast core of loyalists seem to like it that way. But Stratton across the valley has developed rapidly in the last decade in the textbook way of a modern ski resort. Resort village, slopeside lodging, golf course for summer visitors, and a high-speed gondola with a very futuristic name, Starship XII: Stratton has cut bait with the past and cast its line toward the future. It has even been swept up in the most nouveau trend in America skiing—Japanese owner-ship. A few years ago, Stratton became the first New England ski area to be bought by a Japanese company.

What does it all add up to? First of all, the reality of tourism as southern Vermont's economic future is unambiguous. As August St. John, a Manchester resident, suggested to me a couple of years ago in an interview for a magazine article: "This is a new Vermont. Don't expect to see farmers coming to town with manure on their legs. Vermont is now big tourism business."

Don't think for a second, though, that all that tourism is turning southern Vermont into a Green Mountain Disney World. Visitors come to southern Vermont for its natural beauty and old-World spirit, and even the most aggressive developers don't want to blow that off. In one of those wonderful ironies, tourism money is helping to sustain the past even as it erases it. It has instilled new vigor in old inns like the 1811 House in Manchester Village and the White House in Wilmington. It has led to the renovation of the Equinox, the grand sprawl of a hotel in Manchester Village.

Yes, patches of southern-Vermont farmland have succumbed to second-home development. But southern Vermont is still a pretty place of rolling hills and the occasional big mountain, a place of old homes and winding roads, a place where a skiing tradition more than a half-century old is still in evidence. There is no real wilderness left here—for any sense of wilderness you need to head for the far north—but southern Vermont isn't exactly a pristine paradise paved over. It is, simply, a well-settled countryside, with some pockets of settlement dating back three years, others dating back 300 years or more.

And what of the skiing itself? You can find a smattering of spine-chilling runs, but in general, this is cruise country. Mt. Snow might be the ultimate ego-boosting mountain, and Stratton, though generally steeper, isn't far behind. (Stratton used to have tougher skiing, but recent widening and grooming have softened it somewhat.) Okemo, along with Sunday River in Maine, virtually redefined in the 80's the concept of Eastern cruising, made possible by the most advanced snowmaking and grooming technology in the world.

One appeal of Southern Vermont for skiers and other visitors is obvious: It's close to civilization. The big cities of the northeastern seaboard are all within four hours' driving time. That means the weekend and holiday crush can be considerable, although Mt. Snow and Stratton have beefed up their lift capacities to meet the demand. Mt. Snow and Stratton can combine to put close to 50,000 skiers an hour up the mountain, exceeding the combined lift capacity of the six northern Vermont ski areas—Bolton Valley, Jay Peak, Mad River Glen, Smugglers Notch, Stowe, and Sugarbush—that I've covered in this book.

The result on busy weekends is more skiers actually skiing—a situation that I often find uncomfortable even if the lift lines aren't especially long. But if that gets to you, you can always head for Manchester, where Ralph Lauren and Anne Klein are on sale for a song.

MT. SNOW

Based on memories of about 20 years ago, I had the impression of Mt. Snow as basically a soft-skiing place catering to a weekend get-a-date crowd—sort of Eastern skiing's version of Gidget Goes Hawaii. I figured that the place probably hadn't changed much, except maybe that the Gidget-era fashions had been replaced by something more Madonna-ish.

Then Rick Kahl, Editor of *Skiing*, got my ear. He insisted that Mt. Snow was a terrific area. I said, "Rick, I'm sure you're right." Seeing as he's the guy who pays me to ski the world's great mountains in order write about them for his magazine, Rick *always* gets to be right. Privately, though, I was doubtful.

When I returned a couple of years ago after a long hiatus, one thing was obvious: Mt. Snow wasn't what it had been before. Or, more accurately, Mt. Snow skiers weren't what they'd been before. The Gidget gang now had company; a family-oriented bunch had diluted the singles' scene. Get-a-date was just as likely to be get-a-diaper-or-day-care.

Sure, the singles crowd can still, literally, party the daylights out of the apres-ski hour at Cuzzins in the base lodge. Sure, the weekend party scene in the area can still scale the heights of deacadence. But that has still left room for families to establish a comfortable foothold, and Mt. Snow has done an effective and imaginative job of making kids' and teens' programs work.

So while I discovered that the clientele had a new look, I also discovered that, in an important way, the ski area looked very much the same. Mt. Snow was still tapping into its original concept: It was still a moderately priced, weekend get-away spot aimed largely at people in the New York metropolitan area. And Rick *was* right in that respect—Mt. Snow does a great job in making the concept work.

What attracts families and singles now, at least as far as the skiing goes, is just what attracted the dating-gamers a couple of decades ago: lots of ego-boosting skiing. The skiing is as I remembered: skewed to the soft side. Wide, moderate-pitched trails stretch down the front of the mountain like a profusion of white dreadlocks. There isn't a lot of variation among them—Mt. Snow is, by and large, a pretty uncomplicated ski area. But variety isn't the point. Mt. Snow is made for showing off, whether it be junior-high classmates trying to outdo one another or potential lovebirds trying to wow one another with their grace and dexterity.

Mt. Snow does have some challenging terrain tucked out of sight on its North Face. But if I want challenge, there are other places I would seek out before Mt. Snow. Mt. Snow is a place to come to in order to restore confidence: 70 of 84 trails are rated novice or intermediate.

Also attractive is Mt. Snow's accessibility. It's just 28 miles off I-91 in southernmost Vermont, meaning that weekenders from Providence, Hartford, Springfield, Boston, and New York (almost) can hit the road after work on Friday and be at Mt. Snow at a reasonable hour for dinner. And when the weekenders show up, Mt. Snow is ready for them: Its 18 lifts, half of them quads and triples, can get more than 25,000 skiers an hour up the mountain. And that doesn't include the six lifts at neighboring Haystack, which can be skied on a Mt. Snow lift tickets. Such an abundance of uphill transport goes a long way to reducing lift lines, but it also puts a lot of skiers on the mountain, many of them skiing at the ego-boosting speed the trail layout permits.

Just getting a good weekend crowd, though, hasn't been enough to satisfy the Mt. Snow people. So they have concocted a variety of mid-week "theme" packages—things like Teddy Bear Ski Weeks for kids and Romancing the Snow weeks definitely not for kids. The packages generally give you a wide variety of lodging options to choose from, which points up one last attractive element to Mt. Snow—lots of places to stay. You like slopeside condos? Mt. Snow's got slopeside condos. You prefer a modest and moderately priced hotel or motel nearby? Mt. Snow's got that, too. This being long-settled southern Vermont, there are plenty of New England inns, plain to fancy, in the area.

A MT. SNOW STARTER KIT. For a few reasons, I'd recommend that you start your ski day early at Mt. Snow. One is that you *can* start early; Mt. Snow is one of two Vermont areas (Killington being the other) that opens some of its lifts at 8 A.M. If you're someone who appreciates privacy in your skiing, the time to find it at Mt. Snow is before 9 A.M., when the groomed snow is still groomed.

In addition, most of Mt. Snow's skiing is eastern-facing. Trails on the front of the mountain are exposed to the morning sun. More sun, better snow, fewer people—do you need any more reasons to get to the mountain early?

You have two base-area choices: the main base and the Carinthia base. The main base has been spiffed up considerably since the Gidget era, and it's got more of just about everything than the Carinthia base: more dining options, more space to eat, more services (e.g., tickets, ski school, parking-lot shuttle buses), more parking. On weekdays, it's pretty much the place to go, since Carinthia is largely shut down except for weekends and holidays.

On weekends, though, head for Carinthia. It's smaller size makes it more manageable, less crowded, and gives you a headstart on skiing a side of the mountain that usually takes the main-base skiers a while to reach. This is an against-the-flow philosophy: As the main-base skiers begin working their way toward Carinthia, you can be working your way toward the main base, getting there as the morning rush-hour lift lines begin to shorten. And if you really want to get away from the weekend crowds, head for Haystack.

MT. SNOW FOR NOVICES. Mt. Snow might have the best selection of novice terrain of any ski area in Vermont. It's got a terrific teaching arena in near the base area completely out of the flow of other skier traffic and serviced by—count 'em—three lifts ranging from 500 to 2,100 feet. As you master the shorty (the Mixing Bowl double), you graduate up in length, still staying pretty much out of the main skier flow. A separate base lodge here—the Sundance lodge—pretty much devoted to novice skiers and kids (though, like Carinthia, only open on weekends and holidays). This was the way learning to ski was meant to happen: starting easy, progressing gradually through longer, more challenging terrain, not intimidated by better skiers.

It doesn't end there. Once you've mastered the Sundance teaching arena, you can move over toward the Carinthia area, where longer, though not much steeper, terrain awaits. The Fairway double chair also services almost exclusively novice and lower-intermediate skiing, so that the only time better skiers ride it is for transportation back to the main mountain. And once you've mastered Fairway, take a ride to the Carinthia summit and try either *Long John* or *Deer Run*, two easy meanders through the woods.

Actually, you can ski either Long John or Deer Run from the summit, but if you're still working up your skiing confidence, I'd recommend against it. There are a lot more skiers and a lot more trail intersections that make the summit confusing. Making a wrong turn onto something you don't want to be on is easy. So if you're looking for something more challenging, I'd suggest working your way all the way over to the other side of the mountain—the best way is to take the *Switchback* traverse that leads from the top of the Fairway double—to *Snowdance.* Yes, it's a blue-rated run and a bit steeper, but it's so wide that you can easily traverse out of trouble.

MT. SNOW FOR CRUISERS. "Mt. Snow for cruisers" is essentially a redundancy. Mt. Snow is a cruising mountain by definition. Ego-boosting, too—there's even a trail called *Ego Alley.* Almost every trail on the front side is within view of a lift, so if showing off is part of your gestalt, Mt. Snow is *really* your kind of place.

As I've said, Mt. Snow was one of the first ski areas in the East to begin cutting its trails extra wide, to the point now where some of its trails are divided by lines of trees no more than one row deep. Little woodsy, narrow-trail skiing here.

The archetypical Mt. Snow trail is *Exhibition*, the lift line beneath the Yankee Clipper Quad. It's a top-to-bottom, wide-open blast straight down the moderately pitched fall line. Just ride your skis through big, giant-slalom turns. It's got a couple of rolls to it that kids seem to avail themselves of for those tips-up kind of jumps that only kids seem to make. It's fun but popular—a highway full of skiers on a weekend day.

To me, a more interesting cruise combination is *Upper Canyon* or *Upper Choke* to *Snowdance.* Both of the "Uppers" are narrow by Mt. Snow standards and much less skied than Exhibition. If there has been a wind, you can sometimes find fresh snow blown in on them. Snowdance, by comparison, is anything but narrow—it's one of the widest trails on the mountain made interesting by lots of rolls and hummocks, both natural and artificially created. It also seems to get a little less skier traffic, partly because it's a little bit out of the main trail system.

If you're looking for fresh bits of snow (groomed or powder), Mt. Snow can be a fun place for poking around. Between the Standard and Yankee Clipper lift is an entwine trail system that skis more like a series of snow chambers separated by tree islands. The trail names are *Ledge*, *Lodge*, *Choke*, and *Standard*, and it's hard telling which one you're on, but if you do enough poking, there's a good chance you find yourself in one small chamber that's hardly been skied. The other side—that is, the

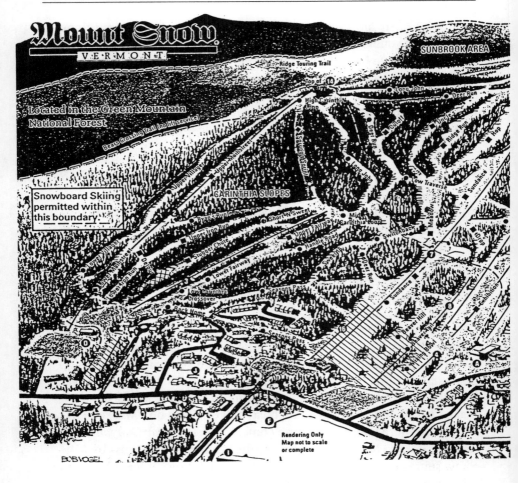

side to the left of the Yankee clipper quad as you disembark—is strictly open cruising. If Exhibition or Ego Alley is well occupied, swing over through *South Bowl* to *Sundance*. It's a trail combination that isn't quite as flush to the fall line as are Exhibition and Ego Alley, but they're so wide that you've got a pretty good shot of finding good snow near the edges.

For my money and time, the Sunbrook area, on Mt. Snow's southwestern flank, produces some of the best cruising on the mountain. The runs are short and skewed toward the easy side—in fact, one of the hardest things about Sunbrook is poling across the flats from the main summit to the Sunbrook summit. What I like about Sunbrook—in addition to the

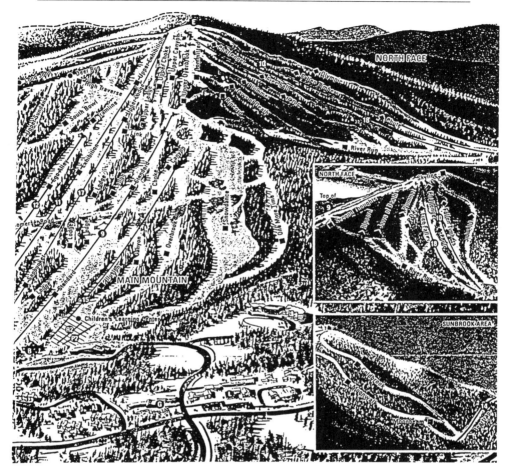

Mount Snow, a reduced view of the trail map

fact that it soaks up the afternoon sun—is that that terrain, in less than
1,000 vertical feet, features more variation than you'll find on the front
side of the mountain. Trails like Little Dipper and Thanks, Walt wind
their way to the bottom in a succession of undulations, narrow at times
and wide-open at others. because a relatively small percentage of Mt.
Snow skiers find their way over here, a sense of calm that's hard to find
on the front side pervades Sunbrook. If you want to get away from the
crowds, Sunbrook is your best chance short of going to Haystack.

Speaking of crowds, one of the keys to enjoying the front side of Mt.
Snow is good lift-line management. You basically have two summit lift
choices—the Yankee Clipper Quad and the Summit Triple. Even if the

Quad line is more than twice the line at the triple, get in it. Simple math: the lift carries 3,000 skiers per hour compared with the 1,800 by the triple. And once a la quad, you're just eight minutes from the top, compared with 14 minutes on the triple. If *both* lines are monstrously long, the Sundance triple gives you almost as much vertical footage and invariably has a shorter line. And if that strategy fails, you can get some pretty good skiing off the Standard or Ego Alley doubles, where lines rarely get very long. My preference would be Standard, since it puts you onto trails more out of the mainstream of skier traffic.

HALFTIME. Mt. Snow's lodges might come up short in ambience—none has much of a view, for example—but there are plenty of them, with four operating on weekends. What's more, the main base lodge alone has four separate food outlets.

On a busy weekend, the place to go, for decent food and elbow room, is the Carinthia base, which serves basic burger fare. If you happen to be at the main base, the "scramble" system at the cafeteria, with food stations rather than a single, long line, seems to do what it was designed to do—get people in and out relatively quickly. For a little privacy, clunk your way up a couple of flights of stairs, where you'll find additional seating. If you aren't into food scrambling, Cuzzins Deli serves pretty good sandwiches, and there's a sun deck right out front for consuming them.

The lodge at the summit serves basic cafeteria food in a dim dining area—not much to recommend, except that lunching here saves a trip down to the bottom and back up if you've committed yourself to skiing the North Face trails for the day. If the lift lines aren't long, it certainly is worth having lunch at the base instead—the eight-minute quad-chair ride makes the top-to-bottom-to-top round trip pretty quick.

MT. SNOW FOR ADVANCED SKIERS. The North Face. That's pretty much it, folks, except for a few short, steep pitches here and there. The North Face offers experts good skiing, but it is limited. The vertical rise is barely 1,000 feet—a little short for my tastes. Also for my tastes, the ski area makes too much snow on the North Face. Why not leave one of the three more-or-less parallel steepies—*Ripcord, Jaws of Death, Plummet*—as a natural-snow trail? This is, after all, a northern-facing slope, where natural snow can stay fresher longer. Whatever, manufactured snow is the predominant surface here, and it can get slick.

A large dosage of comedy pervades the North Face, due to the fact that it tends to attract skiers (young skiers in particular) who are not nearly the masters of this terrain that they imagine themselves to be. I understand what inflates their assessment of their own abilities: With confidence soaring after cruising the front, they come to the North Face certain that they can ski anything. Free Fall. . . Jaws of Death. . . no problem!

Without question, Comedy Central is *Free Fall*, which runs under the Challenger lift. Lift lines have a way of attracting show-offs, and typically imagined ability far exceeds reality. So Comedy Central—that is, Free Fall—is typically strewn with skiers in various states of dishevelment and disarray. That makes for a good show when you're riding the lift, but it also makes for lousy skiing—too many skiers and terribly formed moguls. That's why I prefer neighboring Plummet, which has a nice variation in its pitch and fall line before funneling into a bottleneck near the bottom.

Another good trail that is virtually unskied is *P.D.F.*, which branches to the right off of Free Fall. Part of the reason for its relative anonymity is the obscurity of its entry. If you aren't hugging the right of Free Fall and if you aren't on the lookout about a third of the way down, chances are good you'll miss the trail opening, as many people do. If you do find it, you'll be rewarded with skiing devoid of the hard moguls and crowds on Free Fall.

One more under-skied gem is *Challenger*, largely because its entry, too, can be tough to spot—a little slip between the two North Face lifts. Hard-to-find and narrow—maybe those are the reasons Challenger sees relatively few skiers. Narrow, a little windy, generally with fresh snow, with few moguls—maybe those are the reasons Challenger is attractive to me. It does however, dump you in the end onto the last steep mogul face of Free Fall, although I've found that if you work your way across the trail and take the trail fork branching away right of the lift, you're apt to find softer snow.

Fallen Timbers is another neat trail, partly because as you begin to ski it, the exposure offers a terrific view to the northwest and Somerset Reservoir. In most places, the trail is wide enough so that part of the trail can be groomed, part can be allowed to turn to moguls. Groomed or bumps? On Fallen Timbers, you can have a little of both, making it perhaps the best trail to start out on when you venture over to this side of the mountain.

SNOWBOARDING. *Un Blanco Gulch* is billed by Mt. Snow as a

snowboard park "loaded with spines, wedges, a competition-size half-pipe, and other tricky terrain for you jibmeisters!" Snowboard parks are a growing trend at ski resorts these days, and most, including Un Blanco Gulch, remain works in progress. Typically, they require a lot of maintenance, a poorly maintained half-pipe isn't much more than a glorified snow ditch in my book. That said, Mt. Snow probably does a better job than most of keeping its snowboard park in good shape, in large part to keep trick-happy riders from wreaking havoc on a mountain full of knolls and hummocks to tempt jibmeisters with a zest for big air.

For wide-open cruising and occasional air time, Snowdance is hard to beat; it's a little flat, but several whalebacks add a touch of undular interest. For a steeper cruise, check out Fallen Timbers or Olympic on the North Face side. As for the front side, you can bomb around with ego-gratifying ease just as skiers do, but just keep in mind that if you do take advantage of those knolls and hummocks to put air under your board, just keep in mind that Mt. Snow is often a crowded mountain, and that going for big air is often asking for big trouble.

THE POST-GAME SHOW. Cuzzins at the base calls itself a deli—and it is a deli during lunch—but come the apres-ski hour, the singles gang fills the place to overflowing on weekends. They're there to jump-start a weekend party scene that wil later move on somewhere else—perhaps the nearby Snow Barn—and churn on late into the night.

If you're not necessarily eager to tap into the dedicated party scene, there are more than 50 restaurants in the Mt. Snow and Wilmington area, making it something of a pig-out paradise. The one place that's earned the lion's share of the acclaim is the Hermitage, an inn that doubles as a cross-country touring center. The Hermitage wine cellar is of big-city-restaurant caliber, and where else can you find an inn that raises it's own game birds?

Don't expect to score much insider ski information at the Hermitage, though. The place is a little too tony, and perhaps a touch touristy, for that. You're more likely to find a local crowd at Deacon's Den—one, because it's close to the mountain; two, because it serves decent pizzas at a fair price; and three, because there's live music on weekends. But Deacon's and the Hermitage are just bookends of the dining scene; there are many good choices in between.

One reason for all the choices is that the Wilmington area does a fair tourist business throughout the year (there is little local industry here but tourism). One of the big summer/fall attractions is antiquing. So if you don't care to ski, there are several trash-to-treasures stores in the area. I'm not guaranteeing it, but since the summer antiquing is usually brisker, merchants are more likely to surrender a bargain or two in winter.

Places to stay? The White House in Wilmington is a wonderful, though pricey, spot if you're a country-inn type. If you've got kids, and you hate driving in the morning, stay at the Snow Lake Lodge a half mile from the mountain. The rooms are barracks basic, but the place has things like video games, a good-sized pool, and large-screen TV, etc. to keep kids—who stay free mid-week—occupied.

MT. SNOW DATA
Pluses and Minuses:
Pluses: Lots of cruising, high lift capacity, relative proximity to major cities, variety of lodging and dining. Minuses: Shortage of expert terrain, weekend crowds.
Key Phone Numbers:
Ski Area Information: 802-464-3333
Lodging Information: 800-245-7669
Snow Phone: 802-464-2151
Location: **9 miles north of Wilmington on Route 100. Mailing address: 429 Mountain Rd., Mount Snow, VT 05356.**
Mountain Statistics:
Vertical drop: 1,700 feet
Summit elevation: 3,600 feet
Base elevation: 1,900 feet
Number of trails: 127 (including neighboring Haystack)
Lifts: 2 quad chairs, 9 triples, 10 doubles, 3 surface lifts
Average annual snowfall: 155 inches
Snowmaking coverage: 82% (490 acres)

OKEMO

Okemo is one of the real business success stories in recent New England skiing history. Here was an area that, until the 80's, was "run pretty much as an old men's club," as one local put it to me. In other words, not much was going on here to interest anyone other than Ludlow-ites and a handful of loyalists.

Then Tim and Diane Mueller, who had earned their resort-building credentials in the Caribbean, bought the place in 1982. New lifts were installed (eight in eight years), along with one of the best snowmaking/grooming operations in the East. (Only Killington makes snow on more acreage than does Okemo.) New base facilities and ski-in/ski-out homes went in. Okemo might not have been classically a "skiers'" mountain— that is, one with a good variety of challenge for skiers of every ability— but a trail network was conceived to make the most of what was there. In other words, Okemo was transformed from old men's club into the prototypical weekend cruisers' destination.

Maybe it was the Vail-like clock tower—a true, destination-resort embellishment—that sealed the deal. Whatever, the transformation worked. The Muellers had followed a formula evoking the spirit of the movie, *Field of Dreams*: Build a ski area with guaranteed good snow on terrain that can be enjoyed by the majority of skiers, provide good on-mountain accommodations, and the skiers will come. And keep coming and coming. Okemo can now draw more than 6,000 skiers on its busiest weekend days.

One other attractive part of the Okemo formula was not the Muellers' doing, and that's the town of Ludlow, less than a mile away. Granted, Ludlow isn't the most scenic New England town in a postcard, Main-Street-and-church-steeple way. The underbelly of a down-on-its-luck mill town still shows through the recent tourism sheen that the ski area's success has brought to the place. But the immediate juxtaposition of old town and spiffy new resort is unique in New England skiing, other ski areas generally being several miles from the nearest settlement. I find that refreshing: If the modern-resort polish begins wearing thin, you can head downtown for a dose of true-Vermont piquancy. And it works the other way, too.

To be honest, Okemo's skiing doesn't enthrall me, but that's strictly a matter of personal taste. It's got two shortcomings: one is a shortage of true expert terrain, the other is a shortage of good, long runs. Most of the ski area's black-diamond (as in expert) trails are generously rated so; with all the grooming that Okemo does, almost the entire mountain is negotiable by a confident intermediate. And although the ski area lists a vertical rise of 2,150 feet, the configuration of lifts and trails is such that the longest runs really don't cover much more than 1,600 vertical feet.

Again, those misgivings reflect my own tastes, which obviously aren't shared by the majority of skiers, and the Muellers have a keen ear to the call of the skiing public. Lots of cruising, lots of good snow: Skiers want it and Okemo delivers. The Muellers also have a keen ear to special skier needs; hence the success, for example, of women's weeks at Okemo, along with other specially focused programs.

AN OKEMO STARTERS' KIT. Okemo sets up much better for overnighters at the many on-mountain condos than it does for day skiers. True ski-in/ski-out accommodations are a hard find at New England areas, but Okemo has plenty of them. Probably the best of the lot, at least in terms of skiing access, are the Kettle Brook Condos halfway up the South Ridge slope. A quick ski down from here to the base area, and you're off.

Day-skier parking lots are situated a little inconveniently—across a small road and slightly downhill from the village base. The best thing to do is to pull up to the welcome center, drop people and gear off, and then park the car.

Okemo has one significant drawback: The need for pretty much all skiers (a few slopeside guests being the exceptions) to start the day by riding the South Ridge chairs. The parallel quads service only novice terrain, and are really just access lifts to get to the lifts from which most of the real skiing is to be had.

Not surprisingly, this can result in lift-line back-ups during the morning (around 10:00 A.M.) rush on busy days, when you might have more than 5,000 skiers funneling up the mountain. It used to be worse—one of the South Ridge quads used to be a double. All I can say is, on a busy weekend, Okemo is an area where it really can pay off to start your day early. Here's what I'd do: be on the lift before 9:00 A.M., ski halfway down the South Ridge slope to the Sugar House restaurant for coffee and light breakfast, then head off for one of the upper mountain lifts.

OKEMO FOR NOVICES. Okemo has lots of good lower-intermediate terrain, but its true novice terrain is limited. The South Ridge slopes (prosaically titled *Lift Line* and *Open Slope*), which constitute the main teaching arena, would normally rank high on my novice-skiing list. They are wide, wide open, unusually long for novice trails, and, except for a bit of a roll toward the bottom of Open Slope, gentle all the way. The problem is that South Ridge is the main route to and from all of the upper-mountain skiing. That can mean lift lines at the beginning of the day (as I've suggested above) and after lunch, as well as lots of skier traffic toward day's end, when more advanced skiers come down from the upper mountain. Of course, if you enter ski school, lift lines shouldn't be a problem, and the downhill flow tends to be only a late-day

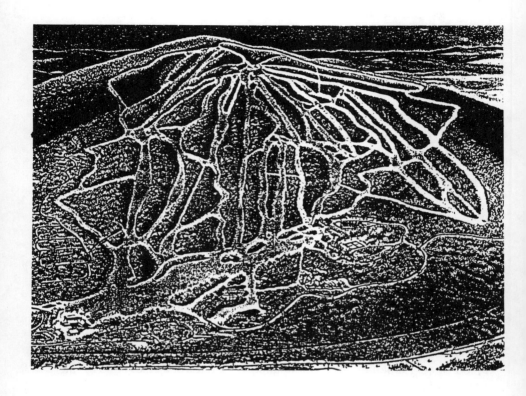

Okemo, an overall view of the mountain layout

phenomenon.

If you want to steer clear of all those faster skiers, your best bet in this area is to bear right from the top of the quads to the combination of *Homeward Bound* and the NASTAR Trail. That's because all the upper-mountain lifts are to your left; hence, the skiers coming down from the mountain tend to stick to that side.

Unless you feel comfortable on lower-intermediate terrain, the upper mountain has little to offer novices. The easiest skiing other than South Ridge is from the Green Ridge Triple. It's possible to find very mellow going here, although numerous intersections can test your trail-selection skills. For example, you can make a relatively easy descent by connecting *Easy Rider*, *Whistler*, *Tomahawk*, and *Beeline*. But wrong turns are possible; for example, missing the turn for Beeline (unlikely, but possible) could dump you onto *Screamin'Demon*—though not as demonic as implied, certainly not a trail a novice would be happy on.

In sum, Okemo is a mountain best enjoyed by lower intermediates on up. When you're ready to cruise Okemo, you're ready to enjoy the mountain at its best.

OKEMO FOR CRUISERS. Okemo is first-order proof of how imprecise the business of rating trails can be. It looks from the trail map as if there are lots of expert trails. There aren't. To put a trail like *Black Out,* for example, in a league with a black-diamond trail such as The Chute at Mad River would be ludicrous. Black Out is a terrific, wide, well-groomed run—a bit steep for the first few turns, but pure cruising territory after that (unless, of course, the area leaves it to turn to moguls, which it sometimes does). The lesson here: Trails at Okemo—as else-where—are rated according to their difficulty relative to other trails on the mountain. If you think you can handle Black Out—check it out on your left, just past the Sugar House restaurant, as you ride up the South Ridge quad—you're ready to handle 90 percent of Okemo skiing. If it looks *fun*, you're ready to have an absolute blast at Okemo.

Let's start with the easier stuff, to be found around the Green Ridge chair. The skiing here is popular, and it's easy enough to understand why: trails are gentle, consistently well-groomed, and contained within their own little pod. You can ski most of the trails to the right of the lift in various combinations, since, as I've described under "Okemo for Novices," trail intersections are numerous. That keeps the Green Ridge skiing from getting monotonous, but probably the most popular run here is *Jolly Green Giant*, the trail with the least variation. It is classically Okemo in its relatively consistent pitch and consistent snow texture, and when I was last at Okemo, it was crawling with kids.

One limitation of Green Ridge skiing is that it's short—the lift barely covers 1,000 vertical feet. But it is possible to extend your runs by skiing down to the base of the Black Ridge chair by bearing right or to the base of the Solitude Peak chair by bearing left. I'd opt for the latter, since the Solitude Peak area tends to live up to its name except on busy days. For my cruising tastes, the best trail combination over here is *Upper Tomahawk* to *Screamin' Deamon*, the top straight cruising with a few pitch and fall-line aberrations, the bottom a trail on which the ski area usually leaves one side to turn to moguls. Great stuff—you can try your mogul-skiing skills out on one side, with the groomed side always available for bailing out. Incidentally, don't combine Green Ridge and

Black Ridge during the post-lunch (1-2:00 P.M.) hour if you can help it; lots of post-lunchers from the Sugar House use the Black Ridge lift for their first ride back up the mountain.

A favorite cruising run? I'd go with *Nor'Easter*, a 1,300-foot-vertical, straight-as-an-arrow shot (actually, a former lift line) from the Northeast triple chair. You can see the end of the trail from its beginning—kind of neat—so that early in the day, when the snow's good and the skier traffic is light, this is the perfect trail to ski fast and non-stop. Another favorite, for completely different reasons, is the combination of *Upper World Cup* to *Lower Chief*, using *Chute* as a connector trail. Upper World Cup has a couple of nice rhythm-changing drop-offs, while Lower Chief has some interesting (and jumpable) crests and undulations to it. You could also ski World Cup's full length, but that's what most skiers do, and the bottom half, while good skiing, is no more than a straight, wide shot.

HALFTIME. The Sugar House is the most popular lunch spot, for good reason. There's little point in skiing to the South Ridge base other than at day's end. But Sugar House has more going for it than just convenience—the food selection is decent, the views through the large, sun-capturing windows are good, and the open-planked walls do a fair job of evoking the architectural character of a traditional Vermont maple-sugaring house. The restaurant is also in an open, sunny location; ergo, great outdoor lounging on spring days. The Sugar House's main drawback is that it's a little small to handle the crowds on busier days.

The Summit House, at the Northeast Summit, is Okemo's most recent addition to on-mountain dining. It's a comfortable, sunny place with good views to the south, and for those who like a little warm-up to their ski day, there is a limited bar as well. However, reporting this comes with a bit of sadness. The Summit House made the Beach House, a little chili-and-beer near the summit, expendable. The Beach House used to be the hub of a funky locals' scene on warm spring days, and perhaps in time the Summit House will assume the same role.

OKEMO FOR ADVANCED SKIERS. The only real pocket of expert skiing at Okemo is the Northwest Summit area. *Outrage* can be a satisfying challenge in its first few hundred feet, but the pitch mellows fairly quickly after the first steep drop-off. The glade skiing on *Double Diamond* is probably the best expert skiing on the mountain and certainly the best powder skiing; after a storm, this is immediately where the local hotshots head. If you're looking for off-trail glades, you can find some skiing through the birch trees off of *Defiance* where the trail doglegs to the left—about 30 turns worth on a fairly mellow pitch.

One shortcoming of the Northwest Summit area is that, like other skiing pods at Okemo, has a relatively short vertical rise—just over 1,000 feet. I like my runs a little longer than that, but over here, unfortunately, it isn't easy to extend your runs by connecting with trails from other lifts. So on Outrage, for example, you can just be getting into your mogul-mashing rhythm when the trail eases up. You can keep on going from the bottom of the chair down Lower World Cup, but that's a big, GS-turning cruise, and there will be two long lift rides back to the summit before you can get back to the bumps. Ah well, if you came to Okemo to tear it up in the moguls, you came to the wrong place.

I give the Okemo people credit on one point: Despite having earned their reputation as a leader in the business of snowmaking and grooming, they've had the sense to leave the expert trails of Northwest Summit to the whims of the natural-snow gods. So when the natural-snow conditions are good at Okemo, the Northwest Summit skiing can be very good; when natural-snow conditions are bad, Northwest Summit can be bad or closed altogether. So if it hasn't snowed recently, or the natural-snow base is thin, expert skiers should be content doing as everyone else at Okemo does: Cruise. Boost your ego on some of the best manufactured snow around, and save your cliff-jumping, mogul-pounding energy for another day at another area.

Actually, Okemo has been an area that has been at the forefront of a relatively recent trend: creative snowmaking and grooming. By that, I mean creating artificial slope contours and hummocks. The hummocks are sometimes simply "whales"—large mounds of manufactured snow that will eventually be spread smoothly across a trail's surface (see "Inside Story: Snowmaking"). But sometimes the groom crew will simply blow and push snow around to add texture and character to a trail. The one trail where a lot of that seemed to be going on the last time I was at Okemo was *Upper Chief.* So depending on how the groomers have configured it, Upper Chief could be a steepish cruiser or a syncopated roller-coaster ride. If you're an expert skier and the Northwest Summit is not up to par, cross your fingers for the roller-coaster. It can be an absolute gas.

SNOWBOARDING. If moguls the Okemo groom crew hasn't allowed moguls to grow too big on Upper Chief, I'd head here; if the rollercoaster effect is fun for skiers, imagine how fun it can be for snowboarders. I've also seen snowboarders behaving like forest-bound kangeroos, hopping their way through the trees of Double Diamond. Catch the lift line at the Northwest Summit area early, and you can find some of the best snow anywhere at any time on the mountain for carving full-throttle, long-arcing turns.

Given Okemo's overall character as a cruising mountain, I'd rate it as a terrific place for anyone just beginning to get the hang of snowboarding. It's made to order for building your confidence and skill before taking on more challenging terrain at resorts farther north in Vermont. However, for more skilled riders who get their kicks from playing with terrain quirks—rocks, stumps, stream beds, overhangs, etc.—Okemo, with its satin-smooth finish, will wear out its welcome all too quickly.

THE POST-GAME SHOW. The liveliest post-game action is at Dad's, where beer flows by the pitcher-load between 4:00 and 7:00 P.M. There is also live music on weekends. For those seeking a quieter, more elegant way to spend their evening after skiing, Nikki's, a mile down the road toward Ludlow, is considered by most insiders to be the best restaurant in town. For my money, one of the best deals going in the Ludlow area is pizza at the bar at Nikki's. We're talking serious gourmet pizza here, at not much more than Pizza Hut prices.

OKEMO DATA
Pluses and Minuses:
Pluses: Good intermediate skiing, superior snowmaking and grooming, lots of on-slope accommodations. Minuses: Limited expert terrain, inconvenient base-and parking layout, need to ride access lifts to get to main-mountain lifts.
Key Phone Numbers:
Ski Area Information: 802-228-4041
Lodging Information: 802-228-5571
Snow Conditions: 802-228-5222
Location: **On Okemo Mountain Rd., one mile off Route 103 at Ludlow. Mailing address: RFD #1, Ludlow, VT 05149.**
Mountain Statistics:
Vertical drop: 2,150 feet
Summit elevation: 3,300 feet
Base elevation: 1,150 feet
Number of trails: 72
Lifts: 4 quad chairs, three triples, 1 double, 2 surface lifts

Average annual snowfall: 200 inches
Snowmaking coverage: 90% (365 acres)

STRATTON

Vail, the giant of Colorado ski areas, may or may not be the archetypical "destination" resort, but it certainly established a blueprint that other resorts have followed. I say this with particular reference to Stratton, because if ever there were a scaled-down version of Vail in New England, Stratton would be it. It's got a little, boutique-crammed walking village, underground parking, lots of modern lodging around the mountain (if not actually ski-in, ski-out), lots of cruising terrain, a gondola. And—yes—not to be outdone by nearby Okemo, it's got a clocktower, a destination-resort de rigueur. It has made a big push for summer business, as Vail has, coming up with a golf course, a tennis school, and other summertime amenities.

If it weren't for the unavoidable accident of geography, Stratton's western-resort sleekness might place it somewhere on the road from Steamboat Springs to Vail rather than in New England. It is even touched by a bit of Aspen/Vail star quality—last time at Stratton, I spotted Treat Williams, John Kenneth Galbraith, and Jill Clayburgh, playing mom to a couple of small fry.

Although Stratton, as a western-style destination resort, is more or less an invention of the 80's, its geographical-displacement theme is not new. When I first began skiing Stratton in the 60's, it always struck me as a kind of weekend/vacation annex of New York exurbia. Stratton skiers tended to be from upper-crust places like Mt. Kisco in Westchester County or Darien, Connecticut. There was always a high percentage of wood-sided station wagons in the Stratton parking lots, having brought to the mountain the families of corporate, old-boy New York.

I don't think new-resort Stratton has superseded old-boy Stratton; instead, the two seem to me to have blended together. The result of this merger is a smoothly operated, sleek-looking, high-end resort backed up by a ski area that holds forth an abundance of well-manicured slopes for intermediate and advanced intermediate skiers. If you are someone who likes trails that ski like World Cup GS courses—long, sustained pitches on the steep side of intermediate—Stratton is for you. It might not seem that way when you look at the stylized Stratton trail map, which makes almost all trails, novice included, appear to be on a pitch approximating

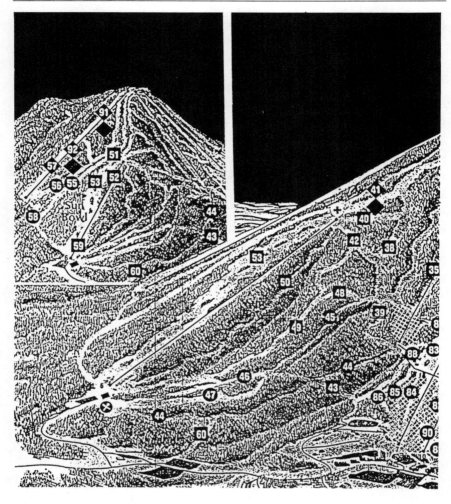

Stratton, a reduced view of the trail map

that of the north face of Mt. Everest. The fact is, though, about 90 percent of Stratton is cruise country.

And the cruising these days is better than ever. It used to be that Stratton's chairlift network effectively divided the mountain into a tougher upper half and a more moderate lower half, with better skiers pretty much spending all day up top. With the installation of the Starship XII lift a couple of years ago, it's now much easier to ski Stratton's 2,000-plus vertical on a single run, a big plus over yesteryear. If you are in southern Vermont on a weekday and your objective is to rack up

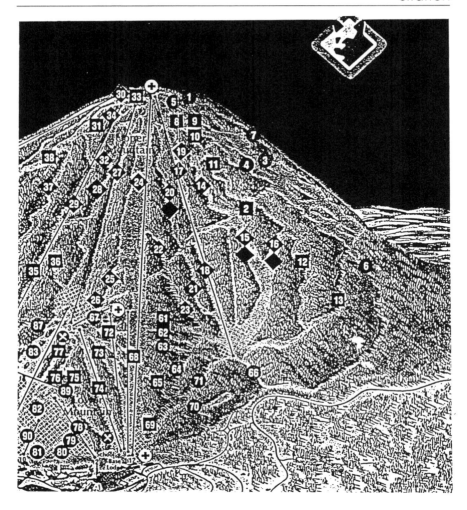

vertical footage, Stratton's the place to go. Starship XII covers the bottom-to-top run in eight minutes, and given the buffed-up nature of Stratton snow, you can whip down the mountain in less than half your Starship-riding time. That comes to—let's see—five runs an hour at 2,000 vertical feet, with seven skiable hours daily. . . Anyone for a 70,000-vertical-foot day?

If I were to find fault in Stratton skiing, it would be in the over-mani-curing of trails. Stratton is a fairly uncomplicated, consistently pitched mountain, and meticulous grooming makes trails ski too much alike one another. My feeling is that, if the natural contours of a mountain aren't varied enough, snow-surface variety would enhance the skiing considerably. I would prefer seeing more trails allowed to turn to moguls or be groomed on a less-regular basis. But this is a matter of personal taste, and apparently a minority view. I haven't got the impression from recent Stratton visits that there is much demand for less aggressive grooming. Most skiers have seemed quite happy with Stratton the way it is.

A STRATTON STARTERS' KIT. You don't necessarily have to arrive at Stratton at the crack of dawn, but I'd suggest you try to show up well before 10:00 A.M. on a busy day. The reason: Once the parking lots near the mountain fill up, cars are re-routed to lower lots across the road. A shuttle bus carries skiers back and forth between the lower lots and the mountain, and I'm a day skier who prefers avoiding any kind of parking-lot shuttle-bus system if I can. As I've said, there is also some underground parking, a nice bonus on bad-weather days, but there isn't much of it, and it goes to the early birds. Also, from the underground lots you can walk a long corridor into the base lodge without going outside—another weather-beating bonus.

You might also considered setting up base camp at the Sun Bowl area. The base facilities here are relatively new (i.e., developed over the last couple of years), and are thus somewhat under-discovered. The Stratton regulars—of which there are many—still tend to proceed by habit to the main base. One drawback is that reaching the summit from the Sun Bowl base requires two lift rides, as opposed to a single, enclosed ride on Starship XII from the Stratton base. On slow weekdays, that's not a good deal; on busy weekends, when the line at Starship XII lengthens, it is the quicker way topside.

STRATTON FOR NOVICES. Stratton has plenty to offer lower-level skiers in an incremental progression up the challenge ladder. The lower-mountain teaching area is relatively self-contained—that is, not buzzed constantly by advanced skiers—which also makes it a nice spot for very young kids.

Even first-timers—with the help of Stratton's first-rate ski school—should master the teaching slope quickly enough, at which point, the next step up is to one of four lifts that reach from the base about a third of the way up the mountain. In general, the least crowded of these lifts tends to be Standard, furthest to the right, although Tamarack, furthest left, provides the best access to the more interesting novice terrain. *Lower Tamarack*, for example, leads into either *Mark's Run* or *Daniel Webster*, both short but neat little trails through the woods. The drawback of the Tamarack lift is that it can get crowded when better skiers use it as a first leg in an alternative lift routing to the top when the Starship line is long.

The Standard lift services primarily one slope, *Lower Standard*, which is wide open and often full of skiers who have taken the trail for its full, cruisable run from the top. (Lower Standard, incidentally, is marked as an intermediate run on the trail map, but it rates no higher than novice terrain in my book.) The Suntanner lift, similarly, services primarily a single trail, *Suntanner,* which is one of the great show-off trails at Stratton. It, too, is generously rated as an intermediate trail, primarily because of a steepish final segment. But it's so wide that the last bit should be negotiable by confident novices; with the trail in full view of the base lodge, the ego is more likely than the body to suffer injury.

Perhaps the best thing about Stratton for novices, however, is that it has a nice, easy trail network on its right, upper flank. At many other areas, it always strikes me as unfair that novices must be relegated to the lower part of the mountain. The view and the mountaintop experience are a part of skiing that every level of skier ought to be able to enjoy. Well, at Stratton, the trail cluster of *Wanderer*, *Mike's Way*, *East Meadow*, and *West Meadow* provide that opportunity. The Meadows are just as their name implies—wide, wide open, with great views to the northwest. If you feel you can handle *Drifter Link*, an intermediate trail but an easy one, you can spend all day on these trails, using the Snow Bowl triple as your access lift, rather than skiing the uneventful lower section of Wanderer to the bottom. Bottom line: This is some of my favorite novice terrain in all of New England.

STRATTON FOR CRUISERS. For the most part, trails rated with black diamonds at Stratton can be considered advanced intermediate. If the snow weren't groomed, they *might* rate as expert trails; moguls would toughen up a pitch that I'd put somewhere between intermediate and expert.

Stratton's main cruiser is *Standard*, the Starship lift line, which was turned into an overly wide "supertrail" to accommodate Starship. (Actually, two trails were merged into one.) A lot of skiers obviously love it, but its straight, wide, lack of subtlety, along with its exposure to the wind that is not uncommon at Stratton, place it well down on my list of favored Stratton runs.

For my Stratton cruising, I'd rather put my time in either on the Snow Bowl or Kidderbrook lifts, the decision contingent upon the time of day and the wind direction. Kidderbrook, facing east, is better in the morning or when the wind is from a westerly direction. (If the wind is strong from *any* direction, it's probably best to stick to the lower, more protected Sun Bowl terrain.) Snow Bowl, with a slightly westerly exposure, is better in the afternoon or when the wind is from the east.

Perhaps my own favorite intermediate route on the mountain starts with *Black Bear* and finishes with *Supertrail*, connecting the two via either *Down Easter* or *Sun Bowl Express*. This trail combo features the kind of terrain variation that's hard to come by at Stratton. It begins as a narrowish, winding trail, levels off for a short time as a ridgeline run, then descends onto wide-open Supertrail. Supertrail is an example of how the "supertrail" concept can work with a little design imagination. Tree islands and natural undulations lend character, and selective grooming—i.e., allowing mogul patches to form in places lends variety.

If I am more in the mood for speed than terrain variation, I'll head over to the *Snow Bowl Liftline.* It's pretty much a straight, consistently pitched, on-the-fall-line shot, and I know that I have to keep my speed up; if I don't I run the risk of being plowed over by one of the numerous other skiers who enjoy taking the trail at high speed. Yes—Liftline is a little steep as an intermediate trail, so if I want something mellower, I'll hang a left onto *Drifter.*

If I am looking for a cruising variation on the Liftline theme, I'll hang a left about halfway down onto *Interstate* and then take my first left onto *Lower Spruce.* Lower Spruce tends to get relatively little traffic, since it lines up best for skiers coming down from Upper Spruce—a relatively small bunch, since Upper Spruce is best known for its fearsome moguls. Lower Spruce, however, is usually groomed, and on a powder day can be a hidden stash for intermediates to test their deep-snow skills. And don't worry about the black-diamond designation for Lower Spruce; it's blue terrain all the way.

One thing worth noting about Stratton for intermediate skiers: The average Stratton pitch is a little steeper than other cruising mountains like Okemo and Mt. Snow, and because the snow surface is uniformly well-maintained, Stratton can be a good powder mountain for intermediates. You need that extra pitch for speed in deeper snow and it's nice not having to worry about bumps beneath the fresh snow to throw your balance off. But don't expect the powder to last long; the groomers will turn it to corduroy soon after any storm. And local skiers say that if there is a really big storm—that is, two fresh feet or more—even Stratton might not be steep enough.

HALFTIME. The lunch options at Stratton are a real treat, primarily because there are options. You can settle for standard cafeteria fare at the base lodge, which is perfectly adequate if predictable. More intimate (or more cramped, depending on the time of day) is the small restaurant at the base of the North American chair. It's a good place to go (as opposed to the base) for beating the post-lunch lift lines, since you're already part way up the mountain, with the North American lift or the usually less crowded Grizzly lift to choose from for your summit ride.

A good crowd-avoiding lunch stop is the Sun Bowl base lodge; as I've said, I think a lot of Stratton regulars have been slow getting used to the idea that Sun Bowl exists at all. Or if you want to linger over lunch, try the burgers, salads, and sandwiches at Mulligans in Village. Ski-booted guests are more than welcome.

STRATTON FOR ADVANCED SKIERS. One of my favorite Stratton trails is *Spruce*, primarily because it reminds me that traditional New England skiing is not dead at Stratton. In other words, it's narrow, it's winding, and, depending in the mood of the groom crew, it's strewn with moguls. As a result, it doesn't get skied a lot because most Stratton skiers get spoiled by all the grooming elsewhere. In following New England tradition, the Spruce snow is often inconsistent, but don't pass judgment on the quality of skiing based on the trail's first steep pitch, which invariably features gruesome icy patches. After that, though, the snow and bumps usually improve markedly, and I've usually found my best rhythm by skiing the right side of the final mogul field before the trail crosses *Interstate*. The lower part of Spruce is usually groomed and doesn't seem to get much skier traffic (as I've said), so the snow quality tends to be good. At that point in the run, the rhythm change from bumps to groomed snow is welcome and refreshing.

North American used to be one of Stratton's premier expert runs, but it has disappointed me in recent visits. Maybe that's because it is still popular and gets skied more than it should. Maybe it is because groomed manufactured snow on this steep a pitch has a tendency (at least in my experience) to become slick quickly. Maybe I've just been unlucky in my timing when I've skied North American. Whatever the reason, the trail has seemed to me been slicker—especially near the top where it is narrower—than other trails of similar pitch (e.g., Snow Bowl Liftline) at

Stratton.

I probably shouldn't divulge this, but Stratton instructors have told me that when they want to sneak away for a free run or two—especially when there is powder to be found on the mountain—one of their favorite getaway places is *Switchback*, a sliver of a trail that veers left about halfway down Standard. Standard skiers, presumably locked into their cruising rhythm, tend to pass the Switchback trailhead by. Although in pitch and width Switchback is a rough approximation of Spruce, running parallel to the left, less skier traffic keeps Switchback from bumping up. A smooth surface and little skier traffic are the elements that make Switchback a good powder run. And a good instructors hideaway. If Ski School Director Alois Lechner is wondering where all his employees have disappeared to on a snowy day, let me suggest he check out Switchback.

Two relatively new expert trails are *Bear Down* and *Free Fall*, which branch off to the right from *Kidderbrook*. How different two trails of such similar pitch and character can be! Both are steep mogul runs, but while my experiences on Bear Down have been, in a word, miserable, my experiences on Free Fall have been nothing but pure delight.

The main problem is that Bear Down's moguls are a messy, unruly lot, while Free Fall's, especially along the edges, allow an easy rhythm to be established. Why so? My answer—sheer speculation—is that Bear Down is longer and comes without bailouts, so that a lot of skiers find themselves fighting their way down amogul trail they wish they hadn't been on in the first place. The result: choppy, inconsistent moguls.

Free Fall, on the other hand, branches off of Kidderbrook about half-way down, at which point most skiers are so tuned into Kidderbrook cruising that they blow right by the trail entry. Thus, those skiers who do decide to take on Free Fall are only those few who really want to be there. One other thing about Free Fall that ranks it high on my list of Stratton trails: the trees on the right side have been cleared, and even a few days after a storm, fresh, untracked snow can be found here.

SNOWBOARDING. Stratton knows snowboarding: This is where the concept was invented by Jake Burton, the epynomous founder of the Burton snowboard company, in the 70's, and the world's first snowboards came out of Jake's small shop in Manchester. So to say that Stratton is haven for snowboarding comes with a rich sense of history.

You can't carve a turn on history, however, and Stratton backs up its historical underpinnings with remarkably good snowboarding terrain. I can't imagine runs much better for snowboarding than Kidderbrook or Supertrail: Thy're great for fast, severely banked GS turns, and their natural undulations are perfect for popping off into mid-air at mid-turn. If you can't like snowboarding here, try another sport.

Another place to play around is in the trees to the right of Free Fall. The trees close to the trail are widely spread enough for skiers to negotiate, and the farther right you go, the deeper you get into snowboard-only country.

I'm speaking here, of course, primarily to expert snowboarders; the fact is, Stratton is a great place for first-timers. The terrain steps up nicely, from short easy trails in the Ski Learning Park to mid-length runs like Suntanner to longer, more challenging runs like Standard.

Stratton does, however, have two unfortunate features that snowboarders should be alert to. Black Bear is a great cruiser, but to get from the bottom of Black Bear back to the base requires traversing a long flat—actually uphill at one point—and if you don't muster maximum speed at the bottom (and most skiers and snowboarders don't), you'll find yourself limping home. Similarly Drifter Link on the other side of the mountain is long and flat and unfortunately so; otherwise East Meadow and West Meadow, for which Drifter Link serves as a connector trail to the base area, would be ideal terrain for novice snowboarders, just as it is ideal for novice skiers.

THE POST-GAME SHOW. The apres-ski party crowd at Stratton usually starts out at Mulligans, with three bars under one roof and live music on weekends. Those with a zest for later-night action will probably find themselves heading down the road to Manchester.

There are a couple of advantages to staying at the mountain (rather than in Manchester), other than the obvious fact that it saves driving to and from the ski area every morning—a drive that, from Manchester, can be slippery and steep on a bad-weather day. Advantage #1: If you stay at the mountain, you can use the Stratton Sports Center, with swimming pool, racquetball and tennis courts, weight room, etc. Go get 'em, you apres-ski aerobic junkies. Advantage #2: A free shuttle-bus service links mountain, lodging, and village, so once at Stratton, you'll find your car to be, for the most part, unnecessary. That's another western-resort feature adopted by Stratton, and it's a welcome one.

Also, Stratton Village over the years has developed into perhaps the most complete, mountain-base village in New England skiing. That means plenty of restaurants, shops, and lodging (on the expensive side, to be sure), from which I'll single out one name: Birkenhaus. The restaurant in this lodge is about the closest thing I've encountered this side of the Atlantic to a Swiss alpine gasthaus, mixing fine dining with an authentic touch of gemutlichkeit.

By the way, there is a third base-camp option if you're skiing Stratton: You can stay in Jamaica, nine miles southeast. It's the sensible choice if you're someone who likes the ambience of small-town, semi-rural New England.

STRATTON DATA
Pluses and Minuses:
Pluses: Mountainside village, good dining, good grooming, relative proximity to major cities. Minuses: Shortage of expert terrain, overgrooming
Key Phone Numbers:
Ski Area Information: 802-297-2200
Lodging Information: 800-843-6867 (on-mountain); 802-824-6915 (area lodging)
Snow Phone: 802-297-2211
*Location:***4 miles south of Bondville (15 miles east of Manchester on Route 30) on Stratton Mountain Road. Mailing Address: RR1, Box 45, Stratton Mountain, VT 05155.**
Mountain Statistics:
Vertical drop: 2,000 feet
Summit elevation: 3,936 feet
Base elevation: 1,936 feet
Number of trails: 92
Lifts: 1 gondola, 4 quad chairs, 1 triple, 6 doubles, 2 surace lifts
Average annual snowfall: 170 inches
Snowmaking coverage: 60% (300 acres)

ALSO KEEP IN MIND. . . *Bromley*

Bromley exists in something of a time warp, having changed little (as far as I can tell) since the mid-60's. That's when it caught sight of the future of New England skiing and installed a much heralded "million-dollar" snowmaking system—a breath-taking investment at that time. Laid out on a southern-facing exposure, the ski area was (and still is) blessed with plentiful sunshine—great for skiers, cruel to snow. Bromley beat the snow-melting heat with top-to-bottom snowmaking, years before other ski areas considered the idea feasible, and established itself as the sun-and-snow capital of Eastern skiing. On those cold, high-pressure days, when skies were blue but the temperature refused to climb above zero, Bromley could be (and still can be) relatively balmy in the sun, while skiers at north-facing ski areas suffered through unbearable cold.

Once snowmaking had been installed, however, Bromley had no more futuristic tricks up its sleeve. It was then, as it is now, a traditionalist at heart, perhaps best characterized by the old, red, clapboard base lodge that for me stands as something of a symbol of pre-commercialized, pre-automatized New England skiing. Sure—a few new lifts have gone in and a few new trails have been cut, but Bromley remains what Bromley has always been—a fair-weather, easy-skiing place to bring the family.

It's hard to imagine a better mountain for novices and lower intermediates than Bromley. The lower left and right flanks of the mountain are devoted entirely to novice terrain, each serviced by its own lift. Also, Bromley's fair-weather exposure helps do away with one factor that I find turning would-be skiers off—the cold.

But Bromley for advanced skiers? There are a couple of short pitches that experts might find entertaining, but basically, if you're looking for killer steeps and come to Bromley, you have erred dramatically. This is a place to come with the family, enjoy the sun, and escape the pace and swankiness of Stratton for a day. And it's also a place to take advantage of the apres-ski scene at Johnny Seesaw's, a couple of miles east of Bromley on Route 11 in Peru. With its sit-by-the-fireplace atmosphere, it evokes a mostalgia, as Bromley does, of an era of stretch pants and hand-knit sweaters decorated with reindeers and snowflakes. Dropping by here is a fitting way, in a time-honored New England way, of capping off a day of skiing at Bromley.

INSIDE STORY
FLAKE FARMING:SNOWMAKING
AND GROOMING

The 80's in New England will be remembered as the era of the fake-flake revolution. Without question, snowmaking and grooming have combined to bring about the biggest change in New England skiing in the last 10 years. Once an oddity, man-made snow is now a New England norm. Areas such as Attitash, Bromley, Okemo, Sunday River, and Waterville Valley can cover more than 90 percent of their terrain with man-made snow; Killington which makes more snow than anyone, lays down the artificial stuff on 40 trail miles.

But the big deal here isn't just in how much snow ski areas can make; it's in what they make of what they've made. As the state of the snowmaking art races ahead, the state of the grooming art has matched stride. Together, they have evolved into the relatively new concept called snow "farming." Ski areas don't just make snow; they nurture it, cure it, turn it over, till it, and so on. In this business, snow is no longer just white, fluffy stuff; it's a crop.

Snowmaking has been around for a while, of course—the first rudimentary system being introduced at Mohawk Mountain in New York State in the 1950's. Bromley astonished the ski world in the 1960's by installing a "million-dollar," top-to-bottom snowmaking system. Other ski areas, however, continued to bank on the natural stuff, using snowmaking mainly for patch-up work. That was the case, at least, until the end of the 1970's, when a couple of devastatingly bad natural-snow years made ski areas realize that no snow means no dough; that if natural-snow droughts recurred they might be out of business. Snowmaking became their anti-bankruptcy hedge. After that the forces of competition took over: when an area such as Killington announced an expansion of its snowmaking capability, other areas felt compelled to expand, too.

There are two basic elements to modern snow farming—making snow and managing it. In principle, making snow is not especially complicated: bring together water and air on a cold day and—bingo—you're in business. But if you look at it as snowmakers must—as an art of producing the best quality snow as efficiently as possible—it becomes a complex, multiple-variable problem.

You've seen the snow guns on the mountain firing clouds of snow onto the mountain. The water that goes into that snow cloud begins in a reservoir, usually near the base of the ski area. The water must be pumped from the reservoir to the guns, and since that water must be moved up the mountain—against gravity—a series of relay stations to pump the water may be used in larger systems. Of course you need air, too, both to mix with the snow and to provide pressure to blow it out onto the mountain. So along with the pumps, the other workhorses of the snowmaking system are air compressors.

The water and air get to the guns through pipes and hoses; certainly you've seen that stuff on the mountain, too. Once in the gun, the water must be broken down into small particles in a water-air mixing chamber before being blown onto the mountain. According to Bruce Schmidt, who oversees snowmaking at Okemo, different gun designs break down the water differently—or into different-sized particles—meaning that, depending on the temperature and humidity, certain guns are more efficient than others.

Which brings us to another element in this story—weather monitoring. Areas like Sunday River now employ computerized systems to monitor climatic conditions an almost a minute-by-minute basis. Sensors at strategic spots on the mountain relay temperature, humidity, wind, barometric data, etc. back to a central computer. That kind of system enables a ski area not only to determine whether or not conditions are right for making snow efficiently but also to adapt gun settings to climate changes while snow is being made in order to produce the best results.

Schmidt says that the ideal conditions for making snow come on a moonlit night, with the temperature at about 15 degrees, the humidity about 60 percent, and a slight wind blowing away from the guns. Obviously, you need conditions to ensure that water in the system is cold enough to make snow but not too cold to freeze in pipes and hoses. Less obvious is the fact that the amount of air required changes according to the temperature and humidity, and snowmakers want to be as efficient about using air as water. Running the compressors uses up energy, and energy is money. And not to be forgotten is the human element. Snow guns must be regularly repositioned during snowmaking, and when it gets too cold, the people assigned to that job, the so-called "gun-runners," suffer.

At one time, snowmakers simply coated trails with a more-or-less even snow layer, as if painting or plastering a wall. Now, however, the standard method is to create large mounds of artificial snow called "whales." You've probably skied over a whale or two at an area with extensive snowmaking. The concept behind whale-making is that it allows the newly made snow to dry out somewhat, through evaporation and percolation, in much the same way a farmer might allow hay to cure in stacks in a field before bringing it in to the barn. Why don't ski areas simply make drier snow? For one thing, the drier the snow, the more compressed air required, and air costs money. Also, the drier the snow, the less apt it is to adhere to the trail and the more likely it is to blow off into the wild blue yonder.

Once the snow has been made, it's time for the groom crew to roll into action. As Schmidt puts it, "Grooming is as much a part of snowmaking as making the snow." After a whale has cured for a couple of days—the curing time depending on the weather—it is chopped up and the snow spread on the slope. It still might not be the best snow for skiing; often the first post-whale phase is golf-ball-like snow. But over time, the groomers continue to work the snow, turning it over and working more air into the surface mix, eventually creating the fluffy stuff that's fun to ski.

Grooming people these days have become like kids in a toy shop. That's because equipment companies in recent years have been regularly coming up with new machines and gear to enable ski areas to groom more terrain and do it in more creative ways. Paul Buhler, Killington's Snow Surface Supervisor, lightness and traction are the critical design elements of snow cats—light enough to keep from sinking in the snow, with enough traction to climb steep slippery hills.

The snow cats that Killington uses to groom approximately 600 acres nightly weigh about 15,000 pounds—flyweights compared with earth-moving equipment, such as bulldozers, of similar size. Relatively new to most big grooming fleets are so-called "winch" cats, able to groom very steep slopes. The cats can be anchored at the top of a trail and then be winched down slowly, much in the way climbers use ropes to rappel down steep faces.

Cats pull behind them grooming rigs with names like Power Tiller, Flex Tiller, and Powder Makers, each with a different forte. The Powder Makers, for example, are good for grooming large, flat areas quickly. Flex Tillers, on the other hand, are ideal for uneven surfaces, being able to move snow over rocks, ledges, and other obstacles that might damage the Powder Makers. Flex Tillers, for example, are capable of grooming mogul trails without completely chopping down (or "blading" in groom-speak) the bumps and creating a flat slope.

The march of technology won't quit, of course. A couple of years ago, for example, the big talk in snowmaking circles was a new technology called "Snow Max," in which benign bacteria are used as nuclei to build snow particles. Snow Max allowed areas to make snow at relatively high temperatures, even above freezing. (Not all snowmakers are sold on Snow Max, saying that it is expensive and no more effective than other technologies at lower temperatures.) More recently, Buhler says Killington has experimented with machines that essentially work like vacuums to suck back onto trails snow that has been pushed or blown into the woods.

So who are best farmers? Reputation puts Attitash, Killington, Okemo, and Sunday River at the head of the pack, and I'd go along with that. Of those three, I'd have to say that the best man-made snow I've encountered has been at Okemo. But man-made snow, like natural snow, can vary: you can luck into a good "man-made" day just as you can luck into a good powder day. Other areas that do good snowmaking/grooming jobs are Stratton, Waterville Valley, and Shawnee Peak.

I should add that some trails are great well-suited for snowmaking, while others aren't. Typically, the steeper and narrower the trail, the less suitable it is for man-made snow. Narrowness presents problems for groomers, and if you can't groom man-made snow, with its high water content, it becomes ice in a hurry. Steepness is a problem because the upper layer of soft, groomed snow all too quickly gets pushed to the bottom of the slope by skiers sliding through their turns to control speed.

So I go with this rule of thumb: The steeper the trail (with groomed, man-made snow), the earlier in the day I ski it, before the fluffy groomed layer gets skied off. I'm fairly confident that the groomed snow on beginner or intermediate terrain will stay nicely skiable throughout the day, so that's where I head when the steep stuff starts getting icy.

Chapter 3
Central Vermont

IF YOU WANT A STUDY of central Vermont in three quick lessons, make the 30-mile drive along Route 4 from Woodstock to Rutland. Lesson 1 is Woodstock, a lesson in history. Woodstock might not be Vermont's oldest town, but so well is it preserved that it might leave that impression. Much of its brick and clapboard architecture has been kept in movie-set-perfect condition. More to the historical point for this book's purposes, Woodstock is the birthplace of lift-serviced skiing in America. It was on a hill outside town in 1934 that America's first rope tow was installed. The vestige of those early days is a ski area that makes up for its diminutive size (650 vertical feet) with my favorite all-time ski-area name: Suicide Six.

The drive westward from Woodstock leads in 20 miles to Lesson 2: Killington, the big daddy of New England skiing. Killington is usually the first ski area that comes to mind when people think of Vermont skiing. By its sheer size and the number of skiers it attracts, it tends to reign supreme over everything else in the neighborhood, although Okemo (not far to the south) and Pico to a lesser extent have begun to emerge in recent years from Big Daddy's shadow.

From Killington, Route 4 descends the western slope of the Green Mountain spine to Rutland, the last lesson in this quick study. Rutland teaches about life in everyday, 9-to-5, workingman's Vermont. It is one of those largely unreconstructed, early-industrial New England mini-cities. In Rutland, Victorian and clapboard homes are interspersed with those old-fashioned five-and-dimes where you can buy vinyl-and-chrome furniture and $5.99 jeans that won't fade no matter how many times you wash them. I say largely unreconstructed, because Rutland has more than its share of shopping-mall, car-dealer clutter on its periphery. Rutland is principally a functional town for Vermonter and traveler alike, a place for supplies and repairs before moving on.

Actually, it's probably useful to consider central Vermont not as one region but two: one with Killington and Pico as a hub, one with Sugarbush and Mad River as a hub. I am always surprised, given their proximity, how different in character, skiing terrain, and geography these two regions can be.

Killington, of course, is perhaps the dominant force in Eastern skiing, hosting more skiers per season than any other ski area in New England. One reason is that Killington skiing comes with a virtual guarantee: The massive snowmaking and grooming operation means that when conditions are marginal elsewhere, they're still apt to be good here.

Both Killington and Pico also feature lots of wide-trail cruising terrain, the kind of skiing that has become immensely popular in recent years. That's not to say challenging skiing or narrow, old trails are lacking, but when I want that kind of skiing, I usually head further north to the Sugarbush/Mad River Glen zone.

The Killington/Pico region is also loaded with lots to keep the attention of non-skiers and part-time skiers in the form of restaurants and shops. Count on everything from McDonald's to epicurean high ground, everything from Montgomery Ward in Rutland to Bill's Country Store, a place that sucks in browse-aholics at the junction of Route 4 and the Killington access road.

If you're looking for guaranteed skiing and lots to do—and you don't mind sharing your ski travels with weekenders by the busload—the Killington/Pico hub is hard to beat. But because of such considerable development, on-slope and off, this is probably not the place you'd come if you're looking for a flavor of old New England, traditional New England, or rural New England.

That's where the Sugarbush/Mad River area comes in, anchored in a spirit of tourism-modified rural life. That this area has not become as developed as the Killington area must certainly have something to do with location and geography. For one thing, it's another hour's drive from the big cities to the south, a cumbersome bit of extra travel. Here also the landscape puckers up in a development-discouraging way, with valleys that are tighter and hillsides steeper than in the world around Rutland and Burlington, where rolling countryside rises up gradually to the massifs and summits of Killington and Mt. Mansfield. I get a sense of being surrounded by mountains here more than in any other part of Vermont, with the possible exception of the Northeast Kingdom.

Nothing for me evokes this midst-the-mountains character more than the drive on Route 100 through the Granville Gulf, just south of Warren, where the road twists through a narrow passageway lined by steep, tree-and-rock-covered hillsides and frozen waterfalls. If you are skiing Sugarbush, the drive here after skiing is worthwhile just for the drive itself.

Another distinction of this part of Vermont is an absence of cities. Yes, Montpelier and Barre are in the general vicinity, but I doubt that in more than 20 years of skiing in north-central Vermont I've been to Montpelier or Barre more than a dozen times. They remain forever on the geographical and cultural periphery.

Instead, small and mid-sized towns—Rochester, Hancock, Granville, Warren, Waitsfield, Moretown, Waterbury, etc.—are strung like Christmas-tree lights along the cord of Route 100. Industry—industrial opportunity, for that matter—and farming are minimal because the angular mountain landscape militates against them. Those who have managed to make a living here have done so by prying from the land the few riches it begrudgingly cedes. Marble quarrying, maple-syrup production, a little bit of logging, a little bit of dairy farming—that's about it.

And, more recently, skiing. For the kind of New England skiing I like, the Sugarbush-Mad River combination is as glorious as it gets. Long runs, steep runs. Runs of infinite variety, of variable pitch. Except for limited novice terrain, these two areas have it all. Both areas are also short on snowmaking—Mad River, the standard-bearer of iconoclasm in New England skiing, has almost no snowmaking at all. That might be regarded in the ski business these days as economic suicide, but it also means that when natural-snow conditions are good, the skiing here is sensational. Let new-age ski-area operators say what they will about the quality of manufactured snow—a deep, natural-snow surface is still to skiing what the best Burgundy is to wine.

If there is a spiritual/economic hub of the region, it is probably Waitsfield, a town that tourism more or less built. Oh, I suppose that if it weren't for skiing, there would still be a Waitsfield; after all, there are plenty of structures in these parts (keep eyes open for covered bridges) that pre-date skiing. It's just that without skiing, there wouldn't be much of Waitsfield. Not that Waitsfield is some gaudy, tourist-trapping rialto. It is actually an attractive clustering of shops, restaurants, homes, etc. And its sister town of Warren, just a few miles south, supplements with a little eccentric New England funkiness in its musty, sloped-floor country store,with goods ranging from work gloves to wine.

KILLINGTON

Killington is the resort that won't let itself be out-anythinged by anybody. No ski resort in the East has more trails, more lifts, more snowmaking, more mountains (though Killington is overly imaginative in using the definition of mountain), or a longer season.

So if you like more of everything, Killington's your place. Frankly, I can take only so much, and for my tastes Killington has more than I need of just about everything. A day—especially a weekend day—at Killington can be more of a carnival than I think skiing ought to be, a kind of Texas State Fair with a cast of a thousand snow guns. Killington indeed has it all: great skiing for all abilities, good and plentiful lodging, lots of non-skiing activities. It's just that it has so much of it all that the total experience here can easily become more confusing than I think skiing should be.

No matter how good the signage—and Killington's is very good—the opportunities for getting lost improve every season. In 1990, after Killington began overseeing the management of neighboring Pico, the cumulative stats for the two areas staggered the mind: 147 trails, 27 lifts, 10 "mountains," and six base areas. (I'll review Pico separately later in this chapter.) Throw in thousands of condo units, slopeside and otherwise, and Killington/Pico can at times seem at times as much mountainside suburbia as resort.

The huge sprawl makes for a trail-guide designer's dilemma. The solution has been to create a trail guide based on topographical relief map, but even if you are used to reading this kind of map, figuring out even the most basic stuff—such as which way's up, which way's down—can be hard. The main map is supplemented by an artist's rendition of the area and a series of tables that looks like a page from the *World Almanac.*

I will say this: the Killington trail guide is the most comprehensive of any I've ever seen, with everything from a box explaining how to ski from one sector of the area to the next to a note about whom to call if you lock yourself out of your car. It's just that the basic info that must be imparted for an area so large is encyclopedic.

The Killington sprawl can also make for a family dilemma if you're not careful. If your kids end up at the Northeast Passage base area when the lifts close, and they should have been with you at Rams Head, you're looking at a 10-mile drive (and a trail of young tears) in order to re-unite. All I can say is, be very precise with your fellow skiers at Killington about meeting places and times, and then hope your plans work.

All that said, Killington also has obvious advantages over other areas, along with some exceptional skiing. It is certainly the world's snowmaking and grooming king, with an array of astonishing stats to prove it. The Killington groom crew reportedly logs in the neighborhood of 30,000 hours per season, and the snowmakers create more artificial fluff than any other resort in Vermont.

Killington has put a lot of marketing energy into the annual contest among New England ski areas for the claim of having the longest season. Given its snowmaking capacity, Killington has basically made the contest a no-contest. Killington can typically boast of more than 210 days of skiing a year and logged an astonishing 246 days of skiing—yes, *eight months*—during the '83-'84 season.

Personally, I could care less if the area has two or three trails open in October or May, but that's not where the real pay-off comes for skiers. Getting a headstart on the season usually means extensive trail coverage by Thanksgiving and plenty of skiing in late April. At these times of year, Killington generally has more terrain to ski—and a greater variety of terrain—than anywhere else in New England.

The Killington snow guns also get plenty of help from Mother Nature. Killington lies not just in a snow belt but in a snow belt buckle: the average annual snowfall at Killington is about three times what it is ten miles away in any direction. You may have heard about Killington's notoriety for inflating its snowfall reports—nothing new to ski areas. But even if the ski area might stretch the truth, I can attest to the anomalously heavy snowfall at Killington; I've driven Route 4 over Sherburne Pass near Killington enough times to confirm that natural snow depths are invariably much deeper here than in outlying neighborhoods.

Another thing about Killington is that, for all of its size and hype, its ambition has not o'erlept itself, to paraphrase Macbeth. It has not left master plans to yellow on the drafting table, as most resorts have a habit of doing. When Killington says it is going to do something, it does it. Thus, Killington can't disappoint you. If you read the brochures and the advertisements, Killington tells you what to expect—lots of everything— and that's just what you get.

Now I don't know anybody interested in skiing all 147 trails other than for the sake of some personal, pathological obsession. My way of skiing, which I think is typical of most skiers, involves sticking to the half dozen or so trails that best match my interest and ability and which have the best snow. So on any give day, the typical skier will find more than 90 percent of the ballyhooed trail count to be excess baggage. One benefit of all those trails and lifts, though, is that it spreads skiers out. That's important, given one more stat that Killington can pocket—more skier days than any other New England ski area.

For my Killington dollar, I still find most of the best terrain to be that which has been around longest, the trails that can be skied from the original Killington double chair. I'm also partial to the cruising trails at Rams Head, partly because they tend to get less skier traffic than the blue runs from the Snowdon and Superstar lifts and mostly because they get more sun. This incidentally points up a big asset to the Killington sprawl: Its multiple exposures greatly enhance the chances of finding a satisfactory combination of good snow and good weather conditions (i.e., sun, wind protection).

A KILLINGTON STARTERS' KIT. On an average weekday at Killington, I have found the best place to establish base camp to be the central Killington Base Lodge. If you are strictly interested in beginner or lower-intermediate terrain, you might want to pull in at Snowshed, with the most extensive facilities and services (i.e., restaurants, ski school) of any Killington base area. If you're looking to avoid the population explosion of weekends and holidays, the Rams Head base is the logical starting point. Otherwise, by continuing along Killington Road to its end at the Killington Base Lodge, you land in the best starting point for accessing most of the area's terrain.

One ride up the Killington double chair puts you at the mountain summit, the one vantage point from which you can branch out to any subsection of the ski area. Be ready for a cold ride in the early morning, though; for the first third of the lift ride you stay low in the basin, where morning dampness can take a few hours to dissipate. If you're looking for a warm-up run or two, the high-speed Superstar quad to the left of the base lodge is a good place to go, before the hundreds of skiers who frequent this popular lift scrape off most of the good snow.

A better option on busy weekends or holiday times is to head instead for the Northeast Passage base area at the junction of Route 4 and Route 100 South. Yes—the Northeast Passage triple chair is long, flat, and slow, and it services little interesting terrain. An extra lift ride—or two, or three—might be necessary to get to terrain you'll really want to ski. But the base area is unusually low-key for Killington, making parking and ticket-buying easier, and lift lines are improbable.

The time you might lose in riding the lift is more than made up for in avoiding the hassles and lift lines you'd likely encounter at the main Killington base. You'll also avoid the traffic build-up at the end of the day at the junction of Killington Road and Route 4, where 15 minutes of stop-and-go before getting onto Route 4 are not uncommon, even with traffic cops working the beat on weekends.

KILLINGTON FOR NOVICES. Killington was one of the first areas to acknowledge the discrete charm, and needs, of the novice skier. The development of Snowshed was groundbreaking stuff—an entire sub-area dedicated to beginners and novices. It was an immediate hit, as the three lifts capable of carrying 5,400 skiers an hour up Snowshed's meager 525 vertical feet attests. (For comparison, consider the Bear Mountain Quad's lift capacity: just 2,400 skiers an hour on more than double the vertical rise.)

Obviously, the Snowshed experience does not elicit that private, in-woods sense of skiing New England, but that's not the point. This is a learning hill, and Killington's ski school, notable for its courting of innovations such as the Graduated Length Method (no longer in use), is among the best anywhere.

Killington's trail layout is designed so that novices (not beginners) have a way of making their way down from any of the area's six sum-mits. Smart planning there, but I pass that info along with a couple of caveats. First, the pitch on some runs—e.g., *Juggernaut*, which mean-ders off the back of Killington Peak—is so slight that if you don't keep up your speed, you're likely to end up walking in places, especially when warm weather makes the snow slushy. Second, trails such as *Great Eastern* and *Rim Run*, are widely used by upper-level skiers as connector trails. The bottlenecks that form around the Killington summit can make for slick and disconcerting skiing if you are a novice, even if the trails are rated green.

One other thing to be careful about is sticking to novice trails. At an area with so many intersections, making a wrong turn onto terrain that overmatches your ability is a constant threat. Recognizing this, the area has put up signs and uses a symbol system (i.e., follow the red snow-flakes for the easiest way down from Killington Peak). Personally, I think this is information overload; most of us are used to following trail names, so why not simply have novice routes that keep the same trail name from top to bottom? Perhaps all the extra trail names help boost the official trail count; whatever, having to link together trails of three or four different names while looking out for easiest-route symbols strikes me as an unnecessarily complicated process for novices to deal with.

Among the novice trails that do stick with the same name top to bottom is Juggernaut, at 10 miles the longest officially designated trail in the East. Even for the novice, this is basically a scenic ramble more than it is a ski. I wouldn't recommend it unless your fully committed to a leisurely pace: the ski down and the process of riding the lifts back up is guaranteed to take more than an hour, with little legitimate skiing involved. All you need to do is a little calculation: 10 miles on 3,100 vertical feet produces an average pitch somewhere under 6 percent.

Nothing wrong with that, but if you're a novice who really wants to ski and you've passed the Snowshed test, your next best stop is Rams Head, a short walk across Killington Road. The combination of *Horn*, *Caper*, and lower *Great Bear*, or Horn to lower *Header*, are among the best long novice routes in the East. Another route that ranks right up there is upper *Pipe Dream* to *Wanderer* off the Sun Ridge chair.

KILLINGTON FOR CRUISERS. I've already mentioned my fondness for Rams Head, even if it does lack the sustained pitch I like in classic cruising terrain. Once you've negotiated the first third of *Timberline* or *Swirl*, the two blue runs that flank the lift, Rams Head skiing is pretty much a stroll in the park and might be too tame for aggressive intermediates.

However, Rams Head does make up for lack of pitch with some compelling features in addition to the aforementioned short lift lines and sunny exposure. One of Killington's great bugaboos, given 100+ trails, is its numerous intersections. On busy days collisions and near-collisions aren't uncommon. I'm sure you can visualize the scene: skier stops to look at sign and figure out which way to go; another skier comes bolting through the intersection. Whammo! At especially hazardous nodes in the trail system, Killington ski hosts act as traffic cops to keep the inadvertent slam-dancing to a minimum, but Rams Head has the best solution: Few skiers and few intersections.

Another thing I like about Rams Head is that its trails meander in a style that takes me back to New England skiing of yesteryear, and the width of the trails, at least to my sense of outdoor aesthetics, seems in proper proportion with the surroundings. Compare this with a more modern approach to trail design in superwide, straight-on-the-fall-line *Skye Lark* or *Bittersweet* off the Superstar chair. One other thing decidedly unmodern about Rams Head that I find less than appealing is the length of the lift ride, a 14-minute, mile-plus poke. Yes—the new high-

speed lifts have something to be said for them.

As long as we're on that subject, let's go on to the Superstar chair. Except for precipitous *Ovation*, all of the trails from this high-speed quad can be taken on by solid intermediates, even if some trail sections are labeled black on the map. That's because these trails are meticulously groomed, so if the pitch is occasionally worthy of a black rating, the snow surface makes for easier skiing. Too easy, at times: On *Superstar* in particular, you must maintain peripheral vigilance for out-of-control speed merchants.

Of all the trails from this lift, I think Bittersweet offers the best combo of cruisable terrain and minimal traffic, but the Superstar pod in general is not the place to be if traffic avoidance is your primary objective. The

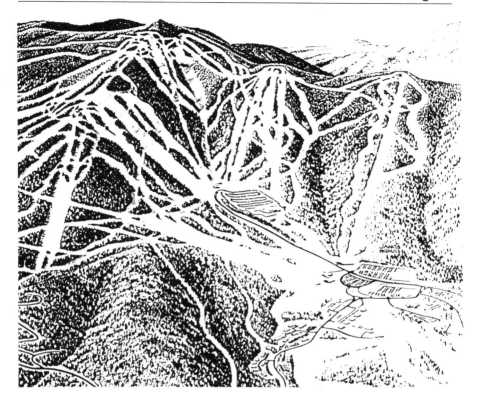

Killington, a rough portrait of a New-England mega-area: this reduced view of the trail map shows the various Killington "mountains."

best strategy is to hit these trails very early, before the crowds appear and when the grooming is still fresh. Put in a quick two or three runs; with the speed of the lift (and assuming a minimal lift line), round trips can easily be completed in 10 minutes. When the lift lines begin forming, move on; because of the volume of skiers that a high-speed lift can dump onto trails, the chances of finding good snow decrease in inverse proportion to the increasing chances of doing an unscheduled slam-dance with another skier.

And where to go? Two suggestions. The Glades chair trails on Killington Peak—*East Glade*, *West Glade*, and *Rime*—are almost ideal in pitch and are inaccurately named: The "glades" are just a few trees here and there that make the trails prettier rather than more challenging. In my experience, the snow on East Glade tends to stay the freshest. The drawbacks here are occasional lift lines and an exposure to weather; when the wind is hard out of the north, you'll want to be skiing elsewhere.

My second suggestion is to head for the South Ridge chair. Stuck behind Killington and Skye peaks, South Ridge is out of the main flow of traffic—the tendency of most people seems to be either to stick to Killington or continue on to Bear Mountain. That's why I've already mentioned South Ridge as a likely place to find powder, but in *Pipe Dream*, it also has one terrific cruiser, flat on top but with a good pitch, included a few yahoo, air-potential rolls toward the bottom. If air is what you're after, keep up your speed and stick to the right of the trail toward the bottom.

HALFTIME. Another eye-opening Killington stat: 11 on-mountain facilities serve lunch of one sort or another. If you're seeking to avoid crowds, the cafeteria and two restaurants near the Northeast Passage base get the least traffic, but they're also the least convenient if getting back to the slopes in a hurry is a priority. The Northeast Passage area itself features little quality skiing, and to get back to Killington's real skiing requires a 17-minute ride on the Northeast Passage triple chair.

On the other hand, if you're seeking to be in the midst of a crowd, the place to be is the base lodge at Bear Mountain. This is one of those spots where being part of the scene is the main thing; getting nourishment is an afterthought. A sun-deck, a high-spirited crowd, loud music, an outdoor barbecue, and the full-view, center-stage action of skiers entangled in the moguls of Outer Limits make for mid-day revelry that gains in momentum as the season warms into spring.

My choice for an easy no-muss/no-fuss lunch is the cafeteria in the gondola summit terminal. It's more spacious than it might look from the outside, its big, south-facing windows let in lots of sun, and the sandwiches-fruit-and-cookies cafeteria food is perfectly adequate. I'm also partial to mountaintop lunching; it means that, rather than standing in line and sitting on a lift with the inevitable post-lunch chills, you can take a run immediately to get the blood circulating again.

KILLINGTON FOR ADVANCED SKIERS. The run that is Killington's rite of passage for skiers who'd like to think they have the right stuff is *Outer Limits*, the showcase trail of the Bear Mountain area. The outstanding characteristic of the trail is its total lack of subtlety—an ultra-wide swatch cut on 1,200 vertical feet of steep fall line, where every winter Vermont's biggest moguls form. To me, the action on Outer Limits is to advanced skiing what arena football is to the National Football League: It's fast, furious, a little bit silly, and something short of the highest standard. The trail is in full view of crowds that accumulate at the Bear Mountain base lodge as well as skiers on the lift or waiting in line. It thus offers a chance to be either cheered by the viewing audience or to be utterly humiliated, and it surprises me how many people take the chance, seeing as the latter fate is by far the more likely.

Ski it once to say you've skied it, but unless the snow has been softened considerably by a fresh snowfall or warm weather, go elsewhere after that. As is the case with other mogul trails that get lots of traffic, Outer Limits tends to develop hard, often strangely configured moguls with deep, back-wrenching troughs. For my taste (and for the love of my vertebrae), a much better mogul trail with much less traffic is *Royal Flush*, which drops off of *Rim Run*, the catwalk connecting the Glades triple chair and Snowdon Mountain. (You can also get to it by taking the top of Royal Flush, an almost-flat cruiser, from Snowdon.) Conditions are just right at about 11:00 A.M. on a sunny day, when the trail's eastern exposure puts the sun's snow-softening effects to full advantage.

Also in the same area is *East Fall*, a narrow, steep sliver bisecting the natural bowl between Killington Peak and Snowdon Mountain. With the recent addition of snowmaking and the recent deletion of some trees to widen the trail, East Fall isn't quite the thrill and challenge it used to be, but it still rates as a local favorite and one of my favorite Killington runs. From the catwalk at the base of the Glades triple chair, East Fall drops off so suddenly that it looks more like a cliff or a mistake than a skiable trail, and thus discourages most skiers. But it's really only the first turn or two that intimidate, and if you start your attack on the trail's left side, you'll wonder what all the fuss was about.

Being narrow and steep and sequestered in the belly of the bowl, East Fall's snow is well-protected from wind and sun. Since few skiers venture over the edge, the snow here can stay fresh for many days after a snowfall. In addition, the trees, especially on the left side, are open enough in places to catch a few powder turns if you can turn 'em quickly.

As long as I've raised the subject of tree skiing, let me throw in a couple of other suggestions. *Big Dipper*, between East Fall and the Killington double chair, is one of those ultra-wide trails that would probably have been better left uncut. It's often closed—too wide to commit the snowmaking effort required to cover it when other trails have higher priority. However, the ski area management had the good sense to leave the left side of the trail gladed, and I've found soft, weather-protected snow here long after things have hardened up elsewhere on the mountain.

As for my second suggestion, I can only say that you take me up on this at your own risk, since deep-tree skiing is supposedly against the Killington rules. As you make your way along Rim Run toward Royal Flush, keep an eye out on your right for openings in the trees. The trees are tight and there is fallen timber—so now I've warned you—but there's great snow to be had before you flush out onto Royal Flush. The last time I did this I was scolded, gently but firmly, by a ski patroller. If the same happens to you, do me a favor and don't tell them you read about it here. (Incidentally, the story I've been told is that this patch of tree skiing has been dubbed "Toilet Bowl" by locals, hence the trail name, Royal Flush.)

I'll throw in one other old favorite of mine, the combination of upper *Flume* and lower *Cascade*. The Flume section, under the Killington chair, is basically cruise country, with a few bumps tossed as the pitch steepens to help promote rhythm in your skiing. Cascade is steep and often has well-formed bumps despite its slant across a double fall line; I have usually found the left side of the trail, toward which snow tends to get pushed, the better side to ski. Alas, this route is hampered by the juncture of the two trails, where you must negotiate around an unnecessary lift mid-station. Neither option—left or right of the mid-station—is a good one; they're both steep, narrow, icy slots, usually populated by fallen or cowering skiers. There is no graceful way around the mid-station, and since it goes unused, I don't see why the ski area doesn't just get rid of the thing.

By the way, if you're seeking powder, Killington is not necessarily New England's best despite it's substantial snowfall, simply because any area that gets that many skiers and does that much grooming doesn't hold onto powder for long. Probably your best powder bet is the South Ridge chair which sees relatively little traffic of either the grooming or skiing variety. The top half is on the flat side, not quite enough pitch when the snow is really deep, but there's plenty of fun to be had in the glades of *Jug Handle* lower down.

SNOWBOARDING. A run that can be a particular blast for snowboarders is Royal Flush especially early in the season, for the snowpack has thickened and moguls have developed. That's because a couple of streambeds run across the trail, forming natural shelves. As a skier, I find these shelves irksome, tip-catching obstacles, but air jocks on boards find that they make terrific launching pads.

Pipe Dream over at South Ridge is another hot spot for the snowboarding crowd. It's a groomed, wide-open cruiser with a distinctive feature—occasional rolls for big-time air. If you're the sort of person who likes fast long turns spiced with occasional air time, you're in snowboard clover on Pie Dream.

THE POST-GAME SHOW. Two things make apres-ski: places to go and people to fill them. Killington has plenty of both. Most of the action is along the access road, and it is usually worth making a stop before getting on your way in order to avoid post-skiing traffic snarls at the intersection of the access road and Route 4.

The place everyone used to go was the Wobbly Barn—aptly named, in that nights of dancing and romancing led to a whole lot of shakin' goin' on. In a recent visit, however, it seemed to me that the Wobbly had become middle-aged, with more emphasis on dining (steak-and-salad style) than dancing. If you're seeking a more local atmosphere for apres-ski, Charity's, across the access road from the Wobbly, is a good choice, a beer-and-ski-talk place.

If you're looking for elegant dining in the area, Hemingway's, on Route 4 between the gondola base and the access road intersection, regularly gets accolades from all fronts—locals, vacationers, and tour guides. The Basin, both a restaurant and deli, can serve up a mean dinner, too, without the grand-restaurant fuss you'll encounter at Hemingway's. For dinner on the cheap, the buffalo wings at Casey's Caboose can do the trick.

Fact is, though, there are dozens of good places to eat—serving all sorts of cuisine at all price levels—lining the access road and the 10-mile stretch of Route 4 into Rutland. If eating is as important to you as skiing, Killington should rank high on your list of New England ski areas.

KILLINGTON DATA
Pluses and Minuses:
Pluses: Size and variety of terrain, snowmaking and grooming, length of season, plentiful dining and nightlife. Minuses: Crowds and congestion, sprawling layout, absence of New England charm.
Key Phone Numbers:
Ski Area Information: 802-422-3333

Lodging Information: 082-773-1330
Snow Conditions: 802-422-3261
Location: **5-mile access road begins 10 miles east of Rutland and 20 miles west of Woodstock on Route 4. Mailing address: 406 Killington Rd., Killington, VT 05751.**
Mountain Statistics :
Vertical drop: 3,175 feet
Summit elevation: 4,241 feet
Base elevation: 1,160 feet (at the gondola base)
Number of trails: 107
Lifts: 1 gondola, 15 chairs, 2 surface lifts
Average annual snowfall: 225 inches
Snowmaking coverage: 60% (395 acres)

MAD RIVER GLEN

The Mad River mystique is a curious thing. It isn't the oldest ski area in New England, even if it acts that way; founded in 1948, it's barely got flecks of gray in its beard when compared with true oldsters like Bromley, Cannon, Pico, Stowe, and others. Nor is it categorically the steepest mountain around, despite its tough-guy rep; you can find plenty of pitches at other areas that are as steep as or steeper than what Mad River dishes out. And it doesn't necessarily have the best skiing around, even if its devotees, who worship Mad River skiing as pilgrims worship at the most hallowed of shrines, might say that it's so. Actually, Mad River skiing can be as dismal as skiing gets—dismal as in non-existent. Mad River is probably forced to close more often due to poor snow conditions more often than any other major area in New England.

So what gives? First of all, Mad River seems old mainly because it won't grow young. Mad River management has generally looked upon change as a kick in the pants of tradition, and tradition is the thread that holds Mad River together. High-speed lifts, computerized snowmaking, mogul-bashing groomers—forget about it. The ski area's managers, it seems, chucked the ski-area equipment catalogs sometime shortly after the double-chair was invented. Who needs any more new-fangled techno-junk! A snoutful of the single chair's diesel exhaust, the metallic clank of the safety bar and foot rest swinging into place and you're off—2,000 vertical feet upward and 40 years backward in time.

Now this business about steepness: What makes Mad River tough is not so much the pitch itself but rather the fact that the pitch never quits. Those 2,000 vertical feet are the most unrelenting, in-your-face verts that I can think of *anywhere* in lift-serviced skiing. (I'm talking here about the single-chair terrain, upon which Mad River's reputation is staked.) It might not all be like the over-the-waterfall drop at the top of *Paradise*, quite possibly the most adventurous trail in Eastern skiing. But this is still the Energizer of Eastern steepness—it just keeps going and going. A flat spot at Mad River is the crest of a mogul.

As for Mad River having the greatest skiing going, anything you might have heard is strictly an expression of a peculiar and particular taste, acquired only if you're willing to go with all the ski area has done to cultivate it. All, in this case, is pretty much nothing. The ski area essentially does nothing—or very little—to alter the hand nature deals it each winter. Beating back progress as is its habit, Mad River is almost entirely without snowmaking. There isn't much grooming, at least on the single-chair runs. Of course, nature can deal some lousy cards (as it has in recent seasons), but Mad River just lives with it. It simply grits its teeth through the natural-snow shortages and the rains that can turn its cherished moguls into ugly welts of blue and yellow ice.

But when the snows come, and come in abundance. . . .or when the spring sun comes to soften those ice-faced moguls. . . .my God. On those days, every hot skier in the Mad River Valley, it seems, arrives at the base of the single chair with some excuse for not showing up at work. The hooky-players come because the moguls are so well-formed—more even and rounded than at other areas because Mad River attracts so many fine, rhythmic bumpsters. They also come because, despite the steepness of the mountain, there is an effortless, natural flow to skiing Mad River. The Mad River trail cutters (notably former manager Ken Quackenbush) took care for the most part to follow the natural contours of the terrain.

Ultimately, though, the skiers come because Mad River's steeps, bumps, glades, rocky overhangs, and other preter-gnarly nasties offer a near-backcountry challenge almost impossible to find elsewhere. A day at Mad River when snow conditions are perfect and when mind and body are in perfect tune to take on the challenge is a day that becomes ever-lastingly implanted in memory.

Sound like I'm foaming over a bit here? It's only because I have had days just like that. Then again, I've had days at Mad River that have simply been awful. You take your chances. And iffy snow conditions are just part of Mad River's downside.

Remember, we're talking single chair here, and Indian-file lift-riding isn't exactly the best way to speed skiers out of the liftline and up the mountain. Also, Mad River skiing makes only a begrudging nod to lower-level skiers, even if there is a nice little cluster of novice trails. Face it: Skiing novice terrain at Mad River is like ordering chicken salad at a steak-and-seafood restaurant. It might be on the menu, but it isn't what anyone really comes for.

Other shortcomings? Base lodge: too small. Parking lot: too small and poorly situated. Ski school: well, there is one. At least I think there is one. There *must* be a ski school. Wait a minute. . . Is there a ski school? Oh yes—I remember seeing in a brochure something about teaching "radical terrain techniques." I guess that's a way of saying that Mad River has never been the kind of place to package learn-to-ski weeks.

In short, something is going on at Mad River that isn't going on elsewhere, and it isn't for everybody. All I can suggest is that, if you haven't tried it, wait for the snows before taking the baptismal plunge.

A MAD RIVER STARTER'S KIT. Before heading for Mad River, I read the snow reports in the newspaper carefully. I might even call the ski area for a snow-condition update. Those are pre-skiing measures I rarely take, but Mad River is the great New England exception. The reason? Just 12 acres of snowmaking coverage. Mad River can't (nor does it have much inclination to) patch up the mountain with artificial snow when natural-snow conditions are marginal. I know that if Mad River's base is less than about 20 inches, or if there has been a recent rain-and-freeze, the skiing can be pretty gruesome, and I'll opt for neighboring Sugarbush North. If marginal conditions exist and I still feel I need a Mad River fix, I'll be sure to pack a pair of rock skis. The rocks, roots, and rubble of Mad River are among the best reasons in New England to invest in gouge-repairing p-tex candles.

Another thing I'll do before going to Mad River is assess the group I'm with. As I've said, there isn't much lower-level skiing here, and what there is is in a small cluster set off by itself. Mad River is one of those mountains that tends to segregate skiers by ability: advanced skiers ski the single-chair runs; intermediates ski the Sunnyside double-chair runs; novices and small kids ski the Birdland-chair runs. If I'm with lower-level skiers who might appreciate Mad River's unique ambience and don't mind spending most of the ski day by themselves on limited terrain, I'll go to Mad River. Otherwise, we're off to Sugarbush North.

The parking scene at Mad River, all in all, is pretty awful. The lot, such as it is, is a clearing in a hairpin crook of Route 17. As much as I can make of it, the parking begins with a vague sense of order that progresses into anarchy as the day wears on. So pick a spot—any spot—taking care not to allow yourself to be boxed in by some late-arriving anarchist.

Be careful crossing the road (especially with kids)—Route 17 is a through road, and the double-hairpins and parked cars can blind drivers to the pedestrian traffic. Look for the walkway leading past the ski shops to the base area; I always miss it and end up sloshing through the snow-melt and mud on the short service road.

One last note about Mad River: It's a good windy-day place to go. The mountain itself is relatively wind-sheltered, and the tree-enclosed narrowness of most trails offers further wind protection.

MAD RIVER FOR NOVICES. Should I bother? All right—quickly then. There is a novice route—at least a route rated as novice—from the Sunnyside summit. It basically involves doubling back on two roads, first *Fox* and then *Upper Porcupine*. Not very interesting, and also potentially hazardous, since there are plenty of opportunities to make a wrong turn and end up over your head, perhaps literally so, in Mad River moguls. Unfortunately, this is the routing to Birdland, Mad River's novice plexus, so all I can say is: Pick your way carefully.

Perhaps the best thing about Birdland is its tilt toward the southeast, making it the sunniest sector of the mountain. And it does make up for its lack of dimension—about 350 vertical feet—with a neat, narrowish, interlocking trail network that reasonably mimics the more advanced trail design on the mountain. In *Panther*, there is even a little bit of novice-level glade skiing—gentle and relatively open.

To be honest, I've always regarded Sunnsyside as a place for Mad River's core of loyal families to deposit their kids. In other words, it's something of a day-care center or, in mimicking the trail design of the rest of the mountain, a version of Mad River with training wheels. It works well in that regard, but I would think adult novices might find Birdland trails a little on the short side, a little on the narrow side, a little on the removed side (set apart from the base area and the rest of the skiing terrain), or all of the above.

Something I don't like about Birdland is that the return route to the base area takes you through *Chipmunk Bowl*, the Times Square of Mad River Glen, if there could be such a thing. *Grand Canyon* and *Porcupine*, two of the more popular Mad River runs, also flush into this mini-bowl, and many advanced skiers try to carry extra speed through here to

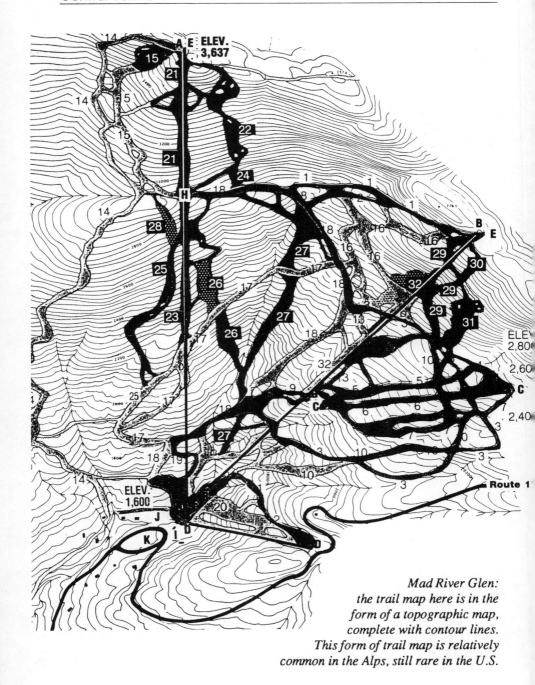

*Mad River Glen:
the trail map here is in the
form of a topographic map,
complete with contour lines.
This form of trail map is relatively
common in the Alps, still rare in the U.S.*

carry them across the flat road that runs underneath the single chair.

MAD RIVER FOR CRUISERS. No one really cruises at Mad River, in part because of the terrain and partly because "cruising" is the sort of neologism that grates on the ears of tradition-minded Mad River skiers. If there is such a thing as cruising at Mad River, it is probably on the mid-section of *Gazelle*, the Sunnyside liftline, which is generally open and groomed. The best intermediate way of getting here, however, is via *Quacky*, which is much more in the traditional Mad River mold, a trail that meanders around tree islands and at times is so enclosed by the tree canopy as to evoke a cocoonish, in-the-woods feel. If you are looking for the cruisable section of Gazelle, be sure to bear right on Quacky and connect onto *Chipmunk*; otherwise, you'll end up having to do battle with a short but steep mogul section. The best way of avoiding problems is to make note of the trail intersections here as you ride the Sunnyside lift.

Mad River has three terrific intermediate runs: *Antelope, Bunny,* and *Porcupine*. Antelope is essentially the only intermediate route from the top of the single chair (although *Catamount*, except for its first steep pitch, is intermediate going as well). Antelope is the kind of trail that grows on you, so stick with it. It rolls, winds, pitches forward, flattens out in such a way as to make no two turns the same and no two runs the same. It is, indeed, the antithesis of a cruising run: Rather than allowing you to establish a smooth, cruising cadence in your turns, Antelope imposes upon your skiing its own, syncopated rhythm. And woe to anyone who tries to ski it fast—it's too narrow and variable for that.

On several of my Mad River visits, Antelope has been closed, for reasons I can't explain, so unless you're ready to take on the first, steep mogul field of Catamount, check with the ski patrol before heading to the top of the single chair. Otherwise, you can do as many Mad River intermediates do: Disembark at the mid-station. There is still plenty of mountain to be hand from here on down—more than 1,300 vertical feet worth—and from here you can access both Bunny and Porcupine.

For my intermediate money, I'd take Porcupine over Bunny, assuming good snow conditions. Bunny tends to shimmy across the fall line a little more than I like, while Porcupine takes a more direct descent. In a way, Porcupine can ski like a toned-down rendition of *Grand Canyon*, the lower-mountain mogul monster. Its pitch is more moderate and its moguls smaller (though the ski area might groom Porcupine, it has allowed moguls to form in my recent visits). You can jump in anywhere (and I literally mean jump in a couple of places) but the farther you traverse across the wide trail opening—that is, the farther you go toward the trail's left side—the easier the skiing will be. As the pitch eases toward the bottom, the trail narrows, finally squirting you through a pair of nozzles into Chipmunk Bowl. I tend to prefer the left nozzle; it's a little steeper and sets up well for a fast, right-hand turn for carrying speed across the road that leads beneath the single-chair lift. One other similarity to Grand Canyon: Porcupine's exposure is such that it tends to gather in afternoon sun to soften the snow.

HALFTIME. Mad River is a place where a lot of people bring their lunch with them. This, I suppose, is commentary both on the kind of skier and the kind of food you're likely to encounter. Let's just say that Mad River skiers tend to be brown-baggers by nature and that the food at the Basebox (that is, the base lodge) cafeteria or the Birdland snackbar is something short of gourmet. A favorite springtime picnic spot among Mad River regulars is the area around the ski-patrol hut at the single-chair summit. The decks—upstairs and downstairs—in front of the Basebox are also prime territory for mid-day solar (and social) activity.

MAD RIVER FOR ADVANCED SKIERS. The *Chute*. Simple name, simple concept, profound results. I love this trail, which only puts me in the company of hundreds of other Chute junkies. Indeed, when the snow is soft, Chute skiing can become pure addiction. No reason even to ski to the bottom; wait at the single-chair mid-station, pray for an empty chair, rush back to the summit for another quick fix.

Why is the Chute not just another, steep liftline? I really think it has something to do with the lift ride—an experience that is like skiing up the trail before skiing down it. Keep in mind that you are on a single chair, so you aren't engaged in the conversation or cuddling you might otherwise experience on a higher-capacity chair. As the chair passes over the trail—seemingly by only a few feet—you can mentally select a line through the moguls in a visualization process akin to what racers go through in their pre-race rituals.

At the same time, I have found that a rare kind of bonding goes on between lift-riders and skiers. The chair, as I say, passes so close to the slope that you feel almost as if you could high-five hot skiers as they fire by. And that raises one last Chute point: When the skiing is hot, so are the skiers. When it comes to mogul skiing, the Chute tends to pull in a gang that can really do it to it.

For all of its straight-on-the-fall-line simplicity, the Chute actually divides into three distinct parts. The first couple of hundred yards are on a relatively easy pitch, allowing you to brush up your rhythm and mogul-skiing basics before the tougher terrain that lies ahead. Part II is a rock-and-ice headwall, something to work around rather than to ski. If there is plenty of snow you can stay underneath the lift, the best snow generally to be found on the trail's left side. Otherwise, you'll do better taking the loop-around to the right, ever so carefully. I've left nice little deposits of p-tex in these parts.

Part III is where the real trail begins, a stream of moguls that just seem to get bigger as the trail goes on. I usually ski the far left side, because this is where I can generally count on finding the softest snow and the most manageable moguls. Toward the bottom the moguls go from big to humongous, and sometimes the best strategy here is just to take a long flyer. The problem is the absence of a good run-out; if you airmail the last few mega-moguls, be ready for a flat landing and skier traffic on your right, coming from *Catamount*.

Speaking of Catamount, it is really an upper-intermediate trail, though its top section is steep and moguls make it ski harder than your usual intermediate trail. Far left, as on Chute, seems generally to be the best line through the mini-bowl of upper Catamount. Partly this is because reaching the center and right means losing a lot of vertical to traversing, and partly its because the left side seems a little more protected from sun-induced melting and refreezing.

Fall-Line is mis-named; it is anything but a straight shot down the fall line. It is a trail of pieces rather than a single unit: a short mogul field, a slot through the trees, another short mogul field, a quick traverse, a glade, another mogul field. Then, suddenly, you're on Porcupine. In a way, Fall-Line is the expert version of Antelope, a trail that imposes upon your skiing its own syncopated rhythm. It is also a trail of multiple choices, as in: right or left of that tree island?

Fall-Line thus disguises its best lines wonderfully, and the choice of lines here is everything. The fact is that no one choice is consistently the right choice: the line that was best yesterday might be trashed today. So I'll offer two Fall-Line strategies. First, never ski it just once. Devote your first Fall-Line to reconnaissance, to investigative research. Take it slow, alert yourself to good snow and obstacles (exposed roots and rocks are Fall-Line specialties), and prepare yourself to get full enjoyment from the trail in subsequent descents. Second, tag along with a group of local skiers, if you can. I can't think of another trail in the East that puts more of a premium on up-to-the-minute local knowledge than does Fall-Line.

Unless, of course, it's *Paradise*, the waterfall/rockslide/whatever-it-is to the left of Fall-Line. In the good old days, Paradise, which until recently wasn't even acknowledged as a trail on the Mad River trail map, was marked by a green-circle, easiest-skiing sign. Funny joke, eh? If you really want to know how easily Paradise skis, I'll mail you the pants that the trees of Paradise tried to shred from my body a few years ago. I won't say much about this "trail" except to say that it's perilous and that skiing it without first asking the ski patrol about current snow conditions is foolishness. If the skiing on Paradise is lousy, you might get down the trail, but I guarantee that the descent will not be fun.

The lower-mountain expert options are three-fold: Grand Canyon, *Glades*, and *Beaver*. Grand Canyon is your mogul option, wide at the top and funneling down to a narrow slip toward the bottom. Like Porcupine (as described above), Grand Canyon tends to ski best in the afternoon, when the moguls have softened.

Glades is a terrific trail once you're there; it's the getting there that can be tough. There are a couple of steep and narrow slits through the trees and around the single-chair mid-station; the better option is probably the little opening to the right from Porcupine, just after the mid-station. However you decide to negotiate this section of the mountain, you're facing a punishingly narrow, usually slick bit of navigation before traversing across into the beginning of Glades. Put up with it; because many skiers don't, the Glades snow can be terrific.

The same can be said of Beaver, which has always struck me as one of the most underutilized trails on the mountain. Shortly after the Glades opening on the left, Beaver opens up on the right. Because it is underskied, its moguls are fairly small by Mad River standards.

SNOWBOARDING. Banned! Snowboarding is much, much too nouveau for the Mad River folks. Snowboarding is a passing fad that will not survive into the 21st century, Betsy Pratt, Mad River's owner, has told me. Of course I don't agree, but I suspect it's not snowboarding's lack of a forseeable future that causes her to snub it but rather a lack of a rooted past. Snowboarding needs to establish a history—a tradition, a lore, a cultural heritage—before it will ever get the go-ahead at Mad River.

THE POST-GAME SHOW. I guess somebody must stop in after skiing at the General Stark Pub in the Basebox. I don't. My apres-ski time is better spent in Waitsfield (see "the Post-Game Show" under Sugarbush), six miles down the road.

MAD RIVER DATA
Pluses and Minuses:
Pluses: natural-terrain skiing, expert skiing, old-fashioned ambience. Minuses: lack of snowmaking, shortage of novice terrain, no on-site lodging.
Key Phone Numbers:
Ski Area Information: 802-496-3551
Lodging Information: 800-828-4748
Snow Phone: 800-496-2001; in VT, 800-696-2001
Location: **On Route 17, 6 miles west of Waitsfield. Mailing address: Route 17, Waitsfield, VT 05673.**
Mountain Statistics:
Vertical Rise: 2,000 feet
Summit elevation: 3,600 feet
Base elevation: base 1,600 feet
Number of trails: 33
Lifts: 1 single chair, three double chairs
Average annual snowfall:
Snowmaking coverage: 10% (about 12 acres)

PICO

Geography dealt Pico Peak a bad hand. I'm not talking about it's 1,967-foot vertical rise or its near-4,000-foot summit, two geo-stats that enable Pico to stand tall alongside other New England ski areas. Those are Pico's real trump cards. No—the bad deal for Pico has always been its proximity to Killington, a couple of miles away as the crow flies. Geography has always compelled Pico to compete with Killington, and it's always been a mismatch. (Almost always, that is, since Pico, founded as a ski area in 1937, pre-dates Killington.) Going up against Killington in the ski business is like taking on Mike Tyson in a boxing ring: Killington is big, hits hard, and is nearly impossible to beat.

For a long time, Pico settled into a niche as a local-flavor alternative to Killington, leaving its neighbor to go after the out-of-state hordes. Pico made its business mainly on Rutland-area skiers, local racers, and

Killington spillover. Pico established itself as a Killington antidote—if you were overcome by the bustle and bluster of the big guy, you went to Pico. It was less expensive and a lot more low-key. Maybe there was less skiing than at Killington, but there were fewer skiers, too.

Then came the 80's, with new investors and grand visions. The idea was to turn Pico into a compact "destination" resort, a concept that materialized into a condo village, sports center, fast lifts, more snowmaking, new trails. The capital flowed in fast—the sports center alone cost $1.5 million to build—and Pico was on its way to resort-dom. Except for one problem: Skiers didn't flow into Pico as fast as investors' money did. So when the financial sting became unbearably painful, who do you suppose came in to supply the balm? Hello, Killington. Killington people were called in to manage Pico, with a merger in mind (that has yet to materialize) and a trail system that would eventually link the two areas. In one respect, Pico did beat Killington to the punch: while Killington moved slowly to permit snowboarding, Pico was quick to open its entire terrain to the shred crowd. But now that Killington has become snowboard-friendly, Pico has lost some of that edge.

Ironically, with all the changes Pico went through in the 80's, it doesn't strike me as a ski area radically changed. Sure, development changed the look of the base area, although for all that's there (150 and some condo units), it's surprisingly inconspicuous. The developers did a pretty good job of understating the resort stuff and keeping it from overwhelming the mountainside. Sure—new, fast lifts vastly improved getting around the ski area. But Pico still comes across to me as a low-key, unpretentious place with a hint of local flavor and a lot of family flavor. And the best of the skiing hasn't changed much; while new wide cruising trails were cut, the 80's change-niks had the good sense to leave Pico's steep and narrowish upper-mountain trail network pretty much untouched. (Trail-clearing resistance from the Appalachian Trail Club might have had something to do with that, too.)

Basically, Pico remains what it has been for as long as Killington has been around: an antidote to Killington. No—I don't think it's a ski area that can truly stand on its own as a "destination" resort. The reason: Although there is a well-balanced variety of skiing, there just isn't enough of it (despite the 2,000-foot vertical) to sustain my interest for several days running. But then that's what Killington is for, and the two areas have been coupled on various multi-day ticket plans. Pretty soon, you'll probably be able to ski from one to the other, though it's some-thing I personally am not looking forward to. After all, Killington already has more than 100 interconnected trails, and who needs more than that? I think it's fine the way things have been: two ski areas of distinctly different character right next to one another.

A PICO STARTERS' KIT. Nothing complicated—you just pull in off Route 4 into the parking lot, and you're on your way. The Village Square (your base of operations) is a fairly simple layout—a walkway between a couple of lodge buildings leads to the main ski-base cluster—ticket windows, ski shop, restaurant. One thing nice about Pico, especially if you've got kids or lots of gear, is that the parking lot and the village area are flat. No scrambling up icy paths or over snow banks here.

Incidentally, Pico has been one of those areas offering free skiing in its first hour (8:30-9:30 A.M.) of operation. This is a policy that a number of areas have dropped recently, and by the time this book comes out, Pico may have followed suit. So call ahead. If the policy is still in force, it obviously makes good sense to arrive early to test-drive the snow conditions. It's especially sensible when you consider Killington as a right-around-the-corner alternative if Pico conditions aren't up to snuff. (For that matter, with Pico's high-speed lifts, you could rack up a several thousand free vertical feet before 9:30 and then just head home.)

PICO FOR NOVICES. True, beginner pickings here are pretty slim. The question is: Where to go after you've mastered the bunny slopes of *Bonanza* (used as much as an open-air day-care center as anything else)? Well, you can move over to *Triple Slope*, wide-open and easy but also short and not nearly as complex as its name might imply. You'll probably master Triple Slope quickly enough, so then where?

I suppose the next place to go is the cruise country off the Golden Express Quad. Most of the skiing here is on the easier side of intermediate and very wide, so you shouldn't have much problem. However, the generally gentle slopes are occasionally interrupted by quick, steeper pitches.

I'll give you an example: Skiing *Expressway* under the lift and crossing over to *The Swinger* is a good lower-intermediate route. But toward the bottom, you might find yourself sucked onto a quick and nasty steep that leads back to the base of the lift. That, at least, is what I've found happening to myself, since the contour of the trail seems to carry me that way. To stay out of trouble, you have to be sure to continue on under the triple chair to the run-out of Triple Slope.

So to be honest, if you have never skied before, you might be better

Pico, a view of the mountain layout

off heading for Killington (if it's not a busy weekend). Killington has a good ski school and a wider array of beginner terrain. After no more than a day or two at Killington, you'll be set to enjoy Pico's wide and (by Killington standards) crowdless cruising runs.

PICO FOR CRUISERS. Pico might not have a lot of intermediate skiing, but it has a nice variation in what it's got. Pico's main cruising country is the trail network off of the Golden Express Quad. Actually, I find its three principal trails—*Prospector*, *Expressway*, and *Gold Rush*—a little too gentle. Gold Rush has perhaps the most consistent intermediate pitch, but Expressway and Prospector flush out onto Swinger, a long, flat stretch on which you can get bogged down if you don't keep up your speed. One thing I noted on my last Pico visit was that this trail cluster seemed popular among snowboarders. There are enough swoops, swirls and small lips on Expressway to make the trail ski/ride like a long half-pipe. Don't worry skiers—the swoops and stuff can easily be avoided.

If you really want to let 'em rip, try the far right—*Fool's Gold* to *Lower Pike*. It's not at all steep and is uncommonly wide by eastern standards. A couple of years ago, I saw a broken-legged skier on one ski—the ski attached to one leg, a cast attached to the other—bolting down this route. That ought to give you an idea of how easy and relaxed the skiing is. On the other hand, if you like more challenge, hang a right off Fool's Gold (just before the Pike juncture) to the Birch Glade lift. Because it's short and oddly located on the mountain (it begins part way up the mountain and ends well below the summit), the lift gets relatively little traffic.

Birch Glade is just as its name implies, but it is neither too steep nor too tight (that is, the trees aren't too close together) to be intimidating. Glade skiing is invariably best after a fresh snowfall, filling in moguls and covering up roots. If it has snowed recently, I'd recommend the glade highly. If it hasn't snowed for a while, or if you aren't confident in glades, you can always hang a left off the lift and join up with Pike below its steeper top section.

Which leads us to Pike, Pico's signature trail, that straight, wide, white slash down the mountain's mid-section. It *looks* like a modern wide cruiser, but it's been around for as long as I can remember (at least 25 years), so I suppose it was before its time. Whatever—it's a trail that becomes easier with every turn. Narrower (though not narrow) and steep at the top, it fans out and grows gentler toward the bottom of the mountain. When it is well groomed in the morning, lots of people ski it, many of them moving at a pretty good clip. That means the top can get skied off long before day's end, so ski it from the top early; later, you can pick up Pike lower down from the Birch Glade lift, as I've described above.

HALFTIME. It would be nice if there were a mid-mountain restaurant near the base of the Summit Express Quad. If you are skiing the upper part of the mountain exclusively, as many skiers do, having to go to the base area for lunch means an extra wait in line and lift ride. I wouldn't be surprised if this shortcoming is largely due to a permitting problem; being near the Appalachian Trail, Pico in many of its expansion plans has encountered a powerful adversary in the Appalachian Mountain Club.

But whatever the reason, lunch is served only at the base lodge. With all the changes Pico's base area has been through recently, it's a little surprising that the base lodge has remained almost totally unchanged. It's a high-ceilinged, big-as-a-barn space with big windows looking straight up Pike. Unchanged, too, seems to be the cafeteria food, but at least it's priced reasonably. Simple, unpretentious, inexpensive—that's what always used to appeal to the local folk about Pico, so maybe the timeless base lodge and its food are indication that, amidst change, Pico hasn't lost touch with its roots.

PICO FOR ADVANCED SKIERS. Pico has some terrific expert skiing from the summit, even if there isn't much of it. (Again, the Appalachian Mountain Club has had a hand preventing the clearing of new trails from the summit.) The easiest of the bunch is *Forty-Niner*, marked as expert terrain but barely so. It's a good trail to ski to get used to the layout and slope of the upper mountain before heading off to the tougher stuff.

The place to head first is Pike, since the snow is apt to get skied up quickly, as I've mentioned in "Pico for Cruisers." Pike really is a cruising trail—straight, wide, and unsubtle—which makes it a totally different ball game from *Upper K.A.* and *Sunset '71*, two old-style New England expert runs. They are the kinds of trails on which no two turns are quite the same due to a constant progression of double fall lines and doglegs, with Sunset the straighter of the two. Both are quite narrow, something I normally like. But the last time I skied Upper K.A., the combination of narrowness and slick artificial snow made the skiing treacherously unappealing. That points up the obvious: These trails are much more enjoyable if natural snow has been plentiful. Otherwise, you'll probably have more fun cruising with everyone else on Pike and Forty Niner.

If you like good, steep mogul trails, *Upper Giant Killer* aims to please. The wide, left-leaning shot is probably at its best on spring afternoons, since its exposure is slightly to the west of north, allowing the moguls to soften in the afternoon spring sun. On days like that, you can spend the afternoon yoyoing up the Summit poma and down Giant Killer until your thighs surrender. Or, with a little orienteering imagination, you can slip through the woods from Upper Giant Killer to connect with Birch Glade—a neat combo of mogul and glade skiing. Turning the tables, you can also use the Birch Glade chair and the Summit poma as a busy-day beat-the-lift-line alternative to the quad.

One final point: Pretty much all of Pico's expert skiing is on the mountain's top half, which is exposed to northerly winds. On days of bitter wind, I'd suggest Killington as a better choice for advanced skiers, since it has good expert skiing at lower, more protected elevations.

SNOWBOARDING. As I have said, Pico—either out of enlightenment or economic need—embraced the snowboard phenomenon earlier than many areas and certainly earlier than Killington. Pico thus has been able to command a degree of loyalty within the local snowboard contingent, and at least one good reason sustains that loyalty: *Pike.* Straight, superwide, true to the fall line and groomed, Pike ranks as one of the best runs in New England for snowboarders who like to lay on edge at high speed, etching deep, carved grooves in the snow. For those who like contours to horse around with, the runs from the Golden Express chair are, as I've mentioned, a snowboarding playground.

THE POST-GAME SHOW. Most of what I've said about Killington's apres-ski scene is applicable to Pico. Except. . . Pico has that sports club, if you didn't get enough exercise skiing. And even if you did get enough skiing, or you aren't into raquetball or weightlifting, there's a sauna, hot tub, and large pool. The club is one of the compelling reasons to stay at the mountain. One other thing: the scene at the base-lodge lounge is much lower-key (i.e., amplified acoustic-guitar music) and much shorter-lived than anything over at Killington. While the Killington crowd is winding itself up, apres-ski Pico-ites are winding down.

PICO DATA
Pluses and Minuses:
Pluses: Low-key atmosphere, on-site lodging and sports center, two high-speed quads. Minuses: Limited terrain, exposure to upper-mountain winds.
Key Phone Numbers:
Ski Area Information: 802-775-4346
Lodging Information: 800-848-7325 (on-mountain); 800-225-7426 (off-mountain)
Snow Conditions: 802-775-4345
Location: **On Route 4, 9 miles east of Rutland. Mailing address: Sherburne Pass, Rutland, VT 05701.**
Mountain Statistics:
Vertical drop: 1,967 feet
Summit elevation: 3,967 feet
Base elevation: 2,000 feet
Number of trails: 40

Lifts: 2 high-speed quads, 2 triple chairs, 3 double chairs, 2 surface lifts
Average annual snowfall: 200 inches
Snowmaking coverage: 82% (144 acres)

SUGARBUSH

Sugarbush could be the best ski area in New England. I say *could be* because it isn't—or isn't yet, anyway. By and large, I suppose most skiers could care less who is in charge at a ski area as long as the skiing is up to snuff. At Sugarbush, though, the ownership issue is of consequence because a succession of ownership changes, I think, has been largely responsible for the ski area's failure to blossom to its full potential.

Let's back up to the glory days of the mid-60's, when Sugarbush was on target to become the Zermatt of New England skiing, if such a thing was possible. There was big skiing—a gondola on 2,400 vertical feet. Sugarbush was unabashedly nurturing a neo-European flair—everybody was walking around with tans that didn't seem to belong in New England, had rich European accents, and went by names such as Sigi and Henri.

And Stein. No one was more tanned, had a richer accent, or lent more accreditation to Sugarbush's neo-European tendencies than Stein Eriksen. Stein was at the crest of his popularity in those days, and the Sugarbush was riding it like a big wave.

But things took a wrong turn somewhere. Stein split, the money started running out, the snow stopped falling, and new owners started coming and going, coming and going. To compound matters, Sugarbush acquired its floundering neighbor, Glen Ellen, renamed it Sugarbush North, and became two financially troubled areas rolled into one. There was perpetual talk of cutting trails and installing lifts that would make the two areas one, interconnected giant, an utterly spectacular ski area. But talk is all it was. The two ski areas are still two.

Meanwhile, the state of affairs started getting ragged. The gondola all but fell apart and had to be removed, to be replaced by a couple of chairs. The revolving door at the top did nothing to instill an esprit de corps among Sugarbush employees, and ticket-sellers and rental-shop fitters could be downright rude.

What's the point in rehashing this unpleasant past? Mainly to set the stage for the good news. Sugarbush is turning around. If your last Sugarbush visit left a sour aftertaste—if you remember it for some of the things I've mentioned above—I recommend your giving the place another shot.

For one thing, its current owners have been in place since 1988 and seem committed for the long run. The best thing they've done has been to install a quad-chair tandem at Sugarbush North that now gets you from base to summit—almost two miles up 2,500 vertical feet—in 13 minutes. The lower of these two quads, the Green Mountain Express, is a high-speed number touted as "the fastest chairlift in the world." I can't validate the claim, but what I do know is that the lift it replaced, a double chair, was undoubtably one of the world's *slowest*—not to mention longest and coldest. It used to be that by the time you arrived at the summit of North, you were one impatient icicle. The new lifts have changed that.

Not that the current owners haven't stumbled. One of their major objectives—that turned into a major headache—was to add more snowmaking at South. That's something that, strictly from a skier's point of view, doesn't necessarily enthuse me; I like the idea that you can have a choice here—North for manufactured snow, South for mostly natural snow. It has also been something that hasn't enthused environmentalists, whose vehement opposition delayed the project for years and cost Sugarbush several million dollars. That financial drag further caused delays in other improvements—e.g., better base lodges—on Sugarbush's drawing board.

Ah well—environmental battles aside, perhaps the best news these days at Sugarbush is a general attitude upgrade. People who work here are actually friendly; there is a true sense of welcome here that has completely displaced the sullenness I regularly encountered in the 80's.

Back to the beginning. Why do I say Sugarbush could be the best ski area in New England? Simple: It's got the mountain. Or mountains, as it were, South with 2,400 vertical feet, North with 2,600, and every foot of it legit. But its more than just a matter of size. These mountains are a jumble of flanks, ridges, glades, long drops, rolling meadows, on and on. The variety here forever amazes me. It isn't enough to say that Sugarbush has something for every sort of skier; it has a choice—several choices—of something for every skier.

A SUGARBUSH STARTER'S KIT. Remember, we're dealing with a choice of two areas—North or South?—the choice being principally between groomed cruising on manufactured snow at North or more challenging, natural-terrain skiing at South. Sure—you can find both types of skiing at either area, but the preponderance of Sugarbush skiing breaks out as I've suggested.

A free shuttle-bus service (departures every half hour) links the two areas, and the ride takes about 10 minutes. But the shuttle-bus system is just enough of a pain to make skiing both areas on the same day unlikely. On rare situations, snow conditions or crowds might lead you to switch from one area to the other, but yoyoing back and forth is unlikely. I tend to pick my preferred Sugarbush and stick with it.

Neither base area is laid out particularly well. Rather than having a single, centrally located base lodge, South has two, undersized, off-center lodges—The Gate House and the Valley House. The Gate House is the first choice of most skiers, being closer to the parking lot and the base of operations for the ski school. So it is possible to avoid the fury of the morning rush by heading for the Valley House, only to do so requires a breath-stealing uphill hoof made extra-tough under a load of ski gear.

Here's what I'd recommend: If you can get away with it, drive up to the Valley House to drop off passengers and gear, and return to the parking lot. I've never been able to figure out whether parking-lot attendants are supposed to stop you from driving up to the Valley House or not, and if you simply act as if it is your inalienable right to drive up there, you usually get away with it. At any rate, if the way is barred, you might as well hang with the masses at the Gate House.

The Sugarbush North parking lots are set on one of the steepest slopes in the world of parking lots. Don't even think twice: Drive immediately to the lodge, drop off all gear and passengers, then park. Even the walk from the uppermost lots can get the cardiovascular pump started. Take a ride on parking-lot shuttle if you don't want the aerobic workout.

Space to boot up is at a premium in the cramped base lodge, but I can usually find it in the room to the left of the stairs on the second floor. On the plus side, the undersized lodge brings all services—ticket windows, ski-school, rentals, shops, cafeteria, etc.—under one roof. That can't be said for South, where services are scattered all over the place. That makes North the more manageable of the two areas if you're trying to outfit a family or large group.

SUGARBUSH FOR NOVICES. No question: North is the preferred choice for novices. South's one novice slope, *Easy Rider*, is a flat, short shot—for true beginners only. *Lower Snowball*, from the Spring Fling

Triple Chair, and *Slow Poke*, from the Gate House Double Chair, are negotiable by confident lower-level skiers despite their blue, intermediate designation. But why bother? There is plenty of longer, wider, more interesting skiing at North for novices and lower intermediates, with faster lifts to boot. In addition, as I've already noted, the North base lodge offers one-stop shopping for skiers needing rentals and lessons, which isn't the case at South.

The novice skiing at North starts at the Ski School Double Chair, just out of the main flow of skier traffic on the ski area's lower left. Unfortunately, *Sugar Run*, running parallel to *Easy Street*, the main ski-school slope, has been turned in recent years into a recreational race arena. If racing is in session (or scheduled), that deprives novices of the chance to test their skills on a somewhat narrower terrain before heading up the big mountain. The race arena used to be on the side of super-wide *Inverness*, where it didn't seem to interfere with anyone's skiing. So it goes.

Is the Green Mountain Express indeed the fastest lift in the East? Let's see—it covers 6,280 feet in 6 1/2 minutes, which comes out to about 11 miles an hour, or slightly slower than front-running pace in the Boston Marathon. Frankly, I could care less whether or not that puts the lift a nose ahead of the rest of the lift pack. What's great about it is that it has made North an immeasurably better ski area, for novice and lower-intermediate skiers in particular. The old double chair used to wheeze its way up the mountain, typically against wind and cold, and basically taking all the fun out of skiing the lower half of the mountain.

Your first choice is *Northstar*, reached by bearing right off the lift and then making every left turn possible. Once you've mastered Northstar, you might give *Cruiser* a go. It is wide, well-groomed, and really has but one steepish pitch, just before you reach the base of the Northridge Double Chair. Whatever route you take, you finish off with *Straight Shot* under the quad. Put it all together, and you get about a two-mile run, none of it on roads or cattracks. For lower-level skiers, that's about as good as it gets in New England.

Walt's Run, from the Inverness Triple Chair, is a very different kind of novice run, but one to sample if you're a novice trying to get a feel for the breadth of variation in New England skiing. Walt's is a meandering, road-like trail through pretty stands of maple and birch, and it seems to gather in a little afternoon sun. It also is without snowmaking and is thus a good introduction to the difference between manufactured and natural-snow conditions. Don't be intimidated by the trail's first big bend; that's it's toughest moment, and everything else is a cinch after that.

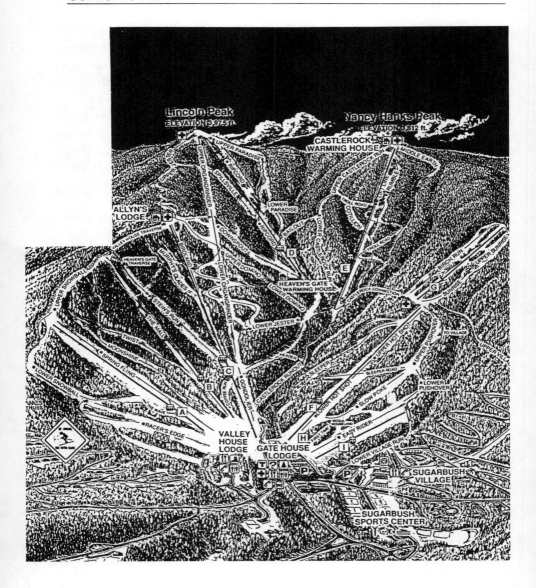

SUGARBUSH FOR CRUISERS. Further ruminations on the joys of quads: when the old slowpoke lifts were around at North, you'd be reluctant to ski top-to-bottom; the lift-riding back up was just too much of a penalty. Now the mountain's full 2,500-plus vertical is legitimately available for skiing. This is true marathon cruising—runs of 3 miles or

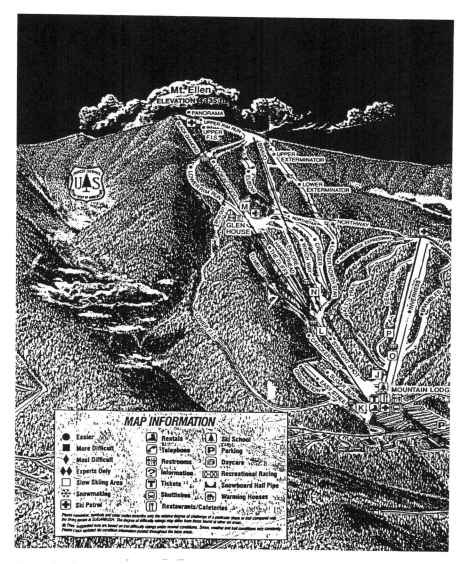

Sugarbush, a reduced view of the trail map

more, runs long enough to make you feel you should have packed a lunch for the ski down.

Start with one of the premier long cruisers in New England: upper *Rim Run* to *Elbow* to *Cruiser*. The worst part is the first part; Rim Run starts on a slick little knoll as it passes by the beginning of *Upper F.I.S.*

(*Panorama* is a knoll bypass.) Grit your teeth, bear with it, and enjoy the view, which to the north and northwest is as good as it gets in New England. The skiing quickly gets much better even if the view doesn't; Rim Run turns into a nice, easy ride through the kind of stunted, rime-encrusted trees you find at New England's higher elevations.

The pitch picks up when you pick up Elbow near the top of the North Ridge double chair. Elbow might seem a bit steep in places for an intermediate rating, but its width makes it manageable. I also have found Elbow to be among Sugarbush's most consistently well-groomed trails, with good snow to be found on the sides even later in the afternoon.

If you plan to ski just the summit chair, be sure to bear right at the opening near the bottom of Elbow that loops back to the base of the lift. But if it isn't an especially busy day, you might as well bear left and keep going to the bottom. Opt for the full length of the mountain; it's hard to find runs this long elsewhere in New England. Elbow empties onto a flat area where route-finding is made a bit confusing by a couple of tree islands. Keep your eyes pealed for Cruiser, although if you end up on *Which Way*, you won't have been cheated; the two trails are very similar in character, both dumping out onto *Straight Shot* at the base of the North Ridge double.

If the North Ridge chair doesn't have a line—and it almost never does—you might want to ride it back up. It is a better deal than the trail map, which shows the lift covering 1,100 vertical feet, implies. I've just got to believe the trail-map vertical is underestimated by at least two hundred feet. Riding the double allows you not only to bypass the lift lines that can form at the two quads but also to bypass the flats both at the top (upper Rim Run) and the bottom (Straight Shot). However, it's obviously slower, and when you can spot through the trees lift-riders on the Green Mountain Express rocketing by you, you might feel a sense of psychological defeat.

Let's go quickly back to the summit. At the intersection of Rim Run and Elbow, most skiers either take Elbow (as I've suggested) or continue on the easier pitch of Rim Run, which makes a big, looping S back to the Summit Quad base. Between Elbow and Rim Run is a third trail, *Lookin' Good.* Most skiers seem to miss it, so that I have often found it to have the best snow of the three trails, especially in the section before it bears left and becomes the quad liftline. By sticking to the high side of the lift line—the left side—you're also apt to find some of the best snow on the upper mountain.

I can't leave North without mentioning a couple of trails from the

Inverness Quad. The width of *Inverness*, beneath the chair, seem make the trail a sun magnet, a blessing on cold days. *Semi-tough*, to the right of the lift, is the antithesis of Inverness—a narrow winder without snowmaking. You may or may not like it—it's narrow, pitch-varying quirkiness is a bit old-fashioned. But if nothing else, you've got to like the pretty, soulful birch glade that marks its beginning.

On to South. The Gate House chair gets a fair amount of traffic—mainly, I suppose, because it's easy to get to after you've bought tickets and geared up in the Gate House—but I find the skiing bland and rhythm-less. However, the chair does provide access to the North Link poma, one of South's undiscovered gems.

All right—I admit that there are drawbacks. The exposure (facing east) isn't ideal; sun and wind tend to beat up the snow, and there is no snowmaking for a quick fix. The poma often isn't running. And it is a poma, which turns off many skiers.

So why recommend skiing here? First, almost no one skis North Link. So while others are waiting in lines elsewhere at the ski area, you can easily be putting in six runs an hour over at North Link.

Second, when there is snow and the poma is running, the skiing can be terrific. There are just two trails, *Birch Run* and *Sunrise*, but with so few skiers, who needs more? Of the two, I prefer Sunrise; it's just a little bit steeper at the top. Don't be turned off by a few exposed rocks near the top; pick your way through them so that you can launch into the wide open, gentle trail that Sunrise turns into. Because of the lack of skier traffic, this can be a good spot to find patches of powder—especially if you're just trying to get the hang of powder skiing techniques—for days following a storm.

In terms of vertical efficiency, it's hard to do much better than the Valley House chair, which climbs 1,250 vertical feet in 7 minutes. By comparison, the Sugar Bravo triple, which runs approximately parallel and reaches slightly higher up the same ridge, takes 12 minutes to cover 1,525 vertical feet. If that sounds like number overload, figure it this way: The Valley House chair takes a straighter, steeper line to the top. I'm not knocking the Sugar Bravo terrain, but I find myself skiing the Valley House chair a lot when I'm at Sugarbush because it gives me a lot of skiing for my time and money.

It also gives me a couple of great intermediate choices. Legitimate choices, too: The main intermediate route, a combination of *Snowball* and *Spring Fling*, is a completely different trail concept than is *Moonshine*, the other top choice. One is a wide open cruiser, with lots of neat rolls at the top (in the Snowball section) leading to a long, straight fall-line shot for the second half (the Spring Fling half).

Moonshine, on the other hand, is a gladed trail, with the trees fairly tight for intermediate terrain. Lack of steepness, however, makes the tightness manageable. Just be prepared for a few of those infamous "unmarked obstacles," especially if it has been a while since a fresh snowfall—grooming machines can't get into the trees.

Despite its less efficient climb up the mountain, the Sugar Bravo chair might be a better option on crowded days. Because the chair is a triple, you can usually make good time working through the singles line. *Birdland*, the trail beneath the lift, is a straight, fast shot, perfect for long, wide-radius turning. *Murphy's Glades* is not a real glade as I would define the concept—that is, it's basically a wide trail with a few trees that add to the trail's aesthetics rather than the challenge. This is not nearly the tight tree skiing you'll find on Moonshine.

Except to take in the view on a nice day, there isn't much point in intermediate skiers in venturing up the Heaven's Gate lift. The only real intermediate way down from the summit is *Jester*, and it's something of a bore—just a half dozen or so big turns back and forth across the fall line. The best intermediate skiing starts from the top of the Birdland chair, so why bother going any higher?

HALFTIME. At North, you'll do better lunching at the Glen House, half way up the mountain, than at the base lodge, although the upstairs deck at the base lodge is a great hang-out on a sunny day. As for South, my preference would be to pack a picnic lunch and eat at Allyn's Lodge, at the Sugar Bravo summit. Allyn's doesn't serve food and doesn't have bathrooms, two shortcomings that seem to drive most people away. What I like is that it's clean, warm, cozy, and uncrowded. If you've got your own food, who needs a bathroom?

SUGARBUSH FOR ADVANCED SKIERS. Upper F.I.S., one of North's featured expert trails, presents a great case for not making snow on super-steeps. The ski area absolutely blasts the trail with the dense artificial stuff, so that conditions are good for spring mogul contests, when the snow softens. Unfortunately, spring is just about the only time the trail is skiable, or at least *enjoyably* skiable. Before that, the hardness of the snow, hardened further by the trail's exposure to wind, make skiing Upper F.I.S. a pretty unpleasant experience.

To be sure, Upper F.I.S. skiing might be reasonably fun after a big dump of, say, two feet of snow, but on powder days, there are other places I'd rather be at Sugarbush. No—I don't think ski areas should make snow on steep trails, especially steep, narrow trails like *Hammerhead*, a through-the-trees sliver lower down the mountain. Man-made snow is denser than natural snow and must be turned over regularly to work air into it. But when groomers can't get to snow on trails because they are too steep or narrow, things can get very ugly.

But forget about that. Let's talk about the good expert skiing at Sugarbush, of which there is plenty. With soft, natural snow conditions, the combination of *Black Diamond* to *Lower F.I.S.* is a personal favorite. Black Diamond, North's Summit Quad liftline, is a good long shot of true double-diamond steepness, and you'd better be ready to turn precisely—the lift towers make a narrow ski trail extra narrow.

After Black Diamond's steepness, the lower half of the liftline, *Lookin' Good*, might come as welcome relief as a groomed cruiser. Look for the right fork before the lift base that takes you to *Spinout*, an undiscovered and underskied little trail that hooks up with Lower F.I.S. I've found some great powder stashes here, and returning up to the summit have found that my tracks were still the only ones through those stashes. As for Lower F.I.S., it isn't steep, but it's fun because it's a trail of singular character—a little narrow, with a little bit of double fall line, eventually turning into a long narrow run-out. There's something backwoods about Lower F.I.S. that I like.

The better expert skiing is certainly at South, which headlines three true classics of Eastern skiing. Classic I is *Stein's Run*, or simply Stein's, as everyone calls it. Stein Eriksen has made a name for himself at Deer Valley, Utah, as a guy who believes in cutting trails flush to the fall line, and he cut his trail-cutting teeth at Sugarbush. Stein's Run is Stein's philosophy at its best (once you've snuck around the rocks and roots at the narrow entryway): a straight, on-the-fall-line mogul blast. The moguls on Stein's always seem to be well-formed, largely because the consistency in the trail's steepness, along with its wideness, allows you to ski long, rhythmic stints.

Classic II is *Paradise*, perhaps the best powder run in the East. As a trail without snowmaking and with a stubbled sub-surface, Paradise requires lots of natural snow to make it skiable—the reason it's often closed. But after the storms come, the skiing can be movie-quality stuff. It's really a series of connected pockets in the mountain, flanked in places with little gladed areas. The trail is shielded well from the wind, preserving the fluffiness of the powder snow. I can honestly say that I have never had a bad run on Paradise, but that's because I have gone by the local code: I ski it sparingly. That is, I think of it as a powder trail and nothing else, so I'd suggest not spoiling your expectations by skiing it if conditions aren't just right.

Classic III is *Rumble*, over at Castle Rock, by no means a trail to suit all tastes. It is so narrow that skiing it feels more like skiing through a tunnel of trees; I'd doubt the trail ever gets more than about 15 feet wide. It winds and falls over rocks, ledges, stumps, and roots, and if there hasn't been a recent snowfall, it is merciless on ski bases. In other words, take your rock skis. What makes Rumble fun is the sheer mental challenge it poses. If you manage to figure out a way to link together five or six clean turns here, you're doing pretty good.

Castle Rock in general is a pretty funky place to ski, very similar in character to Mad River. All the skiing isn't as narrow as on Rumble, but the general features are steeps, terrain variations, ledges, moguls—in a way, in-bounds backcountry skiing. It's not for everyone—the skiing is quirky, gnarly, arythmic. Enough people, however, do appreciate it to attract lift lines, which can grow long quickly at Castle Rock, especially during the 10:30-11;00 A.M. rush hour. The lift is a double chair with 15-second gaps between chairs, making the uphill capacity pretty minimal.

Why no faster lift? The narrow trails of Castle Rock simply can't bear a lot of skier traffic. If you rushed more skiers up Castle Rock, you'd have to widen trails to accommodate them, in which case Castle Rock wouldn't be Castle Rock any more.

I should mention the expert trails (other than Paradise) from the Heaven's Gate chair. The featured run over here is *Ripcord*, a slightly mellower version of Upper F.I.S. It, too is a steepster with manufactured snow, although I've had much better luck on Ripcord finding decent skiing than on F.I.S. Like F.I.S., however, it can catch wind, making it an unpleasant place to be on cold, blustery days. When the snow is soft, a better option is *Spillsville*, which runs alongside Ripcord. Spillsville is sort of a Stein's cut in half—an on-the-fall-line mogul run at half the width of Stein's. Unless it's a powder day and Paradise is open, however, I generally prefer the Valley House skiing to the Heaven's Gate skiing, with *Twist*, a trail that starts out steeply and then connects nicely with the glades of Moonshine, and Stein's being the two main choices.

One last note: Sugarbush does have some good tree skiing—especially at North and in the Slide Brook drainage between the two areas. My rule for off-trail tree-skiing is to find a knowledgeable local to guide you; getting lost or injured in the Vermont woods in winter can, literally, be a deadly proposition. Sugarbush has talked about a guided, off-trail tree-skiing program; if you're interested, check at the ski school desk to see if the program has come on line.

SNOWBOARDING. If you've got plenty of skill and moxey, Castlerock Lift Line is a terrific snowboarding challenge. With small cliff bands, exposed rocks and stumps, steep drop-offs, a strangely contoured fall line, and other obstacles and hazards too numerous to mention. It is a trail with the potential to either exhilerate or injure. If you're not up to it—and, to be honest, few skiers or snowboarders are—the long, groomed descents at North, such as the Rim Run-Elbow-Cruiser combo, is great cruise country. The problem for snowboarders is the flat section near the bottom, so be sure to carry enough speed to maintain momentum across the flats.

THE POST-GAME SHOW. I have a confession to make: I was caught a number of years ago dancing on the roof of the Blue Tooth, the hot spot halfway down the Access Road, on my birthday. Just shows you that the place has been known to get lively enough to get a deadbeat like me going. For lower-key apres-ski, Sam Rupert's, up nearer the ski area, has a nice, relaxed way about it. The food's not bad either. Mooselips, at the junction of Routes 100 and 17, has such an unappealing name that I've steered clear of the place, but I'm told it draws a youngish, lively crowd.

As for dining, the Tucker Hill Lodge is tough to beat, but there are several good restaurants in the area. Low-end dining can be a tough find, though; Beggars Banquet and the Den, both in Waitsfield, are probably the best bets for the budget-minded.

In simplified terms, lodging breaks down to a choice between mountainside condos and country inns in the valley. For some reason, Sugarbush Village (the mountainside village) has never caught my fancy; maybe it's lifelessness has to do with its odd location on the far side of the Sugarbush South parking lot. At any rate, my own choice would be to go with the country-inn-in-the-valley concept, and there are many good variations on the theme.

SUGARBUSH DATA
Pluses and Minuses:
Pluses: great terrain variety, new quad lifts at Sugarbush North, large vertical drop. Minuses: inconvenient two-area arrangement, awkward parking/base-area layouts.

Key Phone Numbers:
Ski Area Information: 802-583-2381
Lodging Information: 800-537-8427
Snow Phone: 802-583-7669
Location: **Sugarbush South: 3-mile Access Road begins two miles north of Warren on Route 100. Sugarbush North: 2 miles north of Sugarbush South via German Flats Road from Access Road; or 3 miles southeast of Waitsfield via Route 17. Mailing address: RR1 Box 350, Warren, VT 05674.**
Mountain Statistics:
Vertical Rise: 2,600 feet
Summit elevation: 4,083 feet
Base elevation: 1,483 feet
Number of trails: 80
Lifts: 3 quad chairs, 6 doubles, 3 triples, 4 surface lifts
Average annual snowfall: 250 inches
Snowmaking coverage: 50% (184 acres)

ALSO KEEP IN MIND. . .*Middlebury College Snow Bowl*

For me, going to ski at the Snow Bowl has an atmosphere similar to going to a neighbor's house for a backyard barbecue. It's so simple, relaxed, and neighborly in the sense that about three quarters of the Snow Bowl skiers on any given day seem to know each other. One other thing I like about the Snow Bowl is that it is an imitation of no one; it follows the beat of its own drummer. It has, for example, a reading room in its small, cozy base lodge, but no bar. It has no base-area lodging and none very nearby—the town of Middlebury is a 20-minute drive away.

The trail layout is a quirky one; the front, northern-facing side of the mountain is plagued by flat spots, including one right off the top of the lift. But there is some interesting skiing; the bottlenecks, multiple fall lines, and pitch changes of *Allen*, for example, can make it like three or four expert trails rolled into one. Although runs tend to be shorter than I like, there is enough of a mountain here to have allowed Middlebury to host the collegiate skiing championships.

One thing the Snow Bowl offers that has become a rarity in skiing is a half-day morning ticket. Clever marketing went into this one: the Snow Bowl folks figured the morning half-day ticket would be an enticement for Sunday skiers who wanted their afternoons open for the drive home.

INSIDE STORY
HOW SWEET IT IS!
ON THE MAPLE SUGAR TRAIL

Sometime in mid-March in New England, when the days grow longer and warmer and the nights continue to be cold, maple-tree sap gets a wake-up call. The warms days allow the sap to run and the cold nights keep it from running too fast. These are the timed-release conditions sugar harvesters have prepared for, and the short sugaring season begins.

Trees have been tapped, buckets, hoses, and collection bins put in place in the "sugarbush"—the collective word for the hundreds or thousands of trees from which each producer draws sap. Enough wood to keep the average home fireplace going for a decade has been sawed up and split to fuel sugarhouse boilers. The sap runs, and the sugarhouse becomes for a few weeks a small hive of industrial and social activity. Two or three weeks is about it, until the sap run is spent and the sap boiled into syrup, to be canned and delivered to market.

These are a few weeks in the life of New England that, despite the condoization of farmland and the modernization of farming in general, hasn't changed a whole lot. To be sure, some sugar producers have upgraded the process by replacing buckets on trees with networks of hoses or use larger, more efficient stoves (called evaporators). But maple syrup production is still largely the business of hundreds of small-time operators, many or most being old-time New Englanders with farming roots, for whom maple sap is the one cash crop of winter. They do things more or less the way they have been done for generations—in part because employing traditiona l methodology is just their nature and in part because they can calculate the basic economies of the business by going with methods their familiar with. The years of experience have taught how to balance costs—wood for fuel and man-hours primarily—and revenues—the amount of syrup they can produce in an average year. Also—or so it seems to me from the sugarers I've talked to—they like the seasonal tradition of the old process, despite annual complaints about the weather not being right, the sap running fast, slow or dirty, the syrup output being too small to be profitable or so great as to drive prices down.

Vermont, of course, isn't the only northeastern state in which maple syrup are produced. However, there are more Vermont sugarers (about

*3,000) producing more syrup (up to 500,000 gallons a year) of a gener-
ally higher quality than you'll typically find in New Hampshire or Maine.
The subtle differences in soil, terrain, trees, and climate are the reasons
behind that. Vermont, for example has a system for rating maple-syrup
quality, a system based mainly on the syrup's color. The paler the color,
theoretically the cleaner the syrup and the higher the grade (as well as
the price). A darker color generally as an indication of more wood
residue in the syrup. I personally prefer the lower-grade syrup—the
darker, mustier stuff—but maple-syrup appreciation, like appreciation of
wines, is all a matter of taste.*

*Now, if you want to put your taste to the test, the best way to do so as
far as I'm concerned is to visit a sugarhouse when the sugaring season is
in session (usually beginning in the second or third week in March). The
Vermont Department of Agriculture publishes a list of sugarers who
welcome visitors, and you should be able to find the list at any of the
Vermont visitor centers that dot the state. A similar list is available from
the New Hampshire Maple Producers, 28 Peabody Row, Londonderry,
NH 03503.*

*But even sugarers not on the state's list aren't apt to turn you away.
Sugarhouse visiting used to be something of a New England tradition,
one that a sugar producer told me has been on the wane in recent years.
It used to be that friends of the sugar producer—or just passers-by—
might drop by for a couple of hours to shoot the breeze and pass the time,
helping to enliven the steamy, laborious business of turning sap into
syrup. When as much as 40 gallons of sap most be boiled away in
evaporators before a single gallon of syrup can be drawn off, days of
stirring, fire-stoking, and taste-testing can run long and slow.*

*So if you're in Vermont (or New Hampshire or Maine for that matter)
in late March, and especially if you're wandering the backroads, look for
steam rising from a small, ramshackle shack. Drop in, especially during
the apres-ski hours, when the sugaring day is beginning to drag on. I'd
be surprised if your company wasn't welcomed, and sampling the fresh
syrup is always part of the deal.*

Chapter 4
Northern Vermont

VERMONT'S FAR NORTH is a chessboard of contrasts. The topography, the relative degree of human settlement, the tendencies of weather, local personality types, local economies—all can change so completely within a matter of miles that driving through the area can be like moving from black square to white, from one environment entirely into another.

Start with Burlington, Vermont's largest city. Lying in the low, rolling meadowlands along the glacial plain of Lake Champlain, Burlington boomed with mall sprawl and sub-division development in the 80's. If you didn't know any better today, you might think you were in suburban New Jersey. By Vermont standards, the Burlington area is flat, climatically mild, and not especially snowy.

Just 20 miles west, though, is the imposing presence of Mt. Mansfield, Vermont's highest peak, and its adjoining ridges and peaks, within which Bolton Valley, Smuggler's Notch, and Stowe are nested. This is ski country—the Stowe area especially, having been one of the original nodes of Vermont skiing. The countryside is speckled with the inns, restaurants, ski shops—the sort of business and industry skiing and tourism tend to attract.

Move west and north from here, though, and civilization begins to fall away. Very quickly you enter a Vermont of a previous generation: farms and wooded hillsides and long stretches of roadway between towns. Stop in a local grocery store, and you're likely to end up standing in line with people in ear-flapped flannel hats rather than powder suits. In the middle of this throwback world is Jay Peak, which emerges from the landscape just when you're wondering if you've made a wrong turn back there somewhere and about five miles before you end up in Canada. Jay Peak is notorious for snagging snow clouds that bypass other places, and when the brown earth of the Burlington countryside is showing through patches of snow, the snowpack around Jay Peak can be five feet or more.

Further west still is the Northeast Kingdom, Vermont's retreat country, a world of fjord-like lakes, mid-sized mountains, and backroads. Despite economic hardship brought on by a lack of industry, the Northeast Kingdom still has a reputation for a fiercely anti-development spirit, and resident and visitor tend to like it here because of the absence of civilization. Hence, there is only one ski area of any note in the Northeast Kingdom, that being modest-sized Burke Mountain.

A contributing factor, certainly, to the chessboard contrast of northern Vermont is the way in which the mountains naturally compartmentalize parts of the land. Things might be close, but there are few short cuts in getting from one place to the next. For example, one can literally ski in a matter of seconds from Stowe to Smuggler's Notch—Smuggler's is right off the backside of Stowe's Spruce Peak—but to drive from one to the other in winter takes close to an hour on a 40-mile loop around the Mt. Mansfield massif.

For that reason, anyone who likes skiing more than one area in a single ski trip would probably do better staying farther south in Vermont. In northern Vermont, you're more likely to commit yourself to a single area, and toward that end, the three principal areas—Jay, Smugglers, and Stowe (with Bolton to consider as well)—hold forth distinctly different experiences. Jay, equal parts American and French Canadian, is big skiing in the middle of nowhere; Smugglers is a self-contained resort combining a strong family push with first-rate expert skiing; Stowe is resort-town, tradition, and a wide variety of skiing wrapped in bustle. If you like action on and off the slopes, Stowe is your northern Vermont choice.

JAY PEAK

Around Jay Peak, there is a localized weather tendency that people like referring to as "six inches of partly cloudy." This is not a truth-stretching invention of the public-relations department, because I've seen it with my own eyes. Start with distant, hazy sun in a gray-blue sky, toss a few flakes in the air, and next thing you know, it's a powder day at Jay.

Jay's northerly latitude and its knack for turning flurries into storms has made it *the* Vermont ski area for anyone who thought natural snow had become an historical, global-warming oddity. Jay claims an average annual snowfall of 296 inches, a figure comparable to snowfalls at major

Rocky Mountain resorts. Ski areas are notorious for inflated snowfall measuring practices, but I've had such good skiing at Jay every time I've been there that I'm willing to believe that the 296-inch figure is right on the mark.

The allure of that considerable snowfall has certainly not been lost on skier population of greater Montreal, the closest metropolitan area (other than Burlington) to Jay. The large number of French-speaking Quebecoise who prefer Jay to ski areas north of the border have made this America's most bilingual ski area. I'm sure the language business can be a nightmare for hotel clerks and ski instructors (though French-speaking employees are numerous), but I find it lends Jay a certain, as we might say *au francaise*, panache. Sure, it *looks* like Vermont, but it can *sound* like Chamonix.

Jay's northerly location influences its character in ways other than language and snowfall. For one thing, Jay is an exposed mountain, the northernmost vertebra in the Green Mountain spine that runs up the center of Vermont. Northern and exposed can translate into cold and windy. On those days when the summit wind is an arctic gale from the north quarter, the enclosed tram can offer welcome protection. Don't count on it though; a not-uncommon northeaster at 50+ mph can force a tram shutdown. If such conditions prevail, Smugglers Notch and Stowe are better northern-Vermont alternatives to Jay.

Jay's location also has it more removed from civilization than any other ski area in Vermont. The closest towns are Jay (6 miles east) and Montgomery (7 miles west), both blink-or-you'll-miss-'em crossroad hamlets. They're the sorts of communities rural enough to have kept alive bartering—e.g., I'll swap the haying rights on my land for a side of beef from your cattle stock. We're talking small-town: I've been told that Montgomery has a community meat locker for local folk who lack electric refrigerators.

There is nothing slickly cosmopolitan about the ski area's base village, either. It's a cluster of functional buildings in the neo-chalet mold (i.e., stucco walls, pine siding, big eaves) and undersized. At last count, the base area's hotel-and-condo bed total was just 800, not a heck of a lot for a ski area that can put more than 7,000 skiers an hour up the mountain. It's no surprise, then, that the ski area's owners have an expansionist master plan, but I've seen many a master plan languish on the drawing table.

What it boils down to is that Jay is a skiers' ski area; you come here to ski and escape civilization, not much else. Nightlife consists mainly of dinner and moon-watching, a combination that will probably prove numbingly ascetic for anyone with even the slightest inclination toward dancing the night away. At Jay, you either drum up your own entertainment or go to bed early to be ready for the next day's skiing, which is what Jay is all about anyway.

Indeed, by my subjective evaluation, Jay ranks alongside Sugarbush and Stowe among Vermont ski areas in featuring a wide variety of terrain for skiers of all abilities. It might, in fact, hold an edge over the other two in its novice terrain; the long flats near the tram base that are somewhat annoying for better skiers are ideal for beginners and kids.

Jay has been called "an explorers' mountain"—an apt description, I think. Its layout is of the sort that allows you to ski trails in differing combinations—that is, combining a section of one trail with sections of others—so that you can ski a segment of the mountain for several runs without skiing the same route twice. In addition, the healthy annual dose of natural snow allows for venturing along the edges of trails, onto gladed runs, between trails, and into the trees. Finally, lots of snow usually means late, long-lasting snow, so that Jay might well be Vermont's premier spring-skiing area.

A JAY STARTER KIT. Jay is a two-base area: the tram base, which is the central location for lodging, dining, ski school, ski and rental shops, etc.; and the few-frills Stateside base (the base of the Jet Triple Chair), with a small, functional lodge, a place to buy tickets, a parking lot, and not much else. On a busy weekend day or holiday, the better choice for drive-in skiers, especially those arriving early, is the Stateside base. (If you need any services, of course—lessons, rentals, food, etc.—you'll need to set up base camp on the tram side.)

Because most skiers park at (or are staying at) the tram base, lines at Stateside's Jet chair tend not to begin forming till around 10:00 A.M., when skiers from the tram side start filtering over. One drawback is that there is no shuttle bus connecting the two base areas, so if you end up at the tram base after the lifts close and you wanted to be at the Jet base, you've got a long, cold two-mile walk or hitch ahead of you. If you're hungry for the tram base's meager apres-ski action, the thing to do is drive from Stateside after skiing.

Conversely, anyone overnighting at Jay—ergo, staying at the tram base—should try to work over to the Jet base as early as possible. You can do this by avoiding the tram: Ride the Green Mountain double chair and cut across on lower Goat Run. The tram is terrific on cold days and powder days, but on crowded days, the line moves slowly. Keep in mind that more than 75 percent of Jay's terrain can be skied without riding the tram, and long lines rarely form at the chairs.

JAY FOR NOVICES. Jay ski instructors tell me that *Interstate* and *Harmony Lane*, the two gentle slopes serviced by the Metro t-bar, make for some of the best teaching terrain they've seen anywhere. They're right for a few reasons. For one thing, both slopes are wide; I'd estimate each, on average, to be about 50 yards or more wide. They're also long; I'd eyeball each at around a half mile from the top of the t-bar to the base. In addition, it's one of those t-bars from which you can bail out at almost any point along the way—a good option for kids and first-timers.

One thing that's also nice about the two trails is that they are right at the base area, in the main flow of the Jay action. Such a layout is not always a good thing, since it brings together skiers of all abilities— novices and better skiers coming down from the summit—on the same slope. That can lead to friction, both physical and psychological. But at Jay, Interstate and Harmony Lane are so wide that better skiers can zoom by harmlessly, almost unnoticed. Given all that space, I think it's a great advantage not having novices or kids shuttled off to some secluded bunny slope, lost there to family and friends for the rest of the day. At Jay, everyone can meet for lunch, between runs, or even for a quick run together.

Jay's major drawback for novice skiers is that it lacks a good variety of novice terrain from the upper lifts. Once you've mastered Interstate and Harmony Lane, the lower half of *Goat Run*, from the top of the Green Mountain chair, is probably the next best route. It has a good, lower-intermediate pitch, but it has a couple of drawbacks. It is used by many skiers as an access route to the Stateside lifts, so especially during a post-lunch rush, it can be populated with more fast skiers than an unsure, lower-intermediate would want to deal with. The other thing is that it's important to keep an eye out for the cut-off left (look for the t-bar terminal) onto *Queen's Highway*, which leads back to the tram base. If you miss it, you'll end up at the Stateside base, where there is little skiing for lower-level skiers.

On a clear day, the tram ride to the summit is worthwile for the view alone, but the lower-intermediate pickings from the summit are meager. (there is the option of riding the tram back down.) Your best bet, if you want to give it a go, is to try the combination of *Vermonter* to *Angel's Wiggle* to *Milk Run*. It's a route with a couple of steeper pitches and tricky intersections, but it's probably the easiest way down. The best thing to do, if you go for the tram ride to the summit, is to let summit clear of skiers before you mount up and head off. (There's a place at the tram terminal to wait inside.) You've got 10 minutes or so before the next tram load, and if you wait a few minutes, you can ski down with the top third of the run virtually to yourself.

JAY FOR CRUISERS. The main cluster of intermediate trails at Jay lies between the Jet triple and the Bonaventure quad chairs. You can also get to these trails from the tram, but really all the tram ride adds is the ridgeline run along *Vermonter*. While the views from Vermonter can be inspiring on a clear day, the run itself is no great shakes and is exposed to mean weather. If you like skiing this trail cluster, you're better off— unless the tram line is short—using the quad or the triple as your main access lift, with the quad lines usually being shorter.

I have a tough time figuring out which trail is which on this part of the mountain, since the trails wind back and forth across one another in a latticework maze. That's neat stuff; it means you can ski the trails in different combinations, enhancing the ski day with sense of variation.

I've found myself more or less following my skis through here, assuming the skis know as I do that all trails eventually lead to the bottom. In fact, this is one of the appealing aspects of skiing this trail cluster. The trails meander in an old-fashioned way, which I find more interesting than the more modern, straight-to-the-fall-line trails. At the same time, they are relatively wide, *Angel's Wiggle* especially, to be able to ski them with wide-radius GS turns.

Because Angel's Wiggle is the widest, it's the most obvious route to take through the maze. As a result, it can be heavily trafficked and is probably the most popular trail on the mountain. If you have a hard time finding elbow room on the Wiggle, there are a couple of good alternatives. You can ski off onto *Paradise Meadows*, a natural-snow track to the right that can be terrific if there's been a recent snowfall. Or, when the Wiggle makes a big wiggle to the right, you can stay straight to *Milk Run*. The difference in pitch and character between Angel's Wiggle and Milk Run is minimal, except that Milk Run gets slightly less skier traffic.

Probably the most underutilized lift at Jay is the Green Mountain chair, where there is never much of a line. That's probably because the lift is old and slow, and it doesn't begin to gain much elevation until after the long Interstate flats. Why bother with it, then? As slow as the lift might be, it still beats waiting in the tram line, which can get pretty backed up

Jay Peak, a reduced view of the trail map

after lunch. It also has two steepish cruisers, *Green Mountain Boy* and *Racer*, short but interesting enough to keep you occupied until the post-lunch tram line begins to dissipate. And in crummy weather—i.e., windy and cold—the lift is lower and on a somewhat more sheltered side of the mountain than the other lifts.

What does the tram have to offer cruisers? *Ullr's Dream*, from the top

of the tram, has just about everything you'd want for big-turning terrain. It's wide, pitched for fast skiing, generally covered with well-groomed snow, and surrounded by terrific views. It's also underpopulated. That's because getting there requires taking the hairpin turn to the right off Vermonter and onto the catwalk that winds around the mountain's backside. Most skiers allow themselves to be sucked straight down

Vermonter. But Ullr's Dream comes with a drawback—a long (and I mean *long*) run-out to the base. On Jay's master plan is a proposed lift up that side (the western side) of the mountain, which would do away with the run-out. It's a great idea, but not one likely to become reality soon.

One improvement Jay already has made, however, has been to cut a couple of intermediate-level glade runs. Bravo! Among the relatively new additions to Jay's trail network, *Stateside Glade*, which runs along the lower half of the Jet triple, and *Bonaventure Glade*, just beyond the juncture of Angel's Wiggle and Milk Run, are nice, woodsy antidotes to the ultra-wide Can-Am Super Trail (see Jay for Advanced Skiers). Stateside is the gentler, more open of the two; Bonaventure is a little steeper, a little tighter, a little more likely to have moguls. Regardless, I applaud Jay for bringing the experience of tree skiing—to my mind, more appropriate to New England than super-trail skiing—to intermediate skiers. Keep in mind that the best glade skiing tends to be best after a fresh snowfall (what kind of skiing isn't, I suppose); the ungroomed snow can get choppy and uneven.

HALFTIME. Ouch. The cafeteria food at the tram base is okay, and the minimal offerings at the tram summit station at least come with a view. But Jay is hurting when it comes to atmospheric lunch spots. Perhaps your best lunch bet is the pizza pub downstairs—good pizza with garage-like ambience. And the made-to-order sandwiches at the Stateside cafeteria make for a good lunch at a reasonable price, although the atmosphere—picnic tables in a warehouse-like setting—is sorely lacking. On a warm, spring day, I'd recommend packing lunch for a trailside picnic; the country store in Jay has pretty good sandwiches and salads at very reasonable prices. As for a picnic site, the summit rocks just outside the tram building are great on a windless day, although reaching them requires a little scrambling. You might also look for spots along the edge of Ullr's Dream, which is wide and smothered in afternoon sun.

JAY FOR ADVANCED SKIERS. You want radical? Jay's got radical. Check out the Saddle, an unmarked (i.e., out-of-bounds) sliver of a chute through the cliffs between the top of the tram and a run called Green Beret. There's about as much room to turn here as there is on the inside of a toothpaste tube. It's so steep that you'll be lucky if you're skiing on snow all the way—your first turn is likely to cause everything skiable to sluff, leaving nothing but an exposed cliff. Enjoy!

Fortunately, since the ski patrol frowns with ticket-taking menace at anyone skiing the Saddle, you needn't feel compelled to ski it in order to earn your Jay spurs. But that ought to give you an idea that Jay can dish it out to the max, if that's what you're looking for.

Advanced skiers who value health and longevity will, of course, be interested in more sensible options. The best place to start, especially on a busy day, is the Jet chair, roughly 1,600 vertical feet of new-breed New England skiing. By new-breed I mean flush-to-the-fall-line trails covered with groomed, manufactured snow—skiing that's smooth, soft, and fast for the first few runs before turning progressively slick and skied-off as the day wears on.

Jet, the trail beneath the chair, is a very popular straight-shot, especially speedball skiers. That means the groomed snow can get slicked out early, sometimes by 11:00 A.M. on a busy day. Before that, though— before the crowds appear and the snow surface gets scratchy—it's a good, steep cruiser, good warm-up stuff. On Jet, the Jay people do something I think should be done more often at other areas: They allow a sector of the trail under the lift to turn to moguls. You can get your mogul legs and rhythm going here without committing yourself to a full mogul run by dividing your time between the bumps and the groomed snow.

For more groomed skiing, slip to the far left of the Jet chair trail system to *Derrick's Hot Shot*. Most skiers allow themselves to be sucked onto *Haynes*, a wider trail just before you get to Derrick's. I don't know why. Derrick's is the more interesting trail—a little narrower, with a couple of turns and fall line variations in it, and with less skier traffic. You may or may not agree that it's the better trail when you ski it, but if you *don't* like it, you can exit, stage right, to Haynes, via any of a half dozen or so connector trails through the trees.

The one trail in this system I wouldn't recommend is *U.N.*, a too-narrow alley of artificial-snow moguls. The moguls I've experienced there, even after a fresh snowfall, were harder than glazed bricks. A mogul trail that *is* a pleasure on this side of the mountain is *Kitzbuehel*, to the right of the Jet triple. It's got a couple of interesting turns to it, along with a double fall that keeps wanting to toss you into the woods to the left.

I'd recommend staying high and right and recommend taking the lesser skied right fork around an island of trees near the top. The right-side snow I have experienced has been better, and the moguls seem less brutish. But I know local skiers who insist that you get the best snow by skiing a tight line along the left side. All I know is that Kitzbuehel provides a good physical *and* mental workout, and if you finish off the run by skiing through *Stateside Glade*, one of a couple of intermediate-pitch gladed trails the Jay Peak people have wisely cut, you'll have pieced together one of the most interesting trail combinations on the mountain.

Not nearly so interesting is the *Can-Am Super Trail* alongside the Bonaventure Quad. For my tastes, the trail is a marketing-driven mistake, a sell-by-numbers kind of trail—150 feet wide! 4,000 feet long! 1,800 foot vertical!—that eastern areas in the 80's seemed to feel was essential to their competitive success in an expanding age of quad-chair, high-traffic skiing. I wouldn't bother mentioning it here, except that you must cross it in order to reach *Lift Line*, beneath the Bonaventure Quad, which *is* worth skiing. As you ride the lift, you might notice, toward the top, good soft snow directly beneath you. You might wonder, "Why hasn't this been skied?" Then, when you try to traverse to it across Can-Am, you'll learn why. Holding a traverse across the slick "super trail" is as challenging as anything at Jay; by the time you've completed the crossing, you've probably lost a few hundred vertical feet just slipping and sliding. All I can say is, stick with it. If you can hold your traverse, the skiing under the chair, which turns to a fine, intermediate-level mogul run as the lift line enters the trees, is ample reward.

Rolfe Barron, a Jay ski instructor, suggested to me that Jay reminds him of a miniature Jackson Hole. There's some validity in the analogy, although maybe it's just the fact that both have trams that makes it seem so. At any rate, it's a trail like *Green Beret* that really bears the analogy out. Jackson is a ski area that turns gnarl into virtue, and so it is with Green Beret. Its entry, a couple of hundred yards from left of the tram summit, seems utterly unskiable. It looks to be nothing but wind-scoured crud decorated with a stubble of rocks and scrub trees.

Stick with it. After the first odd two turns, the trail opens into a little mini-bowl, where loose snow collects in abundance on the right side. This narrows quickly to throat with a large rock as its Adam's apple; either ski around the rock or go for Jackson-caliber air. The trail then bends right into another mini-bowl cache of soft snow before flushing over one last, big-air bump onto Northway. It's one of those trails in which about 2,500 vertical feet worth of variation is compressed into about 800 vertical feet.

Another Jackson reminder is *River Kwai*, beneath the tram line. The twisting-fall-line, between-the-rocks complexity of the trail is also very

Jackson-like, not to mention the very Jackson-like tram passing directly overhead. It's a complexity that almost demands that you ski the trail twice, since it takes one run just to figure out how to ski it. I'd say the best line comes from skiing the steep ridge of moguls on the far right, working left through a rocky narrows where the trail flattens out, then skiing the far left before the trail crosses over Goat Run. The fall line after the narrows tends to flush most skiers onto the right side; since more effort is required to reach the left side, the snow stays fresher longer.

One of the great under-utilized, undiscovered trails at Jay is *JFK*, reached via Ullr's Dream from the tram (and rated, incorrectly I think, as an intermediate run on the trail map). The trailhead off Ullr's isn't obvious (it might not even be marked). Regardless, if you're looking for late-day powder, JFK seems to hold one of the last stashes to get skied out. It's unfortunate drawback is the long, long run-out—a real how-long-can-you-hold-your-tuck tester—after the trail rejoins Ullr's Dream.

Finally, Jay Peak is the true champs of tree skiing, a.k.a gladed skiing, in the East. Cutting gladed trails has been one of the growing trends of the 90's in New England, and Jay has certainly been at the forefront of the trend. In fact, Jay was at the forefront before the trend even started; off-trail tree skiing was one of Jay's main attractions for locals and insiders. Now several of Jay's off-trail tree shots have been turned into gladed trails, disappointing some locals who must now share their once-secret stashes but adding immeasurably to the pleasures of Jay skiing for the occasional visitor.

For my money, the best of the gladed trails is *Timbuktu*, to the right of Derrick Hot Shot. One of the nice things about this trail is that, if snow conditions are less than ideal (as they can often be in the trees, where groomers cannot go), you can traverse out at almost any point onto Derrick Hot Shot. On the other side of the coin, the best snow tends to be to the far right, or as far as possible from Derrick Hot Shot.

If you're looking for steeper, tighter, off-trail trees, they still exist, even if a lot of Jay locals would prefer that I not let you in on them. Well I won't expose all of their secrets, but I will reveal one: the trees to the right of Kitzbuehel. When the snow is deep and light, I've probably had as much fun here as anywhere on the mountain. To the credit of Jay policy-makers, they're pretty liberal in allowing you to ski off-trail in the woods. The basic premises are simply: Don't ski alone in the woods, and don't cross under ropes or enter from a closed trail. Other than that, be careful and have fun.

SNOWBOARDING. For expert snowboarders, Jay holds out a bag of treasures. *Green Beret* and *River Kwai* are full of contours, pitch changes, and funky terrain features that if, especially on a deep-snow day, you can't have fun on these trails, you simply don't know how to have fun. Opportunities for truly serious air time, especially on Green Beret, abound. A less steep trail that is a playground of stumps, rocks, logs, and other terrain quirks is *Power Line*. Look at the trail map and Power Line looks like a straight, boring shot beneath, yes, a power line. It is anything but. Finally for expert snowboarders, *The Jet* (early in the morning, while the groomed snow is still fresh) is a classic for high-speed, hard-carving turns.

The same terrain that entertains cruising skiers should be equally entertaining for cruising snowboarders, but Jay, to my mind, is not nearly the same treasure trove for novice snowboarders as it is for novice skiers. Two reasons: The main learning lifts are t-bars, hard to negotiate as a first-timer on board, and that flat terrain near the bottom is probably too flat for slow-speed snowboarding. You may find yourself spending more time with one foot out of the binding, kicking yourself lamely along the snow, rather than learning how to make a snowboard turn. Even worse for snowboarders can be the long, flat run-out to finish off *Ullr's Dream*. If you don't like the one-foot-out shuffle, you're best advised to avoid trails on the far left of the mountain—e.g., *JFK*, *Beaver Pond Glade*, and Ullr's.

THE POST-GAME SHOW. After the ski patrol has completed its sweep, the rowdies among the red-crossers enliven the base-lodge pub scene for an hour or so, getting plenty of help from lift attendants and other day workers. After that, most of the crew heads home, but one popular local nightspot is the Belfry, an erstwhile red schoolhouse a few miles down Route 242 toward Montgomery. Food is of a steaks-and-potato-skins order—nothing fancy, nothing especially expensive. I'd also recommend the more expensive continental fare at the Hotel Jay's traditional, unpretentious dining room. On Saturdays, there's live music—yes, dance music! At Jay!—at the International Restaurant at the base, although I can't vouch for the quality of the bands. But as I've said, a quiet night in the country is more the order of things at Jay. Incidentally, if you're staying at one of the condos, I'd recommend you do your food shopping in Morrisville or Newport. The grocery pickings in Jay and Montgomery are pretty skimpy.

JAY PEAK DATA
Pluses and Minuses:
Pluses: Lots of natural snow, good terrain variety, spring skiing, quiet country atmosphere, strong French-Canadian influence.
Minuses: Hard to get to, exposure to cold, lack of nightlife.
Key Phone Numbers:
Ski Area Information: 802-988-2611
Lodging Information: 800-451-4449 (resort lodging), 800-882-7460 (area lodging)
Snow Conditions: 802-988-2611
Location: **1 mile of Route 242, 5 miles west of the town of Jay. Mailing address: Rte. 242, Jay, VT 05859**
Mountain Statistics:
Vertical drop: 2,153 feet
Summit elevation: 3,968 feet
Base elevation: 1,815 feet
Number of trails: 46
Lifts: 1 tram, 3 chairs, 2 t-bars
Average annual snowfall: 296 inches
Snowmaking coverage: 80% (230 acres)

SMUGGLERS NOTCH

I am 5'9" tall. At Smugglers Notch I feel as if I'm 6'10". That's not because the skiing, which has a few trails of knee-weakening steepness, inflates my stature by boosting my ego. Rather it's because about half of the Smugglers skier population is less than four feet tall and is still on the rosy-cheeked side of puberty. Perhaps no ski area in America has put more energy into its family programs, the result being accolades from the media (e.g., *Family Circle* magazine's Resort of the Year, 1990) along with a fully booked base-area village when schools (American and Canadian) take time off in February and March.

Smugglers was the invention of Thomas Watson Jr., son of the IBM founder, who in the early 60's had a Vail of the East in mind, largely as an R & R hangout for employees of Burlington's IBM plant. It was Watson's idea to create a Vail-like resort village, but it wasn't until the resort had changed ownership in the mid-70's that the family emphasis began to pick up steam.

In the summer of 1976, the Olympics were held in Montreal, and vacationers in the region were looking for things to do in combination with their Olympic visit. Lights went on in the heads of Smugglers executives: The self-contained resort village was ideally suited as a family retreat for Olympic-weary travelers. What began as a summer concept has since blossomed and spilled over into winter.

So Smugglers can be a combination of camp and non-stop carnival, and I'm willing to bet that more balloon-inflating helium is used up at Smugglers than at any ski resort anywhere. There's a mini-mogul arena near the bottom of the Morse Mountain chair with a ski-through replica of a school house; on one lift ride, a very youthful lift companion told me that the best thing about Smugglers was ringing the schoolhouse bell on the way through. (Not having tried it, I wouldn't know.) A costumed character named Mogul Mouse, who looks like a big piece of lint on skis, presides over much of the activities, most notably Thursday's kids' Olympics and its featured Cookie Race—ski an obstacle course, win some cookies. The apres-ski schedule is crammed with organized events for kids and parents—snow-tubing, bonfires, sing-alongs, dances, and so on and so on.

And yes—there's even a pretty good ski area here.

That's something easily overlooked. Smugglers' family success has, I think, misleadingly skewed public perception of the resort. "Family resort" tends to connote an overabundance of pushover skiing, but Smuggler's high-end trails and tree skiing, mostly on Madonna Mountain, can match up with the expert terrain of any area in the East. On a powder day, Smugglers can attract a bigger crowd of hot-skiing, Burlington-area hooky-players than Stowe or Bolton Valley, its steeps and tree shots being ideally suited to big-snow skiing.

Smugglers is not perfect, however. For one thing, its relatively low elevation (the village is just above 1,000 feet) and exposure leave Smugglers vulnerable to the warm, moist weather that can come off Lake Champlain. That might just be my impression: Smugglers claims an annual snowfall average of 279 inches—a figure I honestly find hard to believe—so the moisture isn't always warm.

In addition, Smugglers lags somewhat behind other major resorts in the East in its snowmaking coverage. The resort claims a 55 percent snowmaking coverage, but that seems high to me, and the quality of Smugglers' snowmaking and grooming strikes me as a notch below the standard at other Vermont ski areas. Another Smugglers shortcoming is its system of older, low-capacity lifts. Saturday lift lines on the Madonna

I and Sterling chairs can be considerable, although perhaps, to be fair, Smugglers doesn't have the breadth of terrain to accommodate more skiers brough uphill by faster, high-capacity lifts.

Finally, the Smugglers layout sprawls widely across its three mountains. You might regard that as a virtue, since the sprawl enhances an in-the-woods character of the skiing—preferable, for my money, to tightly-packed, clear-cut trail networks you might find elsewhere. But skiing the long flats back and forth from Madonna and Sterling mountains to Morse Mountain and the village is time-consuming and tedious. Smugglers has an impressive 2,610 vertical feet, but that's measured from the Madonna summit to the Village, two extremes rarely connected except on the day-ending run home.

Smugglers' principal drawbacks are not things that a good natural snowfall and mid-week skiing can't cure. And they are certainly out-weighed by the quality of the skiing terrain and the success of the family business. I was recently at Smugglers under the worst imaginable conditions—warm, wet, and virtually snowless. Yet the village was sold out (it was school-vacation time), and as much as I could tell, just about everybody was having a good time. That goes to show how effectively Smugglers has nurtured its family orientation—even without much snow, it manages to come up with fun for all ages.

A SMUGGLERS STARTER KIT. There are two distinct base areas at Smugglers—the village base and Madonna Mountain base. If you are a day skier, arriving on a weekday, you'll want to head up to Madonna. I'd recommend going past the main parking lots to the upper parking lot; you can ski down to this lot at the end of the day, much preferable, I think to having to walk down from the base lodge to the lower lots.

On a busier weekday, if you're arriving early, you'll probably want to do the same thing. But a good alternative if the access-road traffic seems heavy is to pull in at the village base. Buying day tickets here is likely to be less of a hassle—the village guests tend to be on multi-day tickets—and the Morse Mountain lift lines tend to lengthen only after the ski-school line-up.

If you're an advanced skier staying in the village and planning to ski Madonna and Sterling almost exclusively, you might want to drive to the upper parking lot—as suggested above—rather than ride the Morse lift. To accommodate kids and novices, the lift is run at an unusually slow speed. Driving might seem gauche, but it's definitely quicker.

Incidentally, it might strike you as odd that the Madonna I chair starts just below the base lodge. Seeking any possible edge over Stowe, his chief rival, Thomas Watson (the original owner) saw an opportunity in being able to claim greater vertical footage. To make the claim, the lift had to extend below the lodge. So for what it's worth, by the margin of a few feet, Smugglers stands taller than Stowe.

SMUGGLERS FOR NOVICES. I admire people of patience, and the ski-teaching crew at Smugglers strikes me as extraordinarily patient. They have to be, dealing as they do with brigades of children. I've watched them coax, tow, push, roll, and carry their young charges down the mountain, seemingly without complaint. On the basis of instructor patience alone, I'd recommend Smugglers as a great place to learn to ski.

It's also got a good teaching arena in the Morse Mountain trail system. What makes Morse so novice-friendly is that its trails are evenly spaced rungs on a ladder of proficiency. Rung 1 is either *Lower Morse Liftline*, wide and nearly flat as anything called a hill can be, or *Magic Learning Trail*, which runs parallel. I'd opt for Magic Learning Trail; it's a little longer than Lower Morse, and sees less skier traffic coming down from the Morse summit.

Rung 2 *is Garden Path*, which wends back and forth across the top of Morse before reconnecting with the liftline. Once Garden Path has been mastered, you can move up to *Snow Snake*, rated as a blue run primarily because of its steepish top. It's not much more than a chance to get your feet wet on steeper terrain, since steep part isn't so long that you'll feel intimidated by it. It mellows out quickly after the first couple of hundred yards. And if the business of learning to ski proves frustrating, you can cool out on *Wanderer*, a narrow, soulful little trail that is really more like a footpath through the woods.

This is not, however, an ideal novice world. For one thing, the Morse chair is run at a painfully slow speed. That's for the sake of the large pre-school contingent, but it makes the lift ride to the top seem longer than long. Smugglers other shortcoming is an almost total absence of lower-intermediate skiing on Madonna and Sterling mountains. *Rumrunner* on Sterling is rated as novice-intermediate, but there is a big, right-hand turn at the top that can be heavily trafficked and tough to navigate. If you grit your teeth and make it through this section, the rest of the trail is fun going.

SMUGGLERS FOR CRUISERS. "Cruising" in the usual sense is not a Smugglers' strong suit. *Chilcoot*, the main intermediate run from the

Smuggler's Notch, a reduced view of the trail map

Madonna summit is a series of pitch changes, flats, and sharp turns, making it a hard trail for developing much turn rhythm or momentum. *Drifter*, the intermediate trail that winds around from the opposite flank of the Madonna summit, is similar in character. They are fun trails in the New England way—idiosyncratic and on the narrow side—but they aren't thoroughfares for wide-radius, high-speed turning.

A little more cruisable is *Black Snake* on Sterling—certainly not avenue-wide, but at least more consistent in its pitch. But Sterling's two other cruisers—*Thomke's* and *Rumrunner*, are more of the sharp-turning, variable-terrain ilk. Rumrunner does widen and straighten out toward the bottom, but it also flattens out, losing some of its zing in the process.

Actually, the best Smugglers cruising can be accessed from the Madonna II lift, which terminates below the mountain's steep upper pitches. This is a lattice-like system of trails—*Link*, *Waterfall* (not as precipitous as implied by the name), *Lower Chilcoot, Dan's Ford*—that offers variety in offering opportunities to ski various sections in different combinations. This is excellent groomed skiing; basically what intermediates sacrifice in riding Madonna II rather than the summit chair is the quirky top section of Chilcoot. The view certainly makes the summit trip worthwile, especially as you ski along the ridgetop section of Chilcoot, but as I've said, it's more syncopated than cruise-control skiing.

I'd recommend the Madonna II arena to intermediates and more advanced skiers for another reason: its lift line is invariably shorter than the line for the summit chair. On a weekend, advanced skiers might want to take a couple of post-lunch warm-up runs here until the 1-2:00 P.M. rush-hour line on the summit chair begins to thin out. But Madonna II skiing comes with an obvious drawback: Runs are short. The lift carries you barely halfway to the top.

Smugglers does make up for its cruising shortage with a wonderful rarity—intermediate glade skiing. I know—skiing in trees is something usually associated with quick-turning hot shots. Indeed, it's probably not for intermediates short in confidence; in the trees, you *do* have to turn aggressively, in patterns dictated by the trees and not your own whims.

That said, Smugglers' glade trails aren't so tight or steep that you'll find yourself pulling twigs from your teeth at day's end. They are, by and large, negotiable by aggressive intermediates. The only designated glade trail with a legitimate expert pitch is Doc Dempsey's from the summit.

So if the snow is soft, I suggest you try out the combination of *Red Fox Glades* and *Three Mountain Glades*, best reached via Drifter from the Madonna summit. The pitch steepens gradually, hopefully matching your increasing confidence, before the glades finish through a stand of large birch trees and the juncture with Link. Don't bother, though, if it's been a while since a fresh snowstorm. Glades are basically ungroomable, and slick-snow tree skiing is no great treat.

HALFTIME. Skiers who spend their day at Morse Mountain certainly have the edge over the Madonna-bound skiers when lunch-time rolls around. For a quick sit-down lunch, the Club Cafe in the Village serves a pretty good sandwich-and-salad-bar; if it's nice and you want to sit outside, you can pick up sandwiches at the Village Center deli. There's pizza and cafeteria food, too—in short, a nice lunching variety.

By comparison, the pickings are cafeteria-slim at the Madonna day lodge (although there is some sit-down service). The lodge has a bit of worn-wood ambience to recommend, but it isn't quite big enough to handle the weekend lunch crowd. On a fair-weather spring day, you might consider bringing a picnic and dig out a space for yourself in the snow around the pond behind the Sterling summit.

SMUGGLERS FOR ADVANCED SKIERS. The head of Madonna's ski patrol once said to me: "You can always tell a Madonna skier. His turn to the right is real strong. His left turn is usually pretty quick." The reason—most trails have been cut across a double fall line, with a consistent cant to the right.

The main exception to this rule is *Freefall*, a relative newcomer to the Madonna Mountain trail system that goes unambiguously in one direction—straight down. It might not seem so upon entering the trail wanders off gently from the Madonna lift line. But the gentle stuff ends with a hellishly steep headwall, on which the area has installed a couple of fence sections in an effort to retain snow coverage. Still, fresh snow often ends up sluffing in small avalanches to the bottom of the headwall, so Freefall can be a rocky, dicey proposition even under the best of circumstances.

You'll probably find the best snow on the left side, which is more wind-shielded, but the fact is that trails this steep have an intrinsic problem holding snow. The best skiing on the trail is actually on the lower half, so bear with picking your way down the headwall; a reward lies ahead.

Actually, Freefall is probably the least interesting among Madonna's excellent array of expert trails. *FIS*—which locals call "Fizz"—is a terrific mogul run with a consistent, sustained pitch. By contrast, *Upper Liftline* is a trail that changes in character with every six turns. The trail flows over a series of rock ledges, and if you stick to the left side—the high side—of the trail, you'll find yourself confronted with 20-foot drop-offs. The right side is the mellower side, but it's anything but a walk in the park. For reasons I can't fathom, a cable running between lift towers is in places just a foot or two off the ground. Why isn't the cable buried, or suspended much higher on the lift towers? Beats me. But beware; it can be dangerous trip cord, especially when concealed under a fresh blanket of snow.

Finally, there is *Robin's Run*, a mercilessly narrow slot that at times seems no more than 10 feet wide as it falls away on a precipitous, westerly facade of Madonna. Smugglers skiers think their fearsome four—Freefall, FIS, Upper Liftline, and Robin's—are a match for

Stowe's Front four, and they might be right. What I like about the Smugglers quartet is how entirely different they are from one another.

Because of their steepness, all are also made infinitely better by a fresh dumping of new snow. As I've said, Smugglers may be the most popular spot among northern Vermont insiders on a powder day, especially a *deep* powder day, when you need a steep pitch to gain skiing momentum.

Storms, of course, are often accompanied by wind. If new snow on Madonna's fearsome foursome has been blasted by wind (the top of Upper Liftline and Freefall are especially susceptible), better soft-snow bets are *Doc Dempsey's* and *Black Bear* over at Sterling Mountain. As a gladed trail, Doc Dempsey's is by nature more protected. And Black Bear, nestled in the drainage between Sterling and Madonna and lined with tall trees can be a relatively wind-free corridor.

One other expert trail I should mention is *Smugglers' Alley*, or "the Alley" as it's more familiarly known. It's the steepest trail on Sterling (except, perhaps, for *Chute*, a 150-yard drop-off known unofficially as "Ballsnapper") and not particularly to my liking. It is quite ordinary—straight, evenly pitched, a little on the short side. But it has snowmaking, so that it offers the best steep skiing when conditions are marginal. When conditions *aren't* marginal, you might poke around for fresh snow in the trees left of the road leading to the Alley.

Poking around for snow in the trees. . . .Smugglers is building a name for itself as one of the best tree-skiing areas in the East and deservedly so. There are great designated glade runs, but those are just for starters. Off-trail tree skiing is the main reason that Smugglers reputation is spreading.

If I were to recommend specific off-trail slots in the trees, the ski patrol would probably slap my wrist, and locals—known to protect their private powder stashes with proprietary fierceness—would probably want to slug me. All I can say is that there are plenty of places to dip off the trails into the trees, and if you can turn 'em quickly, I suggest you hook up with some hot locals to show you where. I should, however, make note of an area called the "back bowls" west of the pond that separates Sterling Mountain from Stowe's Spruce Peak. I've never skied there, but local folk rave about the back-bowl tree skiing.

SNOWBOARDING. As a snowboarder at Smugglers, you have to make a decision right off the bat: Do you want to spend all day on easy terrain, or do you want to spend all day on intermediate and advanced terrain? The need for this decision is that the connector trails between Morse

Mountain (easy snowboarding) and Madonna Mt. and Sterling Mountain (intermediate and advanced) are the makings of an absolute nightmare for snowboarders. They are extremely long and extremely flat; any trail on which skiers spend much of their time skating and poling turns into a death march for snowboarders.

That said, Morse Mountain is, I think, superb learning terrain for snowboarders; it's got just enough pitch and variation of pitch to keep things interesting without being intimidating. The only thing to be concerned about, if you go to the summit of Morse Mountain, is the short, steep ramp you face when getting off the lift. My suggestion is simply this: Let yourself fall and slide easily to the flat. The only thing that can possible get hurt is your ego.

Doc Dempsey's Glades, a rough-hewn series of trees, rock ledges, and troughs, is probably the best expert run on the mountain for snowboarding. There are also some serious (as in 20-foot) drops on *Upper Liftline* for serious aeromaniacs, but this is as close to extreme terrain as inbounds terrain in New England gets. So scout the trail carefully on the lift ride up if you're tempted; chances of getting hurt on Upper Liftline, especially i f snow conditions are marginal, are about as good as your chances of having fun.

THE POST-GAME SHOW. As I've said, all the organized activities, for kids *and* parents, make Smugglers as much camp as resort, especially when the skiing day is done. The mostly-modern Village condos are nothing extravagantly fancy, but if you immerse yourself in the activity-dom, lodging matters little. You won't spend much time in your condo.

If all of the Village action strikes you as overbearing, you can go off-campus, so to speak. For apres-ski beer and a snort of insider info, Brewski's, just outside the Village, is a popular patrol-and-instructor watering hole. I've found the Mexican food across the road at Bandito's to be surprisingly good, and how odd it is to see faux adobe arches inside a Vermont clapboard home. If you want to ski a few days at Smugglers and really want nothing to do with the Village scene, Three Mountain Lodge, a couple of miles down the road, is a good lodging-cum-dining alternative.

SMUGGLERS NOTCH DATA
Pluses and Minuses:
Pluses: Family activities, expert skiing, glade and tree skiing, full-service resort, proximity to Burlington. Minuses: shortage of

snowmaking, small lift capacity, shortage of wide-open cruising.
Key Phone Numbers:
Ski Area Information: 802-644-8851
Lodging Information: 800-451-8752
Snow Phone: 802-644-8851
Location: **6 miles south of Jeffersonville on Route 108. Mailing**
address: Smugglers Notch, VT 05464.
Mountain Statistics:
Vertical drop: 2,610 feet
Summit elevation: 3,640 feet
Base elevation: 1,030 feet
Number of trails: 56
Lifts: 4 chairs, 1 rope tow
Average annual snowfall: 275 inches
Snowmaking coverage: 55% (130 acres)

STOWE

To me, there isn't a ski area that in name alone can match Stowe in connoting the tradition of skiing in America. Stowe is, or at least used to be, home of the Trapp family and the pre-Steamboat Billy Kidd. It billed itself as Ski Capital of the East, and no one was about to dispute the claim. Stowe had Nose Dive, the East's premier downhill race trail. Above all, it had the intimidating presence of four of the most fearsome ski trails imaginable—Star, National, Lift Line, and Goat. The famed Front Four.

When I was cutting my teeth on Eastern skiing in the 60's, Stowe always stood out as a final test on the road to skiing maturity. The Front Four were mine fields of precipitous treachery, and the reward of navigating them successfully with body and equipment in tact was the pure thrill of survival. Stowe was a kind of star chamber for the East's best skiers—if you could make it here, you could make it anywhere. To ride the lift was to experience first-rate theater—a revue of Eastern hotshots strutting their athletic, acrobatic stuff on the most challenging stage around.

There was more to the Stowe aura than just the skiing, too. Stowe had the quintessential mountain-top restaurant in the Octagon—built of red clapboard, low-slung, half-buried in the snow. On warm spring days, sun-soaking revellers on the Octagon deck would use wine pouches as squirt guns to douse lift-riders preparing to unload from the parallel single and double chairs that passed close-by. The Stowe Community Church steeple was the quintessential foreground element in the quintessential winter-in-the-New-England-mountains photograph. The Germans have a word for it—*echt*, meaning genuine, or pure. Stowe, to me, was echt.

Well, things change. Stowe no longer exudes quite the aura of tradition it once did, and part of it has to do with the softening of Stowe skiing. Stowe has evolved over the years into a well-rounded ski area for skiers of all abilities—all for the better, I suppose, except that something of Stowe's star-chamber quality has been lost in the process. Although Goat and Star are as ferocious as ever, some of the teeth have been taken out of National and Lift Line. Widening, grooming, and snowmaking might now make them skiable throughout the season, but neither is quite the monster-mogul run it used to be. Beyond the ski area, commercial development along the access road has certainly brought zest to Stowe's nightlife, but it has simultaneously quashed some of that old-time *echt-ness*.

I don't want to sound overly stuck in the mud, though, because I still rank Stowe as it is today among the best ski areas in the East. As a resort town it's got about everything you'd ever want (except a much-needed stoplight at the critical intersection of Routes 100 and 108, the mountain-access road). Stowe today is just different than it used to be, that's all.

Utterly unchangeable, however, is what bowled me over about Stowe in the first place: the big mountain. Seeing Mt. Mansfield for the first time from the access road on a spring day many years ago, I thought it somehow seemed bigger than any mountain in New England had a right to be. The rocky summit ridges were still coated with their winter rime, creating an image of a huge, white-capped wave cresting over the countryside. I was in awe.

In those days, of course, the only ski trails on Mt. Mansfield were under the steep, up-turned side of the mountain call the Nose, which indeed extends from the ridgeline like a giant rendering of Jimmy Durante's schnozz. If you wanted intermediate skiing at Stowe, you were best off sticking with Spruce Peak, the neighboring but unconnected peak on the other side of Smugglers Notch. Until the gondola was installed on the broad, moderately pitched flanks under the "Chin" of the ridgeline, Mt. Mansfield skiing was, as I've already noted, a tough go for everyman.

Enough of the past. In a roundabout way, I've already given you the basic components of the Stowe layout. There is Stowe, the town, and Stowe, the ski area, umbilically connected by the six-mile access road. Except for the Inn at the Mountain (which in fact isn't quite at the mountain), there is no slopeside lodging at Stowe. Development at the base of the ski area is minimal; at the Mt. Mansfield base, there is an undersized, ill-placed (and, I might add, tradition-rich) base lodge that the ski area is eager to replace, and not much else. Fear not, however, a lodging shortage: inns and motels by the dozens line the access road (a.k.a. Route 108, Mountain Road) and Route 100, the north-south thoroughfare that passes through town.

The ski area itself comes in three distinct parts: The older Mt. Mansfield area, serviced by chairlifts, the gondola area, and Spruce Peak. It is one of Stowe's weaknesses that the three are somewhat disconnected. You can ski from the gondola base to the chairlift base and vice versa, but you skiing the two trail systems in combination is difficult. Spruce Peak is separate enough from Mt. Mansfield so that I had several years of Stowe skiing under my belt before I even ventured over to Spruce. Stowe indeed has a terrific variety of skiing, but the layout tends to segregate skiers by ability: advanced skiers ski the Mansfield chairs, intermediates ski the gondola, lower intermediates and novices stick to Spruce.

Stowe is less than an hour from Burlington, and for that reason is convenient for fly-in weekenders and Burlington locals. That means weekends can get crowded, and Stowe's lift system is such that two lifts—the high-speed quad that replaced the old single and double chairs and the gondola—bear the brunt of the lift traffic. Weekend lift lines at both lifts tend to be long.

But if the lines annoy you, give the non-vertical side of Stowe a shot. Cross-country skiing around Stowe is as good as it gets in Vermont. The Trapp family survived the perils of World War II and the treacle of *The Sound of Music* to settle in Stowe and establish a first-rate touring center. If you're not a track skier, the Mt. Mansfield massif abounds with backcountry trails.

Also abundant (as mentioned) are restaurants, clubs, spas, and all manner of post-skiing diversion. If skiing isn't enough action in a day for you, Stowe is one of the best places in New England to keep yourself entertained late into the night.

A STOWE STARTER KIT. I've said that Stowe comes in three distinct parts. Actually, there are four separate base areas if you throw in the Toll

House base at the Inn at the Mountain—the first base you come to as you drive up Mountain Road. On most days, pass by the Toll House base; its one lift, which serves only the most novice of novice terrain, is there primarily to give inn guests lift access to the main mountain. On a super-busy day, however, you might consider pulling in here, seeing few other skiers do. It will mean a long, slow ride up the Toll House double chair to start the day, and an ultra-leisurely run-out at day's end, but that might be preferable to battling the cramped parking-lot scene at Mt. Mansfield.

As for the Mansfield base, I try to park as close as I can to the old Mansfield base lodge. That's primarily because I like to do most of my Stowe skiing from the Mansfield chairs. But it's also because traffic from both the gondola base and Mansfield base parking lots feed through a bottleneck here. My figuring is that being closer to the bottleneck—rather than the bottom of the bottle, as it were—is a way of avoiding undue end-of-the-day traffic-jam time.

All things being equal, the Spruce Peak base is probably the best of the bunch. It involves less scrambling between parking lot, base lodge, and lifts than do the gondola and Mansfield bases. If you plan to stick exclusively to novice and intermediate slopes, this is definitely the place to go. But if you want more advanced skiing, you'll find yourself having to ride a shuttle bus over to Mansfield. Despite their relative proximity, the Mansfield and Spruce bases aren't, unfortunately, connected by ski trails. You can either hoof it between the two or ride the shuttle—either way, an annoying interruption to the ski day. So in choosing your base area, do so with consideration of the skiers in your group: With an intermediate to expert group, head for Mansfield; with a lower-level group or a group with young kids, head for Spruce.

STOWE FOR NOVICES. Despite its monster-mountain reputation, Stowe actually has some pretty good novice skiing. The *Meadows* at Spruce Peak is the main teaching slope, and it is as the name implies, an open, gentle, snow-covered sward. And once you've got the hang of controlling turns, you might check out *Sterling* from the summit of Spruce Peak. Sterling is, for most of its length, a wide, winding run that gets relatively little skier traffic.

Over at Mansfield, novices and lower intermediates get a pretty fair shake from the old monster by skiing the trail network from the Mountain Triple chair. The chair is under-utilized, and I've found myself skiing over here when the lines at the other lifts back up. You can get an extra 600 vertical feet by riding the Lookout Double, but for lower-

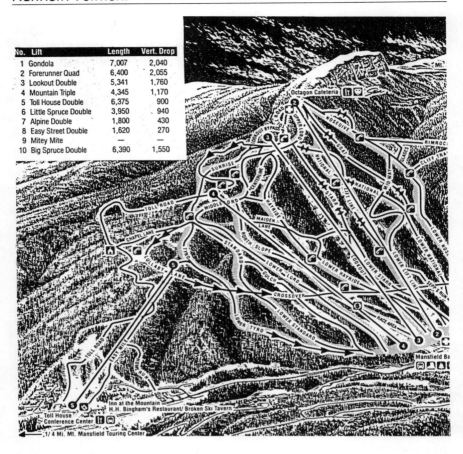

No.	Lift	Length	Vert. Drop
1	Gondola	7,007	2,040
2	Forerunner Quad	6,400	2,055
3	Lookout Double	5,341	1,760
4	Mountain Triple	4,345	1,170
5	Toll House Double	6,375	900
6	Little Spruce Double	3,950	940
7	Alpine Double	1,800	430
8	Easy Street Double	1,620	270
9	Mitey Mite	—	—
10	Big Spruce Double	6,390	1,550

Stowe, a reduced view of the trail map

intermediate skiers, not much is gained. You'll probably find yourself skiing *Toll Road*—the rather uneventful, wrap-around route that winds from the summit to the Toll House base—leading to the top of the triple before finding good skiing anyway. And the knot of skiers that forms at the top of the double—many skiers pass this way coming down from the summit—can intimidate and/or aggravate even advanced skiers.

From the triple, work your way right for the easiest skiing. The combination of *Lullaby Lane* and *Lower Tyro* is the most easily negotiated route, although you might find yourself poling along the pitch-less lower flats. A bit steeper, though hardly any threat to life and limb, is *Standard,* with one short, challenging drop before the flat run-out. If you

like almost total privacy, you might want to stick to the Toll House double chair. On weekdays—and even on some weekends—the area is virtually deserted. You can be assured that with trail names like *Easy Mile* and *Home Run*, you won't be in over your head, here.

STOWE FOR CRUISERS. The gondola terrain is the heart of Stowe's cruise country, with *Gondolier* and *Perry Merrill* being among the best cruisers in the East. They are wide, long, and with just enough pitch so that you can open your cruise throttle without feeling a loss of control.

I am not, unfortunately, the only person who knows of the pleasures of Gondolier and Perry Merrill. They get lots of skier traffic, so the best thing on busy days is to hit them early, when their snow is still groomed and soft. I usually gauge the quality of the cruising here by the length of the gondola line. As the gondola line begins forming—i.e., the tail end of the line appears outside the entryway— I work my way through the singles corral, usually eliminating several minutes lift-waiting time in the process. If the line gets much longer, I assume that the trails are crowded and that the snow on them has become a little scratchy. Time to move on.

But where to? If you want to hop the shuttle bus to Spruce, great cruising can be had on *Main Street* and *Upper Smugglers* from the Big Spruce chair. The ski area recently did some summer ledge-bashing on these trails, clearing a more even path for grooming and snowmaking.

For one reason or another, however, the Big Spruce chair hasn't been running in a couple of my recent Stowe visits, and I've been told by Stowe operations people that on any given day, there is a better than even chance the lift won't be running. So don't head over there unless it isn't; the intermediate runs from the Little Spruce chair are only ho-hum. And if the wind blows coldly from the north quarter (which is often where the cold winds come from), Big Spruce can make for a face-frosting lift ride.

There is also cruising to be had from the Mansfield chairs, but it tends to come in segments rather than in long shots, as you might find on Gondolier or Main Street. Perhaps the most important thing here is not so much trail selection as lift selection, at least on busy days. The quad, the longest and fastest of the chairs, also attracts the longest lines. Entering the singles line can result in a quick trip to the front of the line, but I don't find the singles-line advantage at the quad as significant as at the gondola. Instead, I check the line at the double and triple chairs. The triple chair line is invariably shortest, and though its vertical rise is considerably less than that of the other two chairs, it's a rise that covers the most cruisable skiing of the chair-area terrain.

When lines are short, though, the quad is the way to go. *Nose Dive* is steepest of the intermediate terrain from the quad, as well as the best in my opinion. Actually, the big turns near the top are black-rated and can be rough going, especially when the artificial snow surface gets slick. I've looked down from the top of these turns on a bad day only to think: If this were skiing, I'd quit the sport. But committed to the run, I'll grumpily pick my way around the turns, after which the trail straightens out, the pitch mellows out, my skis begin launching into big, carved turns, and my spirit and zest for the sport are instantly rejuvenated.

On the other side of the quad, you can mix and match trail segments from *Hayride, Lord, North Slope, Gulch, Sunrise,* and *Standard.* Hayride is the steepest; Standard the gentlest. Being able to ski these trails in different combos is great for the sake of variety. But numerous trail intersections on this part of the mountain can also lead to skier-traffic knots, the worst usually just below the double-chair summit. Keep alert to other skiers and be less than concerned about following trail signs. Just be sure to think about bearing left as you get lower on the mountain; going too far right can send you all the way to the Toll House base, definitely *not* something you want to do, while going right in general means a long flat, and even a short climb, to get back to the quad. My mix-and-match favorite: Sunrise (in the morning, for obvious reasons) to Middle Lord to Lower Hayride, but given the complexity of the trail layout, I'm not sure how I make the trail connections when I make that run; I just go with the flow on this part of the mountain, letting trail decisions determine themselves.

HALFTIME. When the weather is right, the Octagon deck is where it's at. I don't know if squirt-gunning wine is still part of the scene, but I know there still *is* a scene. A relaxed scene, that is—if you want something fancier or enclosed when the weather won't cooperate, get your lunch (a Continental melange of burgers, wursts, and salads) at the Cliff House Restaurant at the gondola summit terminal. Big windows at the Spruce Peak base lodge make it the best place for vicarious skiing while lunching, but the food is cafeteria basic.

STOWE FOR ADVANCED SKIERS. And then there were four. You can talk all you want about Stowe skiing, but when you've scrolled through all of the trails here, you come in the end to the four that made Stowe famous: *Goat, Lift Line, National, Starr* (sometimes called *International*). As I've said, widening, snowmaking, and grooming have taken some of the teeth out of National and Lift Line. On my last two visits to Stowe, National was a steep but un-moguled swath of hard, artificial snow. Yes—weather conditions had dictated that (I had come across a couple of rain-refreeze cycles), but the idea of National being anything but a mogul run struck me as incongruous. This is not to say, however, that National is a pushover, and if weather cooperates, the ski area does allow moguls to form, at least on the trail's upper portion.

You're more likely, though to find moguls on Lift Line. It's a ledge-stepping type of trail: big drop-offs interspersed by less steep sections and usually pocked by tooth-rattling bumps. Recent trail work has enabled the ski area to groom Lift Line top to bottom, so don't count on moguls, but if too much mogul-leveling went on here, the ski-area managers would probably be skewered on ski poles by the large contingent of local-area bumpsters. Lift Line's biggest problem—and it's a serious problem—is that the first hundred yards or so are invariably a wind-scoured sheet of ice. I find this one of the scariest parts of the mountain, especially if my edges aren't sharp—give me the steeps and stumps of Goat any day. Like the top of Nose Dive, this is grit-it-out time, with the knowledge that the skiing lower down, either on lower Lift Line or lower National, promises to be much, much better.

I personally have not skied Starr much, not because it's a bad trail, but because conditions must be just right to really enjoy it. And if conditions are right for Starr, they're usually right for Goat, and Goat is a very special trail.

But Starr, first: When you look over the edge of its entry, you see. . . nothing. The trail is so steep at first, it seems to disappear, a visual illusion of steepness usually enhanced by big moguls. Ya gotta turn 'em aggressively here, guys; this is big-time, moguled steeps, and narrow to boot. The moguls at the top can take on strange shapes—trail-entry moguls have a tendency to do that—but hang on. The moguls after that tend to be formed in a good, rhythmic pattern, one reason being that it is almost exclusively good, rhythmic skiers who take the Starr challenge in the first place.

Finally, Goat. Impossibly narrow, ridiculously steep, pitched on a left-leaning fall line. Laced with moguls, ledges, ice bands, and other niceties. I remember many years ago, just after the trail had been opened following a 16-inch storm, coming across a guy halfway down Goat who had blown out of his skis. What do I mean by blown out? He had completely ripped his binding toe pieces from his skis by hitting one of those infamous "unmarked obstacles." This was a day when Goat was on its best, most skiable, behavior, and it was still exacting a brutal toll. Tell you something?

All I can say is, if conditions are less than good, Goat ain't worth it. If conditions *are* good, be ready to pick your way carefully, generally staying toward the left side. If conditions are excellent, Goat is one of the supreme trails of Eastern skiing, a classical physical/mental challenge. Just make sure your bindings are glued on tightly.

Like other areas of northern Vermont (i.e., Jay and Smugglers' Notch) not all of Stowe's expert skiing is on designated trails. "Bootleg" trails—semi-trails cut on the sly by local chainsaw artistes—are a skier's revival of the spirit of the era when Smugglers Notch was used as a cache for contraband liquor during the dry era in the late 1800's. Some unmarked routes run for miles, dropping more than 3,000 vertical feet.

Where those trails are and who cut them, though, is information you must pry from knowledgeable locals. I say that for two reasons. One, I honor the bootleg tradition of preserving the anonymity of the lawless. Two, wandering around Mt. Mansfield without local guidance is begging for trouble. It's a big mountain with big hazards: cliffs, dead-end ravines, icefalls, even avalanches. Dipping into the wrong drainage could land you in Underhill, 40 miles around the mountain from Stowe. If you want to ski the backcountry, make friends with a local. If you want to go off the designated-trail path without venturing into the backcountry, I'd recommend trying the lift line beneath the Lookout Double. Look for a small track that cuts through the trees across the upper part of Lift Line, National, and Starr. The lift-line snow is all natural and the pitch is just the right steepness for some of the best skiing on the mountain for two or three days after a big storm.

SNOWBOARDING. If, as a snowboarder, you're a woods-o-maniac, Stowe is the place for you. There are so many places to poke into the trees—either to have fun, get lost, or hurt yourself—that you could spend weeks here without doing the same line twice.

Here's what I'd recommend, however, long before you decided to venture deep into the woods. First, check out *Nose Dive*. The main body of the trail is great for cruising, and the Stowe people recently cleared out glades along the right side if you want to mix cruising with a few turns through the trees. Lots of snow gets blown in here, and it's often wind-packed; skiers hate the stuff, but good snowboarders simply surf through that wind-whipped stuff. Another place to check out a mix of cruising and tree exploration is *Gondolier*. Look for stream beds along the left side of the trail to dip into and play around in.

For more mellow riding, I'd recommend heading for Spruce. While the lower-intermediate cruising terrain of Mansfield is great, all those trail intersections I've mentioned above are less than ideal for keeping the interaction of skiers and snowboarders under control. Skiers and snowboarders, as we all know, travel in different rhythms and turn patterns, something that can lead to chaos in congested areas. Far better to do the Spruce thing and mellow out.

THE POST-GAME SHOW. The Stowe lodging guide lists over 60

lodging options in the Stowe area, condos to country inns. There are at least as many places to eat and drink. I can't possibly run through all of them, but I will give you two apres-ski-into-evening programs of my own liking. That ought to get you started; after that, you're on your own.

Option 1: The low-key-high-end-after-ski special. If for some reason you prefer apres-ski ice cream to apres-ski beer, drop by the Ben & Jerry's headquarters, 10 miles down the road in Waterbury. You know Ben and Jerry—two regular Brooklyn bubs, relocated in Vermont, getting rich and famous on ice cream. After that, get massaged or mud-bathed at the Topnotch Spa. Go for dinner at either the Trapp Family Lodge for Alpine atmosphere and menu or Villa Tragara—northern Italian cuisine transposed into New England farmhouse. As for a place to stay, the Green Mountain Inn has a legitimate no-two-rooms-alike old-World romanticism about it, and the Edson Hill Manor is imbued with a country elegance, as its manorial name implies, and the kitchen serves up some mean cuisine.

Option 2: The high-life-low-budget-local-luster special. Check in at the Matterhorn on the Mountain Road for your favorite post-game beverage mixed with a little local, inside info. For dinner, StoweAway serves pretty good Mexican food in humble-home surroundings. For live-band dancing, the Rusty Nail packs 'em in. And for a place to stay, the Innsbruck, on the Mountain Road, gives you a decent motel room at a decent price, reasonably close to the ski area.

One last option, or sub-option: Dinner at the Cliff House. It comes as a package deal: The price includes the ride up and down the gondola (although you could ski; Gondolier is lit for night skiing) and a five-course meal. It's expensive, but the food ranks among the best in Stowe, and that's saying something.

STOWE DATA
Pluses and Minuses:
Pluses: Wide variety of skiing, variety of lodging and dining, tradition, proximity to Burlington. Minuses: lift lines, disconnected layout, shortage of on-slope lodging.
Key Phone Numbers:
Ski Area Information: 802-253-7311
Lodging Information: 800-253-4754 (resort lodging), 800-247-8693 (area lodging)
Snow Conditions: 802-253-2222
Location: **6 miles north on Route 108 from Stowe village. Mailing**

address: Mt. Mansfield Resort, P.O. Box 1310, Stowe, VT 05672.
Mountain Statistics:
Vertical drop: 2,360 feet
Summit elevation: 3,660 feet
Base elevation: 1,300 feet
Number of trails: 45
Lifts: 1 8-passenger gondola, 1 high-speed quad chair, 1 triple chair, 6 double chairs, 2 surface lifts
Average annual snowfall: 250 inches
Snowmaking coverage: 73% (350 acres)

ALSO KEEP IN MIND. . . *Bolton Valley*

Bolton Valley is New England skiing's version of the family farm. Head of the farm is Ralph DesLauriers, whose father in 1962 bought 8,000 acres on this spur of Mt. Mansfield with an eye toward logging. When loggers complained that one of the biggest headaches in trying to harvest timber here was an overabundance of snow, a light went on in Ralph's bright mind, setting the wheels in motion to create a ski resort.

As at any family farm, many Bolton duties have passed from father to son—or sons in this case. As Ralph has gone about running the business, extreme-skiing sons Rob and Eric have had their hand in all manner of ski-area chores, from trail-clearing to road-repairing to floor-sweeping. DesLauriers *fils* might be better known for air-mailing 50-foot cliffs in Warren Miller movies, but don't be surprised to see them at Bolton involved in much less sexy undertakings—fixing the plumbing, for example.

Just what has Ralph's vision been in developing Bolton? And just how are Rob and Eric refocusing it? Ralph's basic concept has been to create a mountain-retreat enclave as much as a ski area. Ralph relishes mountain solitude; as he put it to me: "The essence of skiing is to have a sense of the mountains. To me that means no crowds." For skiers, that means a resort village with a modest lodging capacity of 1,350 and what DesLauriers claims is twice the skiing acreage per lift than the industry norm.

For families with small children, Bolton strikes me as a great place for a ski weekend. Lots of novice terrain, a relaxed atmosphere, and the compactness of the resort make it a good, unthreatening place for kids to get their feet wet on skis. A meandering layout makes cruising runs interesting by being ever-changing, but probably Bolton's biggest drawback is its lack of long, sustained, intermediate pitches, despite a vertical rise of over 1,600 feet. There's not a lot of terrain for experts, but Ralph's extreme-skiing sons have been imaginative in clearing out trails through the trees such as *Devil's Playground*, which can be just the diabolical joyride its name implies.

Downhill skiing at Bolton comes with a special bonus: a terrific cross-country network. This is not your usual, run-around-the-golf-course cross-country skiing; trails interweave from the base almost all the way to the ski-area summit. If you've got the right gear (e.g., telemark gear), it's possible to ski the cross-country and downhill trails in combination. I know—I've done it. Or if you're really ambitious and know where you're going, you can ski off the backside to hook up with cross-country trails around Stowe.

INSIDE STORY
TRAILS THROUGH THE TREES

"There are two kinds of tree skiers—the quick and the dead." A ski patrolman said that to me recently, and it's not quite true. I like tree skiing, I'm not especially quick, and I'm living. But the point is made: If you can't turn on a dime and on demand, you're in for a bruisingly unpleasant experience in skiing through the Eastern woods. The trees are packed tightly, the scrub evergreens are spiked with broken branches, and what open spaces there are tend to be infested with huckleberry, puckerbrush, and fallen timber. Trying to turn in the woods when the snow is cruddy—which is to say, much more often than not—is pure branch-slapping, bark-bashing, sitzmarking masochism.

So why bother? I bother because I find Eastern tree skiing as exhilerating a challenge as there is anywhere in the ski world. In the woods is an almost-surreal, wind-free silence, along with an untram-meled freshness of snow and terrain to impart the illusion of skiing as-yet uncharted territory. The orienteering riddles posed by maple-and-evergreen thickets engage the intellect. Best of all, I think, is how the closeness of the trees intensifies the skiing itself—a sensation akin, I would think, to driving a race car in a back alley.

Tree skiing in the East used to be—and largely remains—a renegade (or, as they say at Stowe, "bootleg") thing. A certain underground honor is earned by those New England locals who sneak into the woods in summer with saws and snippers to clear out obnoxious brush and saplings and create in the process hidden, private trails in the trees. Northern Vermont—Stowe, Smugglers' Notch, Jay Peak, Mad River Glen—is the capital of this honorable lawlessness. The bootleggers have also done some good work on old, overgrown trails beyond the ski-area boundaries at Cannon.

But recent years have seen more and more Eastern resorts join the chainsaw-toting lawbreakers and legally clear out gladed trails. Resort muckety-mucks have told me that getting state and/or federal permits to do this kind of trail clearing is far easier than acquiring permits for clear-cutting an open trail. But I think a big reason behind the gladed-trail trend is simply a backlash reaction to the wide-and-groomed-trail trend of the 80's. Resorts, sensing a growing ennui among advanced and expert skiers with the overabundance of groomed stuff, decided to spice things up. New decade, new challenges.

The leaders of the gladed-trail contingent are the northern Vermont areas already mentioned as well as Sunday River and Sugarloaf in Maine. Many areas are also loosening up on previously strict rules against skiing off-trail. The prevailing (although not universal) rule is that as long as you don't cross under ropes or ski on trails that are clearly marked as closed, everything is hunky-dory.

Everything is not, however, hunky-dory at all times in the trees, where, as I've said, the skiing is often lousy or dangerous. That's why I usually save my tree-skiing energy for the day or two after a big storm. On stormy days, you might as well ski the powder you can find on designated trails. After that, after the trail powder has been skied out or groomed out, and after the wind that often comes on the tail end of a storm has pushed extra heapings of fresh snow into the woods, that's when I seek out the best slots through the trees.

Before you do similarly, however, let me impress upon you a few of tree-skiing guidelines:

First, try gladed trails marked on the map first before heading deep into the woods. Typically, these trails have numerous escape routes back to open trails, and when snow conditions are iffy, escape routes are a godsend.

Second, if you want to head off-trail, check with the ski patrol on their tree-skiing policy. Policies differ from area to area. Some areas say flat-out that there will be no off-trail skiing by anyone. Other areas allow it as long as you don't cross closed-trail ropes or boundary lines. Ski patrol at some areas use a discretionary approach—that is, competent, terrain-knowledgeable locals will be allowed to get away with things the average weekend explorer would be reprimanded for.

Third, never go into the woods without someone who knows where they're going. That's a rule I've broken myself, but really only by skiing along trail edges or between trails. I have heard wonderful stories from ski patrollers about rescuing skiers who've taken wrong turns into unfamiliar drainages and have overnighted unexpectedly in the frigid winter woods.

Fourth, ski the trees only after a good base of natural snow has formed. As far as I'm concerned, the biggest hazards in the trees are snow-obscured snags and fallen timber. At least I can see the standing trees I'm supposed to avoid; I don't have that luxury with stuff just below a thin snow layer.

Finally, when you do commit yourself to the forest, take it slowly at first. If I'm unfamiliar with the line, I ski a half-dozen turns or so, reassess the line, and move on. The moment I feel I'm off my charted line or have lost my rhythm, I stop. Instanteously. Bravado, sloppiness, and misjudgment yield few rewards in the trees.

photo, Linde Waidhofer

PART II
NEW HAMPSHIRE SKIING

Chapter 5
Western New Hampshire

AT A POINT ON THE WAY NORTH through the heart of New Hampshire on Interstate 93—somewhere south of Plymouth—you come to a crest in the road from which the beginnings of the White Mountains loom suddenly in the distance. Their main bulk is tinted purple, due to whatever atmospheric trickery causes distant mountain to take on that color on a clear day, and few wear rime-ice crowns of silver-white. I won't say it's exactly a religious experience, but it gives me a tingling sense of affirmation that the big country is at hand.

Indeed, the White Mountains are big—bigger than anything else in New England and more rugged, too. So there is some irony in the fact that ski areas are only of medium size; after all, you'd expect ski areas of a proportion to match the mountains. However, most of the White Mountain landscape is simply too harsh to host a ski area. The summits of the Presidential Range, the main set of mountains that includes Mt. Washington, are windswept rubble and scree above treeline.

If you were to ski these mountains—and there are a few mountaineering types who climb them and do just that—the length of your descent would be considerable and so, in all likelihood, would be your suffering. The weather, simply, can be brutal, even on a good day. People regularly encounter mean, extreme weather at Cannon, with the highest summit of any New Hampshire ski area, and it is still more than 2,000 feet shorter than Mt. Washington.

So New Hampshire skiers must content themselves to ski the smaller mountains and leave the big mountains for scenery. The White Mountains, for the most part, are untamable, which is pretty much what settlers of a previous centuries discovered. The mountains held forth neither an abundance of rich farmland or natural resources. So the region today remain sparsely settled, with a town here and there—Plymouth,

Campton, Lincoln, Franconia—to go with an occasional small city like Littleton. It is nothing like the Green Mountains of Vermont, where small towns are only a few miles apart, and farmland (or what used to be farmland) is everywhere.

Cannon, Loon, and Waterville Valley are a disparate threesome, a fact that works in favor of skiers interested in variety for a multi-day excursion. Cannon has long had a tough-guy reputation, and the weather and skiing can indeed test the best. But reputations tend to be built heavily on flecks of the truth at the expense of a complete picture. Fact is, the weather can be, and often is, pleasant at Cannon, and there is some excellent lower-intermediate skiing along with the tougher stuff.

Loon is a more modern resort, the skiing skewed heavily toward groomed, wide cruising. Waterville skiing is similar in style, but the two resorts are otherwise unalike. Waterville has a subdued stateliness about it, while Loon runs on a faster, looser energy. Put another way, Waterville strikes me as tending toward white-collar, while Loon tends toward blue-collar. As Waterville has grown slowly on the unified master plan of owner Tom Corcoran, Loon and Lincoln, the adjacent town, seem to have sprung quickly into their present being from a more patchwork process.

One thing to keep in mind is that Loon and Waterville are among the several New Hampshire ski areas that set limits on ticket sales. I've found it hard to get a straight answer—or consistently get the same answer, anyway—from ski-resort people about the number of sell-outs that typically occur each season. If ski areas say there are a lot of sell-outs, it sounds as if they're crowded; if they say they rarely sell out, it looks like they aren't popular. Either way, they can't win.

At any rate, sell-outs usually occur on the predictable weekends around Christmas, New Year's, and Presidents Day, along with the occasional Saturday or Sunday during the rest of the season. If you're a day-tripper driving up on I-93 and you're concerned about a sell-out, pull in at the state liquor-store stop near Manchester. You can not only get ticket-status information there, you can buy tickets, even the night before.

CANNON

There is something likeably fierce about Franconia Notch. About as wide as an alleyway, the notch is a storm sluiceway through which weather and wind can be squeezed with explosive irascibility. I'm not saying that it's always stormy in Franconia Notch, but it is stormy enough often enough to have left its mark on the landscape, which is mostly rock and stubbled trees. If you were a tree, this is not a place you'd choose to be, especially in winter. Apparently the hood of my parka didn't care much for Cannon either on my first visit there; I remember having to chase it down in the parking lot as it was trying to ride the big wind out of town. Get the picture of what the weather can be like?

Now you might be thinking: What fool human could take a liking to this place if trees and weather-resistant headgear can't handle it? Well, I'm one of the fools; I like Cannon. I'm not an unwavering loyalist, of which there are plenty, but I am a fan. Truth is, I like the rawness of the place, and those who are Cannon die-hards relish it.

I also like the tradition of Cannon; it is one of the true landmarks in the growth of U.S. skiing. Big-mountain downhill skiing was virtually unknown in the U.S. when the first ski trail, the Taft trail, was cut on Cannon in 1931. A group of local skiers came up with the idea; they had been cross-country skiing through the meadows of Franconia, looked up toward the big mountain, and decided that maybe it was time to reach for higher ground.

So the trail was cut, and the Franconians would hike up it to ski down it. That wore thin after a few seasons; the Taft trail regulars realized that a lift would make their skiing life immeasurably easier. They were apparently as adept at politics as they were at skiing, for they somehow convinced the New Hampshire state government to finance the building of an aerial tramway to Cannon's summit. To put the ambitiousness of that idea into perspective, the rope tow at that time was still a relatively new-fangled concept in North American skiing. The tramway opened in 1938, capable of carrying 27 skiers over 2,000 vertical feet in eight minutes. It was an engineering marvel—the only aerial tramway in America for 20 years.

Cannon grew in stature as the host for national championships and World Cup racing. But through the 70's, the state-run ski area began to grow a little ragged around the edges. Up-and-coming areas like Loon and Waterville Valley began stealing away business, and the state government was apparently less than eager to sink into Cannon the money necessary to compete on an equal footing with the other guys.

Not that the skiing itself suffered; Cannon remained a natural, a mountain of challenge and variety. Where Cannon came up short was in things like modern lifts, modern base facilities, high-quality snowmaking and grooming. The current tram, a 70-passenger replacement for the 1938 original, remained (as it still is) one of the most efficient ways of getting uphill in New Hampshire skiing. But for years, the summit lifts were a pair of t-bars that were virtually unridable when the weather got nasty.

In recent years, the state government has pledged to upgrade Cannon, the most obvious indication having been the replacement of the summit t-bars with a quad chairlift. Some of the base facilities have been spruced up (although I must say that there is a minimalism about Cannon's base facilities—no condos, no muss, no fuss—that I like). A push has been made to promote Cannon's Peabody slopes, an excellent cluster of lower-intermediate trails that have long been overshadowed by the reputation of Cannon's tougher stuff.

Still, some things about Cannon will never change, which is fine with me. The Franconia Notch weather will always have its mean side, Cannon will always wear the mantle of a rugged, iced-tree landscape, the skiing will always present an amalgam of quirks and traditional Eastern challenge. Indeed, perhaps the greatest satisfaction of skiing Cannon is the sense of accomplishment it can bring in coping with the elemental challenges of weather and terrain. That might sound vaguely masochistic, but somehow, to me, it goes right to the heart of what skiing is, and has always been, fundamentally all about.

CANNON STARTERS' KIT. Cannon is one of those areas for which it is important to check a weather report before making your commitment. The wind should be your main deciding factor; if it is blowing hard elsewhere, it can be roaring at Cannon, especially at the summit, making the skiing and the ski conditions pretty unpleasant. If that's the case, you'll probably have a better time of it at Loon. Cold, actually, is not as much of a concern, since the enclosed tram is a fairly comfortable, cold-shielding cocoon.

Cannon has two base areas—the tram base and the Peabody base. In general, advanced skiers pull in at the tram base, while less advanced skiers start from the Peabody base. I think a big part of Cannon's tough-guy reputation comes from the fact that its so-called Front Five—the five challenging trails from the Zoomer triple chair—are the most visible part of the ski area from the highway. The Peabody slopes, long and gentle, are hidden from view on a different facade of the mountain.

The tram base is pretty minimal; a cafeteria and ticket windows constitute the only services. But if you want to get up the mountain and be skiing in a hurry, this is the way to go: the tram ride is seven minutes from base to summit. Peabody is the base to be at if you need lessons, rental equipment, day care, etc.

If you are intent on trying to beat the crowds, it's pretty much a toss-up between the two areas as far as I can make out. In general, however, Cannon gets a little less skier traffic than other areas along Interstate 93, making it a good choice for a busy Saturday, when Loon and Waterville Valley are packed. For one reason, it is the most northerly ski area in the I-93 chain and thus requires a little extra travel for skiers coming from the south. I also think skiers tend to shy away from Cannon because of its reputation for fierce weather and tough skiing. The crowd that does turn out tends to be a mix of hard-core regulars (many over-60 veterans) and budget-minded high-schoolers and collegians taking advantage of state-run Cannon's average ticket price that is about $10 lower than at other major areas.

CANNON FOR NOVICES. Cannon's lower-intermediate terrain might be one of New England skiing's best-kept secrets. Not that the Cannon operators *want* it to be a secret. They've been trying hard in recent years to spread the word about the glories of the Peabody-side skiing. But as I've said, people pass by Cannon on I-93, look at the steep Front Five, and, seeing nothing else, head for Loon or Waterville. So it goes.

The Peabody slopes are serviced by two double chairs; as you look up the mountain, the one on the right is considerably longer and provides access to somewhat more challenging terrain. Unless you are an absolute beginner—in which case you'd probably start on the beginners' slope on the far right—take the shorter lift first.

As you head down, just keep one rule in mind: When in doubt, bear left. Turn right, and you might find yourself on one of the Front Five on the tram side—not where you want to be. For the first run, I think I'd go with *Lower Cannon*, rated an intermediate trail, but wide enough to be manageable for novices capable of controlling their speed. If you find the Lower Cannon going tough, you can always swing around left from the top of the chair and catch *Gremlin*, which runs for much of its length under the chair. check it out on the ride up to determine if it's a good match for your ability.

Another good option, I think, is to take every left-hand turn possible from the top of the shorter double chair and make your way over to *Turnpike* and *Red Ball*. Both trails are wide, very gently pitched despite being rated as intermediate trails, and, being stuck on the far side of the ski area, are both roads less traveled. The last I knew, however, neither trail had snowmaking, a fact that may have changed, since Cannon has been intent on upgrading its snowmaking capabilities. If there is indeed no snowmaking, there are a couple of crowns in the trails where the cover might be thin. Just keep your eyes open; the trails are wide enough to work your way around any rocks or thin spots.

CANNON FOR CRUISERS. I regard *Vista Way* as a true New England classic. Along with *Tramway* and *Upper Canyon*, it is one of three, wide cruisers cut through the summit stubble growth of Cannon, all of them quite similar in pitch and character. So my election of Vista Way as the best of the three is probably more on personal than objective reasoning; I've simply had more good runs on it than on the other two. Skiing along Vista Way when the low clouds roll in and the wind begins to blow, with the ice-encrusted trees along the trail's edge blending into the grey-white color scheme—to me it is the essence of the bracing, elemental character of skiing in New England. Part of the reason that skiing Vista Way in such conditions can be enjoyable is that it's hard to get in trouble; the trail is wide and without any unusual hazards.

After Vista Way wends left to join up with Tramway, I'll be honest: I get a bit confused. The flow of the mountain tends to throw you onto *By Pass* or *Middle Canyon*—almost interchangeable as far as I can make out. What I've found—as you might find, too—is that Vista Way (or Tramway, for that matter) allows you to develop such a nice skiing rhythm, as long as the visibility is adequate, that I don't feel like stopping here. So I go with the flow, and usually that means By Pass.

However, I've also found that I sometimes get sucked left onto *Links*, which leads either to the quad chair or onto *Lower Hardscrable*. This, by the way, should be a weather checkpoint. If it's windy and cold, you might want to continue down on Lower Hardscrabble; if the weather's pleasant, you might as well do a little summit cruising by taking the quad back up.

Lower Hardscrabble is nestled into the trees a bit and is a natural-snow trail. It drops down the Peabody side of the mountain which can be (though won't necessarily be) more wind-protected. If there has been fresh snow, Lower Hardscrabble can be a good trail for finding a few pockets of powder (probably wind-compacted, but powder nonetheless). Just keep in mind that this routing commits you to the Peabody side of the mountain, and you'll find an extra chair-lift ride necessary to get back to the tram and the summit.

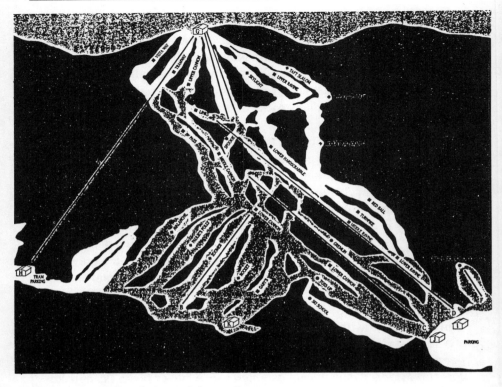

Cannon, a reduced view of the trail map

But back to By Pass or Middle Canyon, both of which have a more open and exposed character to them than the Links-Lower Hardscrabble connection. As I said, the best thing is to go with the flow; your moment of decision will come at the juncture with the Front Five trails.

Here is a lesson in what grooming can do to change the character of a trail. Usually, one or more of the five is groomed, providing a steep rush to the bottom. I've skied *Paulie's Folly* when it has been groomed, and it's a real trip: a process of connecting wide, fast giant-slalom turns while trying to maintain speed near the bottom to carry over the flats that lead back to the tram base. (Without adequate speed, your chances of making the tram without walking or skating are not good.) If Paulie's Folly (or neighboring *Avalanche*, which also may be groomed) has been allowed to turn to moguls, it is an entirely different trail indeed—expert stuff all the way. So the thing to do is to stop here on your way down By Pass and check the surface status. Continue left on Lower Canyon if neither of the steeps is groomed; *Rocket*, on which you can usually find good groomed snow, is probably your best bet for a run back to the tram base if Avalanche and Paulie's Folly are mogul fields. Just keep in mind that the further left you go as you survey the Front Five, the longer the flat run will be to get back to the tram.

HALFTIME. We're talking state-run cafeterias here, so don't expect haute cuisine. Cannon is a ski area where brown-bagging makes a lot of sense. There is actually an airy, high-ceilinged openness that I like about the eating area at the tram building cafeteria; in atmosphere, it comes across to me as something like a big schoolroom from the 30's, without the blackboards. But if it's a clear day, you might want to take your brown bag to the cafeteria at the tram's summit building. That way, you can take in the view while eating and be skiing immediately *after* eating— always a good strategy, I think, for fighting off the inevitable post-lunch chills.

CANNON FOR ADVANCED SKIERS. You like moguls? *Zoomer* has got 'em. Zoomer rates right up there with trails like the Chute at Mad River and Lynx at Wildcat when it comes to big-time, jaw-breaking moguls. What makes Zoomer a terrific trail, though, is not the size of its moguls but the variety of its skiable lines. There is a subtle knoll in the middle of the trail that seems to create variable fall lines. Ski on the left side (the lift side) of the trail, and you're apt to find more jagged moguls and deeper troughs. Work your way to the far right (something I don't find easy, since the fall lines don't seem to feed naturally toward that side of the trail) and you're apt to have a different ski experience entirely. All I can say is: experiment. Ski Zoomer a few times, trying different lines, before either you master it or it masters you.

What you typically find at Cannon is that many or most of the advanced skiers spend a good part of their day skiing the Front Five from the Zoomer triple. It's a well-balanced trail cluster, with Avalanche and Paulie's Folly, steep and straight; Zoomer with its monster moguls; Rocket, a good high-speed cruiser and perfect for occasional mogul relief; and *Gary's*, the soft touch of the bunch. The Zoomer chair has one shortcoming: It's too short. If there were an extra 200 to 400 vertical feet to it, it would be absolutely perfect expert terrain. But so it goes; not much can be done to change that. What it means is that if you want long runs, you've got to head for the tram and head for the top.

And what to ski from the top? You can always feed into the Front Five by taking one of the cruise routes (e.g., Vista Way to By Pass) as described above in Cannon for Cruisers. But at some point, you really ought to put in a run or two on the combination of the *Taft Trail* and *Hardscrabble*. This trail pairing is really almost a history lesson as much as a skiing experience. This is skiing the way it used to be in New England a quarter of a century ago and more: narrow, winding, varying and unpredictable snow conditions. The Taft-Harscrabble combo is less a trail than it is a series of trail segments. Veering back, forth, and down the fall line, it always intrigues with the question: What could possibly be in store around the next corner? It can be a real test in route-finding skills. Passing the test means finding pockets of loose snow hanging around the trail corners and edges. Failing the test means nailing the exposed rock and stubble and the patches of ice that are invariably to be found somewhere along the route.

SNOWBOARDING. Here's a choice if there ever was one: If you want to bomb straight down the fall line, try *Profile*, the run beneath the Cannonball Express Quad to the summit; if you want a virtual bobsled run on a board, head instead to *Upper Cannon* and its hairpin turns. If it were my choice, I'd head straight for Upper Cannon—banking through those hairpins is a true gas.

More adventurous snowboarders might want to head across the ridge that leads out from the end of the Taft Slalom Trail toward Mittersill, a neighboring ski area that has been closed for several years. There are a couple of things to keep in mind here: first is that many of the Mittersill trails are pretty overgrown, and may be hard to negotiate. Also, unless you hike back up from the Mittersill base, you'll have to make arrangements for a car shuttle to get back to the Cannon base. But if your somebody who likes the funky, unpredictability of what is, essentially, backcountry snowboarding, Mittersill is the place for you.

THE POST-GAME SHOW. It strikes me that Franconia hasn't changed a whole lot since the days when the first Cannon skiers were hiking up the Taft trail. There are fewer than 20 places to stay in the Franconia area, almost all of them bed-and-breakfasts or country inns. This doesn't necessarily make Franconia quaint; in fact it is a rather plain little town. But what I like is that it seems utterly lacking in pretension.

The Franconia Inn is a rather elegant place, the sort that has a dress code for dinner. I prefer a more casual elegance (if there is such a thing), which can be found Lovett's Inn, where the food is terrific to boot. One thing that's kind of neat about the inns of Franconia is that most are

connected by a cross-country network. What you won't find in
Franconia is abundant nightlife; if such activity is in your plans, you'll
do better staying down around Lincoln and Loon, about 10 miles south.

CANNON DATA
Pluses and Minuses:
Pluses: Low ticket price, balanced terrain variety, relatively un-
crowded. Minuses: Cold, windy weather, limited base facilities.
Key Phone Number:
Ski Area Information: 603-823-5563
Lodging Information: 603-823-5661 or 800-648-4947
Snow Conditions: 800-552-1234; in NH, 823-7771
Location: Exits 2 and 3 from Interstate 93 at Franconia Notch.
Mailing address: Franconia, NH 03580.
Mountain Statistics:
Vertical drop: 2,146 feet
Summit elevation: 4,180 feet
Base elevation: 2,034 feet
Number of trails: 26
Lifts: 1 aerial tram, 1 quad chair, 1 triple, two doubles, 1 surface lift
Snowmaking: 66% (100 acres)
Average annual snowfall: 160 inches

LOON MOUNTAIN

Loon is one of the 80's success stories in New England skiing. Here's
the Loon recipe for ski-area success: Mix convenient location (2 1/2
hours from Boston, right off Interstate 93) with lots of modern lodging,
throw in a fast base-to-summit lift to service mostly groomed, cruisable
terrain, and give people plenty to do when the skiing day is done. Allow
to simmer through the 80's and serve to the many Boston-area skiers who
come firing up I-93 on weekends.

Whether you go for this presentation or not is a matter of personal
taste; although I find Loon skiing fun, I don't find it varied enough—or
offering enough challenge—to make the fun last through an extended
visit. To be honest, one of the things I like best about Loon is its non-
skiing side. The Mountain Club, an attractive hotel/condo complex with
sports clubs and restaurants, is certainly the best ski-in-ski-out facility in
New England.

But back to the skiing: I suppose Loon can get by with a shortage of variety and challenge because it's mainly a day ski area and weekend resort rather than a place to which people come for a full week of skiing. As much as I can tell, the weekenders from Boston and the day-trippers from Manchester and Concord (about an hour's drive from Loon) all seem to be pretty content with what Loon has to offer. Long lines at the gondola are the main complaint, but the skiing seems to satisfy, and I'll concede that there is certainly enough at Loon to sustain my interest for a day or two.

Success, of course, hasn't come without growing pains. For one thing, Loon remains no more than a modest-sized ski area despite aspirations to expand to neighboring South Peak. Environmental concerns have roadblocked, at least temporarily, the intended expansion. So Loon has had to get by with terrain that is somewhat undersized for the number of skiers who crowd the slopes on busy weekends.

Although its vertical rise is 2,100 feet, Loon is one of those ski areas that doesn't seem to ski to its full height because of the way the terrain divides into smaller segments. And yes, Loon does limit its ticket sales, but in my judgment, the 6,000-skier limit exceeds what Loon's trail layout can handle comfortably. If there's a sell-out—or even the threat of a sell-out—you don't want to be at Loon anyway; head north to Cannon instead.

While on-mountain expansion has been held back, off-mountain expansion has encountered just the opposite problem. When the Lincoln mills, for years the mainstays of the local economy, closed in 1979, the writing was on the wall that tourism would be the new economic messiah. Land around Lincoln was cheap and zoning almost non-existent, so resort construction—condos, restaurants, shops, etc.—proceeded apace. The lodging numbers for the Loon-Lincoln area has now swelled to something like 14,000 beds (the various figures I've been told have ranged between 13,000 and 17,000) within a six-mile radius of Loon. Considering Loon's 6,000-skier limit, you have to wonder about the wisdom of allowing so much lodging construction.

Not surprisingly, there have been calls recently for a building moratorium, although the economics of the lodging glut have effectively seen to that anyway. If you're looking for a condo bargain at a New England ski resort, Loon might not be a bad place to start your looking. Even if you're interested simply in a place for the weekend, good deals can usually be had; you don't have to be a math genius to figure out that when there are 14,000 beds for just 6,000 skiers, it's a buyer's market.

To be honest, the 14,000-bed figure surprises me. You don't get the sense at Loon of being in the midst of a large suburban sub-division. The valleys are deep, the woods seem to close in tightly around you, and Lincoln, despite its numerous boutiques and restaurants, is still a far cry from North Conway or Manchester, Vermont. I won't say that Lincoln is quaint, but it's attractive enough and a manageable place to get around in.

There also has been an admirable effort to retain some of the spirit of the mill world of yesteryear. Rather than dynamite the old paper mill, developers have converted it tastefully into a shopping/restaurant/theater complex. The old narrow-gauge railway is used to shuttle skiers the few hundred yards between Loon's two base complexes, and I'll bet there are plenty of kids who spend more of their day riding the rails than riding their skis.

LOON STARTERS' KIT. Your Loon day might conceivably start the night before. When Loon is expecting an especially busy day—possibly a sell-out—tickets can be bought the day before, from 2:00 till 10:00 P.M. Tickets can also be bought through Ticketron, reserved with something called a Loon Card (for frequent Loon skiers), or reserved if you are staying at one of several Loon-area lodging establishments participating in the reservations program. I frankly don't know how the Loon people sort all this out, but if you're worried about being burned by a sell-out, you might want to buy tickets well in advance.

I've been told that Loon sell-outs occur about 20 times a season, on Saturdays and holidays. That sounds high to me, but whatever—my own inclination, as I've said, would be to make tracks to Cannon if the specter of a Loon sell-out looms. I've never been at Loon on a sell-out day, but I've been there for near sell-outs, and I know that the lift lines and trail congestion can be severe.

The Loon layout is pretty simple, so that you basically have just one decision to make when you pull in to the parking lot: left or right? If you're traveling with lower-level skiers or small kids, turn right to the Governor Adams base area; that's where most of the easier skiing is and it's also the less crowded of the two bases. In fact, starting from the Governor Adams base can be a good crowd-avoiding strategy for all skier levels; on busy days, a substantial lift line can form at the gondola during the morning (9:30-11:00 A.M.) rush period. By riding the West Basin double chair and cutting across to the East Basin double or the North Peak triple, you can get topside by bypassing the gondola.

147

Assuming it isn't an exceptionally busy day, however, and you're with a with a better-skiing group, you might as well set up base camp near the Octagon area and the gondola base.

LOON FOR NOVICES. Loon has a fine skiing pod for beginners with a terrible name—Kissin' Cousins, which sounds to me like the title of a grade-B Elvis movie. Oh well, you don't ski the name; the terrain is much more important, and this is one of the better beginner nooks in New England. There is even a free pony lift over here for kids and absolute first-timers.

Loon has done a nice job of designing its trail network so that there is novice routing from all lifts except for the North Peak triple chair. From the gondola, stick with Bear *Claw*, which seems to start off in the wrong direction as it winds around the backside of the rock outcroppings near the summit. Don't worry—it gradually works its way back to and across the mountain's frontside.

The pitch of Bear Claw is certainly gentle enough for most novices to handle, and it is nice to get to the summit for the view and the length of the run. The main drawback to Bear Claw is that it does attract traffic, mostly skiers en route to other trails. That means several trail intersections—follow the Bear Claw signs and you won't get lost—the most troublesome of which is Grand Junction, an aptly named convergence of several trails.

Grand Junction vexes the Loon people as much as it does skiers; extra trees have been cleared to improve sight lines and ski patrollers are usually stationed there to crack down on speed demons. I'm not sure how effective all of this is for traffic control, but whether speeders are reprimanded or not, the fact is that a lot of skiers do pass through here, a possible cause of intimidation for some novice skiers. Once beyond Grand Junction, however, lower Bear Claw is a delight, a nice meandering trail through the trees. If all you want to ski is this last, pleasant section, you can get to it from the Seven Brothers triple chair.

LOON FOR CRUISERS. Loon suffers from trail count inflation. You might think that 41 trails sounds like a pretty healthy number. But then look more carefully: Seven trails become 14 by being divided into "upper" and "lower" sections. Another four or five trails are really no more than connector trails—roads and cat-tracks to get from one section of the mountain to another. And a few trails (e.g., *Pickaroon*, *Lower Flying Fox*, and *Lower Picked Rock*) are parallel trails with more or less

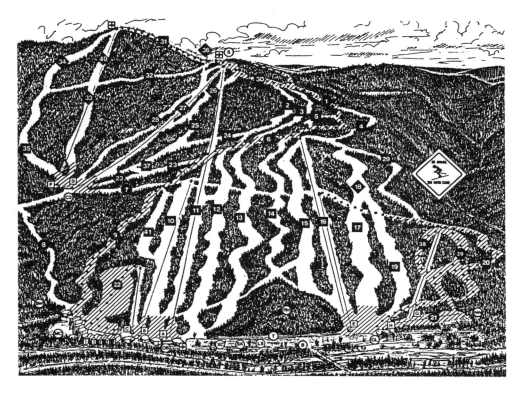

Loon Mountain, a reduced view of the trail map

the same pitch and character.

I raise this point less as a matter of criticism than as a way of giving you an idea of how Loon cruising works. Loon's main cruising terrain from the gondola comes down essentially to three or four variations on a similar theme. Trail selection becomes more a matter of assessing the factors that can change from run to run—i.e., snow quality and skier traffic—rather than on the intrinsic qualities of each trail.

Upper Flying Fox and *Upper Picked Rock* are the two most cruisable routes that cover the mountain's top half, each on the narrow side and each with a quick, steepish section to keep you honest. In my Loon experience, more skiers end up on Upper Flying Fox, suggesting that Upper Picked Rock should be your preferred route. But for all I know, skier preferences might flip-flop when you're skiing Loon. So I'll leave it to you to make the call at the juncture where the two trails diverge from *Exodus.*

The upper sections of the two trails officially become the lower sections at Grand Junction, but rather than take *Lower Flying Fox* or *Lower Picked Rock*, I'd slip across on *Bear Claw* to *Pickaroon* (the gondola lift line), *Seven Brothers*, or the *NASTAR Trail*. I won't guarantee that these three trails will have better snow, but that's been the case in my Loon experience. In fact, some of the best (if short) high-speed cruising on the mountain can be had simply by skiing these last three trails from the Seven Brothers triple chair. I've found that putting in five or six quick runs here after lunch is a good way of getting the blood circulating again and avoiding the post-lunch gondola crunch.

More first-rate cruising is to be had from the longer of the two West Basin double chairs. The runs are on the short side, as they are from the Seven Brothers chair, but there is a little extra pitch over here; *Upper Rumrunner* features a neat mini-headwall to test your carving ability and speed control. From there you can continue with Lower Rumrunner, as most skiers do, but a better option is Coolidge Street. For reasons I can't possible comprehend, Coolidge Street is virtually ignored by skiers who head instead to neighboring Lower Rumrunner. The trails are almost identical—nicely pitched, straight, and flush to the fall line—but in my experience the snow on Coolidge Street, with fewer skiers to trash it, is invariably better.

HALFTIME. For atmosphere, the best spot on the mountain is the Camp 3 Lodge, the small log cabin at the North Peak base. There is a throw-back feeling about the place, the feeling you might expect to find at a base lodge 30 years ago—small, intimate, and woodsy. Because North Peak is set slightly apart from the main ski area, there isn't the sense of by surrounded by all the resort buildings and bustle.

If you want to take a little extra time for lunch, it's relatively easy to head into Lincoln. There is a free shuttle bus to carry you back and forth from town, just a mile away, and since lunchtime is usually slow time for restaurants in town, you're apt to get seated and served promptly.

LOON FOR ADVANCED SKIERS. There might not be a whole lot of expert skiing at Loon, but the three trails from the East Basin double chair—*Angel Street, Big Dipper, Triple Trouble*—are fine stuff. The pitch is fairly steep at the top, but eases off nicely; if there is a drawback here, it is that the runs are short and over all too quickly. Triple Trouble is the one trail of the three without snowmaking, and consequently can have the best skiing when natural-snow conditions are good. It can be icy at the top, at its juncture with Big Dipper, and the fall line here seems to pull you in about five different directions. My suggestion would be to traverse, as high as possible, to the far right of the trail. There, if natural-snow conditions are good, you can often find some of the best snow on the mountain. If natural-snow conditions aren't good, spend more time on Angel Street, which is groomed regularly.

The best strategy for the East Basin threesome is to scope out the conditions as you ride the lift. If things look less than inviting, you can always pop over on *Haul Back* to the North Peak triple chair. The two main North Peak trails, *Flume* and *Walking Boss*, are more recently cut, and hence wider, than the East Basin trails. That makes grooming them easier if tough snow or weather conditions makes grooming necessary, and the North Peak snow conditions tend to be more reliable.

I'm not, however, as fond of the North Peak skiing as I am of the East Basin skiing. I find Flume—wide, steep, and groomed—strangely lacking in character. It is also the sort of trail that invites people (myself included) to ski too fast, and a couple of hard-to-distinguish knolls and lips can send the unwitting speed demon flying. I've watched from the chairlift as skiers have taken Flume straight from about halfway up to the bottom, and I've felt my heart flutter with fear. Skiing Flume *can* be fun, but there is a numbing sameness to it once you've skied it two or three times.

Walking Boss is a little more interesting—not especially steep, but with mogul fields here and there adding to the challenge. What a difference a few moguls can make: Unlike Flume, which is basically a wide, straight, unvarying line from top to bottom, the combined effect of Walking Boss's slight arc, its width, and sporadic moguls create several different skiable lines in the trail. Snowmaking is also a part of the Walking Boss package, meaning that the moguls can be hard, as tends to happen when moguls are carved from the dense, manufactured stuff. The Loon groom crew does an admirable and merciful job of chopping up the Walking Boss moguls if they become especially unmanageable.

SNOWBOARDING. Loon, especially on crowded days, would be far from my first choice as a snowboarding mountain. Because the trails tend to be narrow and because of numerous trail intersections, the potential for unpleasant skier-snowboarder encounters are numerous. The fact is that snowboarders and skiers move with different rhythms and turn patterns, a fact that comes to the fore at Loon. No one, whether on skis or snowboard, likes being forced to stop, change direction, or make choppy, unnecessary turns to avoid others. Unfortunately, I've seen too much of this sort of skier-snowboarder interaction at Loon.

That said, a couple of Loon trails do set up nicely for snowboarders. *Walking Boss*, like a wide, rolling river, is pure snowboarding delight; you can ski fast, turn big, and occasionally get air under your board without having to be too concerned about skier collisions. Walking Boss is wide enough to accommodate plenty of traffic moving at different speeds and in different turning patterns. Another rolling river—less steep and narrower than Walking Boss—is *Blue Ox*. It's best reached from the West Basin I chairlift, and, sliped between more popular *Picked Rock* and *Rampasture*, it's often surprisingly uncrowded.

Finally, for steep cruising, I'd suggest the combinations of *Angel Street* and *Basin Street* from the East Basin chair. Just be sure to get there early; the snow on Angel Street's steep pitch at the top gets skied off early, and I can't imagine a less pleasant experience than being on a board on a steep, icy pitch.

THE POST-GAME SHOW. There is lots here, depending on your post-skiing tastes. As I've already said, I like Loon's Mountain Club. It is legitimately a ski-in-ski-out facility (many places stretch the ski-in-ski-out claim), and with restaurants, sports club (a nice, big pool included), indoor parking, etc., there is pretty much everything you'd want or need. Loon likes to say that you can drive to the Mountain Club on Friday, park, and not have to use your car again until Sunday afternoon. Of course, you pay for all this convenience, and with plenty of bargain lodging available in the general area, the Mountain Club prices might seem especially steep by comparison.

Loon has done a pretty fair job of lining up post-skiing activities; among other things, you can hang out at the sports club, go skating on a small, outdoor rink, or sign up for a sleigh ride. Of course, you can also do what many Loon skiers seem to like doing, which is to swing into Lincoln and go shopping, catch a movie, or grab a bite to eat. There is no restaurant in Lincoln that stands out in my mind—Woodstock Station down the road in Woodstock often generates a lively, locals-heavy evening scene—but there are several restaurants that can produce a reasonable meal at a reasonable price. And if you feel like quitting the skiing day early and taking a nice drive, the Kancamagus Highway, which can be bumper-to-bumper leaf-peepers in the fall, is as pretty a road as there is in New Hampshire.

LOON DATA
Pluses and Minuses:
Pluses: Lots of lodging, including on-mountain hotel, good interme-diate skiing, convenient location. Minuses: Weekend crowds, lack of expert terrain.
Key Phone Number:
Ski Area Information: 603-745-8111
Lodging Information: 800-227-4191; 603-745-9976 in N.H.
Snow Conditions: 603-745-8100
Location: **On the Kancamagus Highway, 2 miles east of Exit 32 off I-93. Mailing address: Kancamagus Highway, Lincoln, NH 03251.**
Mountain Statistics:
Vertical drop: 2,100 feet
Summit elevation: 3,050 feet
Base elevation: 950 feet
Number of trails: 41
Lifts: 1 four-passenger gondola, 2 triple chairs, 5 doubles, 1 surface lift
Snowmaking: 85%
Average annual snowfall: 125 inches

WATERVILLE VALLEY

Waterville Valley messed with my mind at an impressionable age. It was the place that gave me brief, false hope that I might have it in me to become a ski-racing jock. I first went there with a school group when I was young and when Waterville, as a ski area, was even younger, in its second or third season. I spent the day skiing with a member of the school's racing team. He skied fast, so I skied fast. Big, sweeping, long-carving giant-slalom turns. Speed! I thought I was ready for the World Cup. Man, was it fun.

To make a long story short, Waterville tricked me. It was less my ability (my racing career was mercifully brief and without distinction) than the nature of the mountain that gave me the illusion of my own greatness. Waterville was made for that kind of fast, GS-style skiing. Still is. Waterville, in a way, was ahead of its time in those days. Along with Stratton and Mt. Snow, it was an 80's-style cruise-land—lots of wide, groomed, intermediate runs—alive in the 60's. That kind of skiing might seem the norm these days, but it was hard to find back then. Waterville was ahead of its time in another way, too: It aspired to be an international destination resort before even the *term*, "destination resort," came into vogue and when New England skiing was still hopelessly parochial.

The man behind this ahead-of-the-times stuff was Tom Corcoran, a former U.S. ski team star who had liked what he had seen at European resorts during his race days and didn't see any reason why a New England ski area could have a similar mix of serious skiing and gemutlichkeit. So he began cutting trails (a few old, non-lift-serviced trails were already there) and stringing up lifts in 1966.

Corcoran's ambitions weren't staked on an entirely raw tract of land. Waterville Valley is either a large glen and a small patch of meadowy flatland—depending on your definition—amidst the hard bulk of the White Mountains. Fishermen and summer vacationers had been slipping into Waterville for more than a century before Corcoran made the scene. As a mountain retreat, it followed nature's blueprint perfectly. Corcoran might not have come across a St. Moritz or Chamonix, but Waterville had something important in common with the famed resorts of the Alps: Long before skiing, a tradition had been established of people coming to escape the city and to feel rejuvenated in the fresh mountain air.

With that premise, he began developing a resort village, though (thankfully) not overdoing the Alpine-resort theme with lots of ersatz Tyrolian chalets and clocktowers. Instead, the village of Waterville Valley has risen on a conservatively New England architectural tradition: clapboard siding, brick chimneys, straight-eaved rooves with dormer windows. That sort of thing. It looks like much of Waterville Valley could have been built a century ago, except that it wasn't.

Still, Corcoran wanted to go one stop further on his Alpine-resort ride. He wanted a European-style, world-class racing presence. Racing meant credibility, especially to a former racer like Tom Corcoran. Waterville became a regular stop on the World Cup circuit, and it is coming to be recognized as a center for elite cross-country competition as well.

Enough people seem to have liked what Corcoran has created at Waterville to have established a remarkably loyal clientele over the years, with Boston-area families being well-represented. There is a kind of clean, traditional elegance about Waterville, although I find there is an air of coolness about it, too. Waterville to me has the atmosphere of a quiet, suburban-Boston neighborhood—not a surprise, perhaps, since that's the sort of community from which a large percentage of Waterville skiers come. This is anything but a hard-partying place at night; as far as I can make out, Waterville's idea of a fast nightlife is a candle-lit cross-country skiing tour.

The main drawback I find with Corcoran's scheme is that his ski mountain (technically Mt. Tecumsah, not Waterville Valley) is limited. Although the ski area's vertical tops 2,000 vertical, there is less skiing than you might expect. There is great cruising as I've already mentioned and a couple of fine mogul runs, but I wish there were more of it, more variations. Officially there are 255 skiable acres, but the total seems to me much less than that.

But what do I know? Waterville has an amazing number of loyalists who come weekend after weekend every winter, so apparently there is enough variety in the skiing to satisfy them.

WATERVILLE STARTERS' KIT. Weekend early birds score big at Waterville. The lifts open at 8:00 A.M. on weekends to help stretch out the morning rush crunch at the liftlines. I know Waterville regulars who ski almost exclusively between 8:00 and 10:30 A.M; with the speed of the High Country Express detachable quad, they can get in almost a full day's worth of skiing on the day's best snow, and still have the best part of the day ahead of them. If you're in High Country line waiting for the 8 AM rope drop, you'll be in the company of the knowledgeable Waterville hardcore.

Parking convenience is not Waterville's strongest suit. The parking lots are a series of terraces reaching up a steep hillside to the base lodge, and even if you manage to arrive early enough to park on the top terraces, the walk to the base lodge still seems a slog. On a busy weekend, I think it is probably easier to park at Town Square in the village and take the shuttle bus up to the mountain. It runs fairly regularly, and the ride up to the mountain takes about five minutes.

WATERVILLE FOR NOVICES. Although I've said that Waterville is short on variety, the variety of terrain for lower-level skiers is surprisingly good. Many ski area's use the same terrain for learn-to-ski classes and for kid's programs, a grouping that does always work well. But Waterville is different: It has a distinct kid's area—Kinderpark—and the Lower Meadows double chair for beginners. Best of all, both are slightly separated from the rest of the ski trails, so that you don't have lots of faster skiers zooming through.

Often, lower intermediate runs tend to be pretty straightforward. Wide-

Waterville Valley, a reduced view of the trail map

open, gentle, on an unvarying pitch—count to 20 and it's over. *Valley Run* is different, really one of the best trails of its kind in New England. For starters, it's long, flanking the mountain's eastern side. Actually, there is long and longer: Of the two chairs here, the triple extends a bit further than the double, bringing into the game a last, somewhat steeper section of the trail. Valley Run tends also to be warm, protected from wind in a crotch between two mountains and exposed to the morning sun.

But what I like best about Valley Run is its undular variation. Ski the right side—the lower side—all the way down, and you have pretty much a straight, lower-intermediate shot. Stick to the high left side, and there a couple of places to dip back right on slightly steeper pockets in the trail. Ski it a few times and experiment with different lines.

For families and lower intermediate skiers, Waterville even comes with an added bonus—a whole other mountain. Snow's Mountain, located near the village, is really more what I would characterize as a ski hill—580 vertical feet—rather than a mountain, but what's in a name? Snow's has no snowmaking and often isn't open if skier traffic doesn't warrant it. In fact, I've never skied it, though I have scoped it out. But locals tell me it's a great place for families to take a picnic and spend a relaxed day away from the bustle of the big mountain.

WATERVILLE FOR CRUISERS. Sometimes doing what insiders *don't* do is better than following their lead. I was skiing recently with a Watervile local, and we were talking about the difference between *Tippecanoe* and *And Tyler Too*, the two ultra-popular intermediate runs on Waterville's northern flank. There wasn't much difference between the two, my skiing partner conceded, at least in terms of pitch, width, grooming, and so on. But Tippecanoe, said my friend, tended to get more traffic just because long-time Waterville regulars tended to go that way. For that reason, we headed down And Tyler Too.

Actually, in recent years, those two parallel trails have nearly become one, indication of a trail-widening trend that I think is out-of-proportion with a mountain the size of Mt. Tecumsah. Waterville cuts off ticket sales at 7,000, a pretty substantial number, and it is trying to mold the mountain to accommodate that number easily. That was obviously a big reason behind putting in the High Country express, and faster, higher-capacity lift. But once you rush lots of skiers up the mountain, you've got to make more room for them to get down without running into each other. And so, wider trails.

That said, there is one cruising run at Waterville that I find truly outstanding. Here's the routing: *Tree Line* to *White Caps* to *Sel's Choice*. Tree Line is just a quick squirt around a tree island from the top of the quad. Most skiers seem to take off on *Express*, the trail right under the lift. As a result, I've always found it full of slick spots. But by hugging near the trees on the right side of Tree Line before it empties back onto Express, I've always seemed to be able to find a little corridor of good snow.

Then comes the bad part: Waterville's flat spot, about 200 yards worth past the Schwendi Hutte restaurant. Skiers don't like it. The Waterville people don't like it. And since big wind fences have been constructed here to reduce wind shut-downs of the high-speed quad, this trail section is somewhat lacking in aesthetic value as well as pitch. But what are you going to do? Get another mountain? So grin and bear it—and tuck it to avoid skating and poling. The best is yet to come.

After the flat, White Caps takes on a nice, even intermediate pitch. I find it easy here to establish a turn cadence. Just past the summit of the World Cup triple, hang a left onto Sel's Choice, one of my two favorite runs on the mountain. It's rated as an expert trail because of a couple of steep pitches, but grooming makes them ski fairly easily. Sel's is wide and fast but with two or three nice pitch variations to test your ability to hold a clean, smooth turn as the terrain forces you to adjust your balance. It skis like a good giant-slalom course, in fact, and that's just what it is. World Cup GS races have been staged here regularly. All things being equal, I'd allot probably a quarter of my Waterville ski day to Sel's Choice. If it were a windy, stormy day, I'd probably spend even more time here, using the World Cup Triple as my means of getting uphill. The triple is slower than the quad, of course, but by reaching only about two thirds of the way up the mountain, it's more wind-protected.

On busy days, it can also be less crowded. Base-to-summit high speed quads are a great concept—so great, in fact, that they become the favorites of the masses quickly. On busy days, the best crowd-avoiding strategy is to ride the World Cup triple and cut right on *Terry's Trail* to the Northside Double. The chair allows you to mainline Tippecanoe and And Tyler Too if you want. It also throws a couple of funny, old-style trails, *Tangent* and *Periphery* into the package. Both are narrow and strangely lacking in character otherwise; they are the sort of trails I find myself drifting down, looking for a place to link together a couple of turns, and next thing I know, there's no more trail. But so few people ski Tangent and Periphery that they are nice place to get away from it all and provide a change of pace from the two, wide cruisers. Just watch out for the occasional icy patches that, for some reason, seem to appear here more regularly than on other trails.

One other trail to keep in mind—perhaps for an early run or two, to catch the morning sun—is *Oblivion*. It begins with a steepish pitch followed by a sharp left turn; if you hug the left side of the turn, you might find a couple of moguls to try out. After that, the trail becomes pretty much of a run-out, a bit on the narrow side, until it connects with Valley Run. The Oblivion-Valley Run combo may not challenge you— except for Oblivion's top section, as I've described it—but it makes for a good, long run, a good warm-up for the day.

HALFTIME. I won't say that you should avoid the main base lodge dining area at all costs. It's got a little old-fashioned coziness to recommend it. But being cozy is one thing; being cramped and crowded on a busy day is another. To avoid feeling cramped, you can head upstairs for full-service dining at the World Cup Bar and Grill. But if I'm going to put in the time and money for that extra modicum of elegance, I think I'd prefer do it in the more atmospheric digs of the Schwendi Hutte, the mid-mountain restaurant. In keeping with Corcoran's alpine-resort concept, the Schwendi Hutte, in name as well as atmosphere and fare, is an effort to re-create, quite effectively, the kind of on-mountain dining establishment popular in the Alps.

If you were to do it with true Alpine-style, I suppose you'd wolf down a massive helping of pig's knuckles, spaetzel, and red cabbage—and wash it down with a liter of beer—as I remember watching, with perverse admiration, an instructor in Garmisch do once. But don't worry: you can eat far more modestly at the Schwendi Hutte, filling up on soup, pasta, sausage, or salad and do what European skiers would do—wash it all down with a bottle of wine.

Probably the best lunch spot on the mountain, though, is the underutilized Sunnyside Up cafeteria restaurant, near the base of the Sunnyside Triple. My assessment of the situation here is that flow of Valley Run tends to suck people to the base, and that the restaurant is set off just enough from the trailside to escape the notice of many skiers. Whatever—it is a good, quiet place to grab a quick lunch, and there's also an outdoor barbecue when the warmer days of spring roll around.

WATERVILLE FOR ADVANCED SKIERS. Waterville has a few trails on the front side of the mountain rated as expert—Sel's Choice, for example, which I've described above—but I don't think there is any *real* expert skiing on this part of the mountain. Just a few steepish pitches here and there. If you come to Waterville dedicated to skiing legitimate tough stuff, you'll pretty much end up spending the day on the Sunnyside Triple.

The featured trail over here is *True Grit*, a classic, wide mogul run used regular for training and competition by the young stars of Waterville's active freestyle program. I like watching these kids ski, but I'm not so fond of the line they ski, usually on the lift-side of the steeper top section. Some of those kids might be small, but they manage to carve out some big bumps, and when the bumps are big and hard, they aren't for me. I'll search instead for a tight line of fresh snow on the far right of that steep section, which I can usually count on finding.

A nice alternative to True Grit is *Gema*, which runs parallel. It has one crummy section—a short, usually slick, rhythmless mogul field where the trail swings left near the top. There is a knoll on the trail's left side that seems to throw a wrench into the skiing; all of a sudden, there seem to be about five different fall lines working against one another. At any rate, pick your way through it, the skiing gets quite good after that.

Gema has virtually the same pitch as True Grit, but because it gets skied less, the moguls are smaller and the snow often fresher, and when conditions do get nasty, the Waterville groomers chop it all up and let the moguls form anew. What I like doing is skiing the first two thirds of Gema and then cutting over to the last moguls of True Grit, which are manageable enough to make me feel like a hero when I ski them.

I often think the measure of a great trail is when it is the choice getaway spot for ski patrollers. These are the people who know the mountain best, so where do they go when they want to have fun? In the case of Waterville—if there has been a recent snowfall, that is—they head for Lower *Bobby's Run*. Bobby's is often not open a) because it has no snowmaking (though that may change) and b) because I think those ski patrollers like saving it for themselves. At any rate, it is a good steep pitch with few moguls (since it's skied so little) and thus is perfect for those days when there's a foot of fresh powder. If it isn't open on a day like that, I'd suggest you check with the patrol for an opening time (if there's going to be one), to be sure you're there for the drop of the rope and first tracks.

SNOWBOARDING. Waterville has created a snowboard-only terrain garden on *Lower Sel's Choice*, and while it seemed, on my last visit, to be still a work in progress, it showed great promise. Among the obstacles for snowboarders to "bonk" is a burried bus. It's this sort of terrain—and the snowboarders that it attracts—that makes clear to me that snowboarding's roots reach as deeply into the world of skateboarding as they do into the world of winter sports.

Other than that, Waterville's wide, groomed trails are made to order to wide-arcing carvers. If I were to single out one trail to recommend, it would probably be *Gema*, from the Sunnyside Triple, just after it has been groomed. Another good choice is *Upper Bobby's Run*, which runs more or less parallel to *White Caps*, beneath the High Country Express quad. Skiers tend to get sucked onto White Caps; making a quick jog to the right puts you on under-populated Upper Bobby's.

By the way, if it is a powder day, plan to spend most of your time not riding the high-speed quad. That flat spot near Schwendi Hutte that is a pain to skiers is pure misery for snowboarders when the snow is slow. You really aren't giving up much terrain by spending most of your time riding either the World Cup triple chair or the Sunnyside triple.

THE POST-GAME SHOW. If you're looking for convenience in apres-ski, the place to go is the World Cup Bar and Grill, upstairs in the base lodge. If you're looking for a little more local color, head a few miles down the road to Campton and the Mad River Tavern, which looks a bit like a couple of old New England houses that ran into each other and became a bar/restaurant. It's also not a bad place for a simple, reasonably priced meal and so it draws a crowd, Campton not being a place that suffers from restaurant overload.

If you stay in the village at Waterville Valley, the hotel and condo accommodations are perfectly adequate and, despite a few traditional New England facades, pretty modern on the inside. The Snowy Owl is the hotel for those on a more modest budget; those who live higher stay at the Golden Eagle Lodge. If you want a little local color at a fair price, you might want to stay in Campton at the Mountain Fare Inn, a bed-and-breakfast run by Nick and Suzy Preston. The Prestons coach Waterville's freestyle program, and the inn is often a stopover for visiting freestyle hotshots.

WATERVILLE DATA
Pluses and Minuses:
Pluses: Good, high-speed cruising, top-to-bottom high-speed quad, good cross-country terrain. Minuses: Limited terrain, lack of

nightlife.
Key Phone Numbers:
Ski Are Information: 603-236-8311
Lodging Information: 800-468-2553
Snow Phone: 603-236-4144
Location: **11 miles on Route 49 from Exit 28 on I-93**
Mountain Statistics (all mountain statistics refer to Mt. Tecumsah; Snow's Mountain statistics are not included):
Summit elevation: 3,835 feet
Base elevation:1,815 feet
Vertical rise: 2,020 vertical feet
Number of trails: 48
Lifts: 1 detachable quad chair, 3 triples, 4 doubles, 3 surface lifts
Average annual snowfall: 140 inches
Snowmaking: 96%

ALSO KEEP IN MIND. . .*Bretton Woods*

Bretton Woods's terrain is both its drawing card and its drawback. It is perhaps the most consistently easy-skiing mountain in New England, the sort of place to bore expert skiers senseless within a few runs. At the same time, that gentle terrain, along with excellent snowmaking and grooming, is perfect for families, especially for those with small kids. In terrain and character, Bretton Woods doesn't intimidate—just the sort of area you'd want if you're trying to interest a reluctant friend (e.g., that new girl friend who insists that skiing is a cold and dangerous sport) in taking up the sport you love.

The trail map indicates a couple of black-diamond trails on the mountain's 1,500 vertical feet, serving only to make the point that trail-rating is a relative and subjective business. Black-diamond skiing at Bretton Woods would rate as intermediate skiing almost anywhere else.

The main Bretton Woods bonus is the view of Mt. Washington, so close that on a clear day you'd almost feel you could poke the summit weather station with your ski pole. Another bonus is a well-groomed cross-country network. And a third bonus is the lack of development; although there are townhouses and hotels surrounding the ski area, the outlying countryside remains pretty much unblemished. Don't necessarily expect to have Bretton Woods to yourself on weekends, though; despite the limitation of its terrain (or perhaps because of it) and despite a ticket-limit policy, the ski area can draw a good crowd on weekends.

INSIDE STORY
COST CONTROL:
FINDING THE BEST NEW ENGLAND DEALS

Ski-area operators like saying that the expense of skiing isn't out of line when compared to the cost of other recreational activities such as golf. I don't know about you, but I'm not entirely convinced. When I look at daily ticket prices pushing $40, when I think of the cost of lodging, equipment and clothing, when I consider what it can cost to take a family skiing for a weekend—it strikes me that the expense of skiing is pretty steep.

That is, it can be steep. If you're willing and able to be somewhat flexible in your plans, you can escape at least some of the high costs of skiing. Let me suggest a few guidelines that can get prices down as low as $50 per person per day for lifts and lodging—in some cases, with lessons and rental equipment thrown in.

- *Ski late in the season or early in the season. Late-season skiing is usually better than early-season skiing because snow bases have deepened through the course of the season and because the March snowfall is often the heaviest of the year in New England. Either way, if you're willing to ski before Christmas or after the middle of March, you can find extraordinary deals. Mt. Snow is one of the New England kings of pre-Christmas packaging; lodging and lift ticket packages can be found for under $40 a day per person. And there are some packages in which lessons and equipment rentals are virtually thrown in for free.*

  By the way, the early and late strategy works well for buying equipment, too. Many of the best deals can be had during the pre-season, when ski shops are trying to rid themselves of last year's inventory. If you can live with the stigma of skiing last season's gear—something that has never bothered me—you can get first-rate equipment for less than half price by shopping pre-season.

- *Ski mid-week. Most resorts offer three- or five-day mid-week packages that, if you go for the budget option, can bring your* *combined lodging and lift costs in at under $50 a day. You can book packages through a resort's central-reservations system. There are, however, a couple of things to keep in mind. One is that if you go for a five-day package, it's a bargain if you ski all five days. If you end up taking a day or two off, there are no refunds, meaning that if you end up paying for a day or two of skiing that you don't use, the deal isn't such a great deal. The second thing to look for is packages with various lodging options. Places like Attitash, Killington, Mt. Snow, and Stowe often give you several lodging choices—country inns, motels, hotels, and condos—within a package's price range. My feeling is that just because you're saving money doesn't mean you should be forced to stay in some dive ill-suited to your style or needs.*

- *Look into special weeks. Many areas feature them: kids' weeks, seniors' weeks, lovers' weeks, and so on. In some cases the bargains are considerable, but be careful. Be sure a) that everything that comes in the special-week package is something you want, and b) that the package is a legitimate bargain. If you're not careful, you might find you're paying an extra $50 for a welcome cocktail or a meal you don't eat, or you might find that a regular mid-week package is actually priced more reasonably than the special-week package.*

- *Look for age-group specials. Kids under 12 can ski for free—and usually share your lodging for free—in many package deals. College students with I.D. often get discounts, as do over-55 skiers. One of my favorite New England deals is Mad River's student special: $49 a day gets you lift tickets, lodging, and breakfast and dinner. Skiers over 70 can ski free on weekdays at almost all resorts; it used to be a universal policy, but a few resorts found so many 70-plussers showing up that they began charging a minimal— e.g., $5-10—day rate. Just remember that for whatever age group special you're trying to plug into, you should be prepared to show I.D. and to speak up for yourself. Unless you ask for the special and show your I.D., you're going to end up paying regular prices.*

- *Not all deals are money-saving deals. Many specials are based as much or more on convenience than they are on price. For example, if you do your own shopping for air-fare and rental-car deals, you can probably come up with a better over-all deal than you'll get in a typical fly-drive package. If you're after maximum savings,* *probably the best strategy is to go for the lift-and-lodging package and make your own arrangements otherwise. Multi-mountain passes—e.g., One Pass, the Ski 93 Pass in New Hampshire, the Ski Vermont's Classics package—save you the pain of having to buy a ticket every morning, but they don't necessarily save you money. The daily ticket prices at some areas that can be skied on the pass are lower than the average daily price for the pass. For example, if you get the five-day One Pass for $125 and ski only Cannon, Balsams/Wilderness, and Cranmore you're paying more than you would if you bought daily tickets.*

One last note: Ski resorts are keen on two things—trying to convince us all that skiing is a family sport and trying to attract new skiers into the sport. For that reason, bargains are often available to families and first time skiers. Many, many resorts offer bargains deals where kids stay and ski free; the cut-off age is usually six, but at some places at some times the age limit goes as high as 12. Be sure to ask when you book your reservations. All resorts have some kind of learn-to-ski program, usually in which lessons and equipment rentals are thrown in for the price of a lift ticket.

Chapter 6
Eastern New Hampshire

IF YOU'RE CURIOUS about the different ways in which tourism can affect a mountain town, compare North Conway and Jackson, New Hampshire. Jackson has followed a rustic route: renovated country inns, small restaurants, a lot of clapboard houses and stone walls, even a covered bridge. Jackson is quaint (ouch!) in a tourist-attractive way, its heart bleeding quiet old New England.

For the most part, North Conway is—and it's hard to put this diplomatically—a strip. North Conway is outlet boutiques, shopping malls, traffic lights, motels, fast-food stops, and, at rush hour on a typical ski weekend, a five-mile traffic jam. Yes—some of the old-style stuff that makes Jackson Jackson still exists in North Conway. North Conway has its nice restaurants and country inns, too. It's just that all that other stuff overwhelms any residual charm.

Now, I don't want to dump too heavily on North Conway. It serves a few useful purposes. For one thing, it can be a bargain center—inexpensive lodging, inexpensive dining, inexpensive outlet clothing. It's also a good information center. North Conway ski-shop employees, bartenders, shop-owners, etc. are among the most knowledgeable sources of insider info regarding where the skiing is good and the snow is best—for cross-country and backcountry as well as alpine. Finally, North Conway acts as something of a junk magnet. Most of New Hampshire ski country's golden-arches, home-of-the-whopper Americana has condensed in North Conway, leaving the rest of the rugged countryside largely unaffected.

And the countryside *is* rugged. The geographical extremes of this part of New Hampshire absolutely obliterate fond images of gently rolling New England. North Conway's elevation is around 500 feet, while the summit of Mt. Washington, about 10 miles away by crow flight, is 6,288 feet—more than a mile higher. Even in the Colorado Rockies, where valleys are at about 8,000 feet and summits top off somewhere above 13,000, an elevation gain much greater than that is hard to come by.

A skiing tradition here runs deeper than pretty much anywhere else in New England—anywhere else in the U.S., for that matter. Skiers began climbing into Tuckerman Ravine on Mt. Washington's southwestern shoulder in the late 20's, and the climbing and skiing of Tuckerman's remains today one of New England skiing's great spring rites.

When ski lifts came into vogue in the 30's, places like Black Mountain and Mt. Cranmore were among the first to jump on the bandwagon. Among the original and most durable lifts was Mt. Cranmore's Skimobile, a wonderfully inefficient and anachronistic device that was only recently taken out of service. Mt. Cranmore has another claim to historical fame: Hannes Schneider, acknowledged as the forefather of modern downhill skiing technique, set up ski-school shop here when the specter of World War II chased him from his native Austria. His son, Hubert, now in his 70's, still teaches at Mt. Cranmore.

Taken as a whole these days, eastern New Hampshire skiing is a hodgepodge, which is to say, it packs a bit of everything into its portfolio. The major areas are Attitash and Wildcat, as dissimilar as two areas within 20 miles of one another can get. Attitash draws on the modern resort concept: snowmaking, base-area lodging, and groomed-run skiing, gearing itself largely to weekend and vacation business. Wildcat is old-fashioned in an almost ascetic way: the base facilities are minimal, the skiing tends towards the rough-hewn and ungroomed, and local skiers tend to favor it. Throw in small areas like Black Mountain, King Pine, and Mt. Cranmore, add extensive cross-country skiing in Jackson, combine with the ferociously rugged Mt. Washington backcountry, and you've got your basic something-for-everyone mix.

ATTITASH.

Imagine taking a ski resort like Sunday River and scaling everything down about 30 to 40 percent. Smaller mountain, fewer lifts, less lodging, but a similar idea: Beautifully groomed, manufactured snow, a mountain made for cruising. Family crowds on weekends, solace on weekdays. If you can picture that, you have a pretty good idea of what Attitash is all about.

Of course, you might think that if Sunday River has more of just about everything, why bother with a place like Attitash? I'll give you a few good reasons. One is that—almost directly as a function of size, as much as I can make out—Attitash seems a somewhat warmer, friendlier place than the bigger guys. Two is that Attitash is generally a bargain; it offers some of the best package deals in New England. Three is that, on a clear day, the view is special: more than 5,000 vertical feet of Mt. Washington, right across the valley.

This last stat, however, points up one of Attitash's shortcomings: its low elevation. The base elevation is just 550 feet. That means the natural-snow conditions are often less than great. It also means that the cold, damp air that can linger in the low valleys in winter tends to linger here longer. And whether its because of the lower elevation, or the steepness of the ski area's lower front facade, or the height of the ever-green trees that overhang trails, there are parts of Attitash that always seem dark to me.

Low elevation does work in Attitash's favor in one respect: It's more wind-protected than New Hampshire areas like Cannon, Waterville, and Wildcat, which are notorious for attracting wind. The darkness has it's plus side, too. One cause of the darkness is Attitash's due-north exposure, helping preserve the snow late into the season.

Also helping to preserve the snow are the Attitash snow "engineers," the guys who make it and groom it, and they're among the best around. One thing Attitash does an excellent job of—you'd hardly be aware of it, but take my word—is summer grooming. Rock, stumps, ledges, and so on have been removed and smoothed over, so that Attitash can open most trails with just six to seven inches of cover. In fact, Attitash is essentially a purely manufactured snow area. They don't even open trails unless there is a sufficient manufactured base.

How good is the snow at Attitash? Well, the U.S. Ski Team has used the area for early-season training. I figure that if it's good enough for the best, it ought to be good enough for you and me. And the toughest quality test for manufactured snow is the early season, before base depths can be built up and while temperatures are still on the warm side. Attitash manages to pull it off; as the U.S. Ski Team can tell you, the early season snow can be very good.

Attitash's lifts, unfortunately, aren't quite up to the standard of the snow. For a mountain with just 1,750 vertical, the ride to the summit is remarkably slow. Of course, this might be one of those delicate balancing deals. Attitash is not a big mountain, and its trails aren't especially wide. If the lifts were more efficient, trails might be overcrowded. Nevertheless, I've been irrevocably spoiled by the high-speed lift revolution of the 80's, so that a long, slow lift ride these days seems *very* long and *very* slow.

ATTITASH STARTERS' KIT. One Attitash idiosyncrasy is a parking lot across Route 302 from the ski area. When I first visited Attitash, I did what seemed logical: I parked and crossed the road. But had the road been busy with weekend traffic, lumbering across in my ski boots would have been suicidal. There had to be a better way.

And there is, of course. An underpass leads directly to the base lodge (at the eastern-most end of the parking lot), and I strongly recommend using it. In fact, despite being on the wrong side of the road, the Attitash parking lot is one of the most conveniently located in New England. However, if you arrive early on a weekday, there is a small lot on the North Conway side of the base lodge—on the same side of the road—that's even more convenient.

There is nothing complicated in the base layout here, which is probably why Attitash tends to be popular with families. It's hard for kids to get lost. There's one base lodge, one main set of ticket windows, and all lifts begin at more or less the same base area. And although the road is right there, the layout is such that it's unlikely kids will wander on to it. Simplicity can, however, have it's drawbacks. On those busy weekends, when everyone is booting up in the same base lodge, buying tickets at the same set of windows, and trying to get up the mountain on the same lifts, things can get congested.

Speaking of buying tickets, Attitash recently installed computerized turnstiles at its lifts, enabling it to offer pay-per-lift-ride tickets (called "Smart Tickets") in addition to regular daily tickets. It works like this: You buy a Smart Ticket with a certain number of points electronically stored in it. Each time you pass through a lift turnstile and insert your ticket in a turnstile slot, points are deducted until you reach zero.

For most skiers, the daily ticket is probably still the best way to go. But if you're only an occasional skier—you just like taking a run or two a day—the Smart Ticket, which can be used throughout the season, makes a lot of sense.

ATTITASH FOR NOVICES. Novices and lower intermediates get a pretty good deal at Attitash: Three lifts—half of the Attitash total—and a pod of skiing on the area's far right pretty much all to themselves. Two runs over here are actually among my own Attitash favorites: *Inside Out* and *Councilor's Run.* They're wide without being too wide so that you have a sense of trail skiing, they're protected from whatever wind there might be, and the sun filters nicely through the trees on fair-weather days. The best thing, though, about the two trails is the freshness of the snow. This being an out-of-the-mainstream part of the mountain, few skiers except novices venture this way, and even late in the afternoon, the corduroy pattern left on the snow by grooming machines is still visible in places.

One drawback here is that both trails finish on a flat, well away from the base lodge. To avoid walking, you must cut right halfway down onto *Alleyway* (look for it where Inside Out and Councilor's Run part ways). That sends you under the lift and onto lower *Thad's Choice*. Now you are in the mainstream of skier traffic, cutting across it, in fact, as you make your way back toward the base lodge. Be wary of faster skiers bearing down from uphill; the width and ease of the slope here tend to encourage speeding.

ATTITASH FOR CRUISERS. There is an intricacy to Attitash's trail network: Trails swoop and roll, wind around rock ledges, slip through gaps in the trees and across subtle indentations in the mountainscape. It is a mountain of constant rhythm changes, and if you're the type of skier who likes long, consistently pitched runs, Attitash is going to disappoint you. On the other hand, if you like your skiing rollercoaster-style, you'll think Attitash is terrific.

For the most part, I'm one who appreciates Attitash's terrain variation; it gives substance to an otherwise modestly proportioned mountain. But it can get frustrating, too. Every once in a while, I get the urge to get on a trail and just rip for a minute or so, and Attitash simply isn't the sort of place that satisfies in that way. So it goes.

The best place to start the day at Attitash is *Saco*, a straight left off the top of the Summit Triple Chair. With its tilt toward the east, Saco absorbs a good bit of the warming, morning sun. (Incidentally, the Attitash summit is often a good place to head for on a cold morning, something I wouldn't say of many areas. Because of the valley dampness that I've already mentioned, the summit at Attitash can be warmer than the base.)

Saco has one nasty section—a narrow right turn around a rock face. The skiing here is made more unpleasant by the fact that it serves as a connector between other trails—e.g., Ptarmigan and Tim's Trauma—and gets extra skier traffic. Bear with it at your own pace rather than try to conquer it; once through this unpleasant bottleneck, Saco returns to its comfortable, rolling self, progressing through a series of wave-like rolls

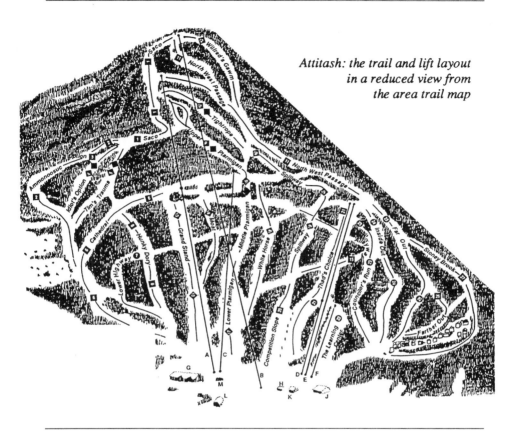

Attitash: the trail and lift layout in a reduced view from the area trail map

to the bottom.

The most popular cruiser at Attitash is *North West Passage*, which winds back steeply under the lift. At least it starts steeply, with a fall line that tends to pull you toward the trail's right side. Combine steepness, strange fall line, and skier traffic, and you've got a trail section that can turn slick in a hurry. After warming up on Saco, it's probably best to do your North West Passage time in the morning, while the snow is still good. In the afternoon, you can still get to the lower sections of North West Passage by skiing the top of Saco and bearing left on a connector trail at the top of the Top Notch Double Chair summit.

A couple of Attitash trails—*Tightrope* and *Wilfred's Gawm*, are generously rated as expert trails. They certainly have sections steep enough to warrant the rating, but Attitash, like many areas these days, uses grooming as an antidote to steepness. As a result, these are trails on which strong intermediates should have no problem. I personally prefer

Wilfred's Gawm because it winds off by itself, mixing in one short, steep segment into its otherwise modest pitch before joining North West Passage about halfway down. Tightrope has perhaps the most sustained, on-the-fall-line shot on the mountain, although it isn't quite wide enough to allow you to open up the throttle. When it eases off, I'd recommend scooting across to *Spillway*, another generously rated expert trail. Spillway is more typically Attitash in its rolls and turns and pitch variations. When the U.S. Ski Team trains at Attitash, it likes using Spillway for giant-slalom workouts because its undular character helps to fine-tune racers' balance and "snow feel."

HALFTIME. The base lodge is clean and attractive in a modern, wood-sided way, with a cafeteria offering the usual choice between food from the grill and food from the yogurt/fruit/sandwich cooler. What's decidedly above-average at the Attitash base lodge is one of New England's best sun decks. Now I'm hardly a sun worshiper. But on a bright, clear, early afternoon, if I buy a beer and settle into a deck chair—the sway-backed sort that inspires instantaneous laziness—I'm running the severe risk of being there for the rest of the afternoon. I'm not alone, because there always seems to be a shortage of available chairs.

ATTITASH FOR ADVANCED SKIERS. Attitash has a few truly steep pitches—*Middle Ptarmigan* and *Tim's Trauma* are the prime examples. The problem, if you're a lover of steeps, is that the pitches aren't long— 300 to 400 feet, and that's about it. Both come up short of perfection in other ways.

Attitash promoted Middle Ptarmigan heavily after it was first cut for the 1990-91 season. The "killer steep" theme of the promotional push predictably attracted a lot of skiers to the trail who really shouldn't have been there, intermediates determined to prove they were a match for the monster. Maybe the crowds will thin out as the newness of the trail ebbs, and the fact of the matter is that Middle Ptarmigan isn't all that hard anyway. Its difficulty comes in the fact that it turns slick in a hurry, and can be dangerous for fallen skiers who take the big, fast slide.

Tim's Trauma is a neat trail, nicely pitched, and stuck on the same side of the mountain as Saco, the side that usually doesn't attract advanced skiers. The Tim's Trauma snow tends to stay fresher than trails like Ptarmigan, especially the upper section of Ptarmigan, which has a severe double fall line and tends to get skied off early in the day. Tim's Trauma is wind-protected and sun-protected—another way of saying it's probably the first place I'd head if there has been an overnight powder dump.

So what's its shortcoming? The trail is, simply, dark. If that sounds like a weird gripe, ski it and see if you don't agree. Take a steep, northern-exposure trail and line it with thickly-packed evergreens, and I suppose darkness is inevitable. Tim's Trauma's darkness is that much harder to cope with given the fact that the ski area grooms the trail, as it does pretty much everything else. There are no moguls for depth reference. Small complaint perhaps. . . the trail really *is* nice, if only you could see it.

On the lower section of the mountain are a couple of underskied trails you might want to check out, especially as conditions start to get slick elsewhere later in the day. *Grandstand* and *Moat* aren't hard to get to, but the general flow of Attitash skiing tends to steer you away from them. Most skiers coming down from Upper Ptarmigan and Tightrope tend to finish out on Middle Ptarmigan or Spillway. But you can reach Grandstand or Moat by bearing sharply right where Middle Ptarmigan begins.

Moat is the first right off the road you'll be on, and I like to ski it as a narrowish, relaxed-day-in-the-woods sort of trail (although I've heard that Attitash has plans for widening Moat). Grandstand is wider and straighter (you can see the bottom from the top of the trail), and it's probably the best trail on the mountain for fast, wide-radius skiing.

SNOWBOARDING. There is no trail at Attitash that sets up unusually well for snowboarders. Just as for skiers, it is a cruisers' mountain for snowboarders. That's obviously great for those who like long, carved turns, but considerable grooming and a shortage of natural snow make Attitash less than ideal for snowboarders who prefer the funky challenges that come with unpredictable conditions and terrain. I will say this: Good grooming and good novice terrain make Attitash a good mountain for anyone interested in testing the snowboarding waters for the first time.

THE POST-GAME SHOW. Horsefeathers in North Conway as a place where locals like to hang out. If you want to meet skiers, locals and non-locals, the place for that is the Red Parka Pub in Glen. You'll have a chance to meet lots of them on weekends. When I was there Saturday in January not long ago—I should say, when I *tried* to be there—people were standing outside because the place had exceeded its capacity for human containment. The Red Parka attracts not just a boisterous crowd but families, too (at least the restaurant does). I can't imagine waiting 45 minutes for a table with a couple of first-graders in tow, but I saw people doing it. There must be *something* worthwhile about the place.

Now for dinner you can always head for the multiple-choice scene of North Conway. But I've found two good places closer to Attitash that come without the North Conway congestion. Margueritaville, on the Attitash side of Glen, serves decent Mexican meals at decent prices. Bernerhof, toward Glen and even closer to Attitash, serves high-end European food in a stylish Victorian-era setting. Local people seem to agree that it's got the best food in the area, North Conway included.

You can also stay at Bernerhof, the stylish-Victorian theme again predominating. If I were on a romantic runaway weekend, that's probably the way I'd go. For convenience, Attitash's base-area condos are perfectly adequate, despite somewhat of a dormitory atmosphere. There are many, many lodging options in the general area, and if you plan to ski Attitash in combination with other areas (e.g., Wildcat), you might want to look into staying in Jackson or North Conway. I'll go into that option in more detail in "The Post-Game Show" for Wildcat.

ATTITASH DATA
Pluses and Minuses:
Pluses: High-quality snowmaking and grooming, friendly atmosphere, bargain packages. Minuses: Lack of long, sustained pitches, undersized vertical rise, location on major roadway (Rte. 302).
Key Phone Numbers:
Ski Area Information: 603-374-2368
Lodging Information: 800-223-7669
Snow Conditions: 603-374-0946
Location: **On Rte. 302, 15 miles northeast of North Conway. Mailing address: Rte. 302, Bartlett, NH 03812.**
Mountain Statistics:
Vertical drop: 1,750 feet
Summit elevation: 2,350 feet
Base elevation: 600 feet
Number of Trails: 28
Lifts: 2 triple chairs, 4 doubles
Snowmaking: 98% (140 acres)
Average annual snowfall: 80 inches

WILDCAT

A name can tell all. Weatherwise, terrain-wise, style-wise, and almost any-wise, Wildcat is one, feral beast. Being a sizable mountain (4,100 feet) just across Pinkham Notch from Mt. Washington, Wildcat is apt to borrow a piece of the big guy's intemperate weather ever once in a while. It shows it, too, towards its summit, where the beast's mane is a sad congregation of wind-and weather-beaten trees. It is the kind of rugged landscape where you might not be surprised to come across one of the eponymous felines, a rare sight these days in the mountains of the East.

There is a ruggedness about the skiing, too; Wildcat certainly ranks in New England's top five on the mogul scale. Even the facilities—the base lodge and the lifts—are a little worn around the edges, not gussied up and domesticated.

That gives you some idea of why Wildcat has a rugged reputation, but it's funny how reputations have a way of manipulating truth. For one thing, the weather isn't intemperate all the time, and it comes with a bonus: natural snow. Attitash's low elevation might offer nice protection from the wind, but Wildcat, with a base elevation about 1,400 feet higher and closer to Mt. Washington, gets more than twice as much natural snowfall. When natural-snow conditions are good, they can be great at Wildcat.

Wildcat's reputation as a rugged-skiing mountain comes from the fact that its best terrain is its advanced terrain. Don't be misled—there is some excellent skiing for lower-level skiers, too. Not a lot, admittedly, but what there is is top-notch.

As for those un-gussied facilities, it would be nice to be able to say that this is all in keeping with Wildcat's rough-guy gestalt. But the truth is that Wildcat has gone through lean times financially for several seasons. Improvements have been made, but the going has been slow, and Wildcat's base buildings have the drab, functional character of state-park facilities. Perfectly adequate, mind you, but nothing to make you want to spend much more time there than you'd have to. And there's not much to encourage lingering anyway, since there is no lodging at the area (except for the Pinkham Notch hostel across the road). When the skiing day's done, you'll pack up the car and probably drive off to Gorham, Jackson, or North Conway, the nearest towns with lodging.

Wildcat is a little shaggy on a couple of other points. While the area claims snowmaking coverage of 96percent, the quality of Wildcat's snowmaking operation is not up to the level of areas like Attitash or

Sunday River in Maine. And its lifts behave like creaky, elder statesmen. Whether that's the reason the two summit lifts are often on wind-hold delays—or whether it's just the persistent wind itself—I don't know. One thing I will say about the lifts is that they are well positioned, compartmentalizing and making the most use of Wildcat's ample terrain. You won't spend a lot of time at Wildcat on wasted lift rides.

So with bad-weather tendencies and rough-edged facilities, why is Wildcat a local skier's favorite? Simple: The skiing is terrific. Wildcat has steepness, challenge, variety, and character. In addition to the inherent variety of the skiing, Wildcat is weather-activated chameleon; the Wildcat you skied yesterday might be an entirely different Wildcat than you'll ski today. In short, even if you know the mountain well, it's hard to be bored, and what more could a good skier ask for?

WILDCAT STARTERS' KIT. It is important to play your weather cards right when heading for Wildcat. Wind is a frequent, often fierce, Wildcat visitor. So listen for the morning weather report from the Mt. Washington summit (most area radio stations carry it regularly). If winds on Mt. Washington are moderate to high, you can bet it's going to be a windy day at Wildcat, too. You might want to opt for more a protected area like Attitash or Sunday River.

Snow is another factor, and a tougher one to call. Route 16 through Pinkham Notch climbs steeply for over 1,200 vertical feet on either side of the notch. If it's snowing and you don't have a car that climbs or descends well in bad winter weather, you might be safer ruling out Wildcat. On the other hand, Wildcat is perhaps the best area in the neighborhood for natural-snow skiing. What can I say? You make the call.

Once you make it to Wildcat, however, the layout is nicely straightforward: no extended access road to incur traffic jams, no multiple-base options to add confusion. A big parking lot and a base lodge—that's it.

Although I've been hard on Wildcat's base facilities, one thing I do like is that the base lodge is set conveniently close to the parking lot. No half-mile scramble up hills and over ice floes required. That said, it can be a bit of a scramble from the base lodge to some of the lift bases. But by then you should be geared up, ticketed up, mapped up, and psyched up, so that finding your way to the lift you're looking for should be a minimal hassle.

WILDCAT FOR NOVICES. With all of Wildcat's tough-guy rep, here's an unexpected rarity: There is a novice route down from *every* lift. Parents: When your seven-year-old accidentally scrambles onto the wrong lift, do not panic. Wildcat is one area at which you can be assured of making your way down safely.

Let's work our way up the ladder. The area served by Snowcat triple, on Wildcat's far right, is nothing but a big open meadow where you'd expect to see cows grazing in the summer. It gets lots of sun (when there *is* sun) and little skier traffic. An excellent beginner's slope really—easy, but with enough subtle rolls in the terrain to make it interesting.

As I've said, a name can tell all. So what would you expect from a trail named *Wildkitten*? Every trail at Wildcat has some sort of "wildcat" name, and you can bet that any trail with "kitten" in its name will have more purr than snarl to it. Wildkitten is indeed a nice, gentle, looping trail reached from the right of the Bobcat triple summit. The only snarl is literally that—a knotted series of trail intersections on the road leading to the trail. Take it easy here: Faster skiers will be zipping through from the upper mountain. And keep left all the way; make a right turn anywhere and, as a lower-level skier, you'll be unhappy. Once you *do* make it to Wildkitten, it's a purr all the way.

From the summit—or from the top of the Tomcat triple, halfway up the mountain—you can take a ride on the nearly three-mile *Polecat*. A basic skiing rule of thumb: short means steep, long means gentle. Very long usually means very gentle. Polecat has a few dips in it and a couple of funky turns, and I wouldn't try it before you're confident of controlling your speed on a gentle-to-moderate pitch.

Basically, though, it's pretty easy. *Too* easy in some places. The flats of Polecat (as locals might like reminding you) can bring new meaning to its name—you can find yourself pushing your way along with your poles at times. So it goes; the *real* reason to enjoy the trail is for the opportunity to be high on the mountain and to enjoy the view. The skiing is just a bonus.

WILDCAT FOR CRUISERS. Actually, novices and lower intermediates probably get a better deal at Wildcat than solid intermediates do. Wildcat is a mountain that likes bumps, probably because a lot of Wildcat *skiers* like bumps. Although that's great for advanced skiers, it's potential misery for groom-happy intermediates. So unless you're will to plunge into the moguls every once in a while, you're going to find yourself battling the beast in Wildcat.

Polecat, as I've mentioned above, is a nice, coasting cruise with a good

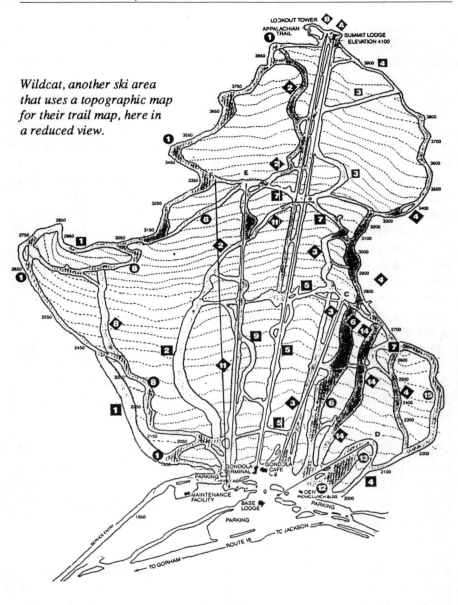

Wildcat, another ski area that uses a topographic map for their trail map, here in a reduced view.

view, but I doubt it's something you'd want to ski run after run. If you take Polecat from the summit of the Tomcat triple, you can cut onto *Tomcat*, which has a nice, steep middle section that's usually groomed. The section isn't long, only 400 vertical feet or so, but it's cut close to the fall line and is evenly pitched. It's one of the few places on the mountain to let out the stops.

A cruiser from the summit? Nothing, I'm afraid, fits the description. Wildcat skiing is old-style New England, and cruising is a new-style concept. The best for intermediates is probably upper *Wildcat* to *Catapult*, a route that winds around narrowly through a series of terrain changes.

Unfortunately, when you come to the base of the Catapult triple (the summit chairlift), you are, well, kinda stuck. Everything from here down passes through advanced-rated terrain. That doesn't necessarily mean anything super-steep, but it does mean challenges. If you want to try moguls, you can cut through on *Catenary* to catch the last few mogul fields of *Lynx*, as that trail begins to ease off in pitch. Or you can bear left instead on *Cattrack* and catch the last section of Wildcat. That leads to some nice groomed skiing on the parallel *Bobcat* and *Cheetah* trails. Because race training for local skiers is held in this area, the snow is usually kept in pretty good shape.

But hey—you can get to the groomed skiing of Bobcat and Cheetah by bagging the summit and riding the Bobcat triple. I'm not saying the ski from the summit isn't fun. But if you don't like the kind of skiing that requires you to pick your way astutely and to keep your throttle in second gear, you might feel constricted.

HALFTIME. As much as I've been able to make out, brown-bagging is pretty popular at Wildcat. This says something a) about the cafeteria food, and b) about the clientele. Brown-bagging usually indicates lots of local skiers and families. As for the food quality, it isn't that it's so bad—it's basic, ski-lodge cafeteria stuff—but that it's your only option. If you don't like it and you don't brown-bag it, you starve.

On the trail map is a note that "outdoor barbecues take place on the deck when the weather is appropriate." That tells you that there's a deck, which is nice, and it tells me that the weather has apparently never been appropriate when I've been at Wildcat.

WILDCAT FOR ADVANCED SKIERS. Horsefeathers, the North Conway bar, annually awards an old ski boot to the ski trail voted best in the region by local skiers. Give it the boot—get it? I suspect that the polling in this case falls far short of League of Women Voters' Standards (or Women's Christian Temperance Union Standards, for that matter). But whatever the legitimacy of the voting process, the result has been remarkably consistent in recent years. *Lynx* at Wildcat has been given the boot time and time again.

These locals know their stuff. Lynx is a long, winding, and ever-changing mixed bag, with moguls being its predominant theme. There is a gnarly top section on which snow can be either fine and nasty—or both, depending on how the wind has worked it. Stick to the sides, and, if there has been fresh snow, be prepared to punch suddenly into wind-packed slabs.

For those who would rather mainline moguls than have to deal with the gnarl of the top, Lynx's second half can be skied from the top of the Lynx double. It's about 1,400 vertical that can feel like about 14,000 vertical in your thighs and back. It's one of those rare trails that sashays across the fall and yet still tends to have moguls with rounded, on-the-fall-line shapes.

Lynx comes in distinct segments: a narrow slip through the trees at the top, a slide across the fall line under the lift, a series of stepped mogul fields after that. In fact, I'm sure that much of the reason that Lynx is consistently booted is that locals appreciate its segmented character; it's a trail of almost infinite variation. So ski it in short spurts, stopping and reestablishing your preferred line frequently. By the time you reach the gentler mogul fields toward the bottom, Lynx should seem (pardon the dumb pun here) like a pussycat—if your muscles haven't already been clawed to death.

Long before Lynx was Horsefeathers' favorite trail—in fact long before there was a Lynx, a Horsefeathers, or even lift-serviced skiing—the favorite trail on the mountain was the *Wildcat* trail. In the 30's, 20 years before lifts would be strung up, the Wildcat trail was a gathering place for some of the East's hottest skiers; it was used for national championships and Olympic trials.

The competitors, from the legendary Dick Durrance of the 30's to Toni Matt, made famous by schussing the cliff-like headwall of Tuckerman Ravine, liked the trail for its challenge. Narrow, winding, and in places quite steep: the Wildcat trail was a good test for the best.

Give credit to the Wildcat people for not doing much to change the trail; they've left it pretty much as is as a kind of memorial to past glories. And when you ski it today, you'll do it under conditions quite similar to those encountered by the racers of yesteryear, since in those days the most anyone did to groom a race course was a little ski-packing around the gates.

The trail comes in three basic parts: a gentle ridgeline a central series of steeps, twists, and undulations in the old New England style, and a lower section that's a bit hard to find in a tangle of other trails. The ridge run has been used for promo photos, its snow-shrouded trees framing Mt. Washington in the distance. Without discouraging you from taking in the view, I'd suggest you also make note of the snow conditions.

If the snow is good, by all means keep on going to the middle section, the real guts of the trail. If the snow is hard, slick, severely wind-blown, or otherwise impaired, you might want to can the 'cat and hang a right on Catapult. When snow conditions are wanting, picking your way down an old-style trail like Wildcat can be a pain—the narrowness just doesn't offer many options for searching around for good snow.

As for the last Wildcat section, it's stuck in among the trail network from the Bobcat triple chair. Wildcat is (or at least used to be) distinguished from other trails here by being without snowmaking. If there has been a recent storm, it's probably your best bet. Otherwise, you might want to bear right near the Bobcat lift summit and ski the fast, groomed manufactured stuff on Bobcat or Cheetah.

If you like center-cut skiing, locals tell me that the *Gondola Liftline* can be pretty hot going. Having not skied it, I'll take their word for it, but I know the conditions have to be right. Much of the liftline has no snowmaking, and the subsurface is pretty rough and stubbly. So wait for the days when the natural snow is deep and soft. If you have to run a liftline, head for the Lynx double chair. The lower section is at a perfect, ego-boosting pitch. If the rest of Wildcat has been rough on you, this is a great place to regain confidence.

SNOWBOARDING. Well-formed moguls are perhaps Wildcat's best feature, yet moguls, no matter how well-formed, are not ideal snowboarding terrain. However, the combination of *Wildcat* and *Catapult* is a good cruiser in the rugged style of Wildcat, meaning that in addition to cruising, you can probably find some quirky contours to play with along the edges. And quirky contours are plentiful all over the mountain, so if you don't mind—or even enjoy—negotiating a route through mogul fields, you just might find Wildcat a snowboarding gas.

THE POST-GAME SHOW. When you finish skiing Wildcat, you split the scene. It's as simple as that. As I've said, there's no reason to hang out much longer at the Wildcat base than for the time it takes to change out of your boots. There isn't even some off-key guitar strummer singing "Country Road" (and other favorites) in an upstairs bar to give second thoughts about sticking around for apres-ski. So head on down the road—right (on Route 16) to Gorham, left to Jackson and North Conway.

Head for Gorham only if you're looking for a cheap meal, a fill-up, or a cheap place to crash. Gorham is a cluster of a few motels, convenience stores, "family" restaurants (defined, it seems to me, as the kind of place that serves chopped-steak platters for under $6 and serves no liquor), and almost no character. Gorham is, however, easy on the budget.

Jackson is the first town you come to heading the other way (south) on Route 16. As I've said, it's got country-inn character. There are a couple of rather elegant (and pricey) hotels, the Wentworth and Eagle Mountain Resort, the kind of places just fancy enough to make me self-conscious about not having polished my shoes as I stride through the lobbies and hallways. My preference would be for the much smaller Inn at Thorn Hill, with a little homier atmosphere and a nice dining room, though it's certainly not the cheapest place in town.

If you want livelier action, North Conway is, of course the place to go. If it's a weekend and you're not staying in North Conway, you might want to wait till after 7 P.M. to avoid the apres-ski traffic. Of course, if you've been skiing Wildcat and have caught the Lynx fever, you are probably obligated to drop by Horsefeathers at some point to cast your vote for the boot.

WILDCAT DATA
Pluses and Minuses:
Pluses: Good advanced terrain, substantial natural snowfall, local-skier atmosphere. Minuses: Wind-prone, minimal base facilities, nearest lodging 8 miles away.
Key Phone Numbers:
Ski Area Information: 603-466-3326
Lodging Information: 800-334-7378
Snow Conditions: 800-552-8952 (in NH only)
Location: halfway between Jackson and Gorham on Rte. 16. Mailing address: Rte. 16, Pinkham Notch, Jackson, NH 03846
Mountain Statistics:
Vertical drop: 2,100 feet
Summit elevation: 4,050 feet
Base elevation: 1,950 feet
Number of Trails: 30
Lifts: 1 2-person gondola, 4 triple chairs, 1 double

Snowmaking: 96% (115 acres)
Average annual snowfall: 170 inches

ALSO KEEP IN MIND. . .*Black Mountain and Cranmore*

These are the region's two little big men. Their vertical rises are
modest—1,100 for Black Mountain and 1,200 for Mt. Cranmore—but
each is worth checking into for a couple of reasons.

Both tend to be locals-oriented places—especially on weekends, when
local skiers are looking to escape the crowds that go to the larger areas.
Both have a lot of history going for them, dating back more than 50
years.

I am not alone in mourning the passing of Mt. Cranmore's Skimobile,
dismantled only a few years ago after a half century of service. People
on the Skimobile would ride sideways up a wooden ramp in cars that
look stolen from a carnival's bumper-car arena. The absence of the
Snowmobile diminishes Mt. Cranmore's unique appeal considerably, but
that appeal regains strength in an enduring tradition as a locals' mountain. Rising right out of the town of North Conway, it is the place where
local moms bring local small fry to learn how to ski, and where local
racers do much of their gate-crashing.

Black Mountain's big plus is a southerly exposure, so that when the
weather is frigid at Wildcat and even at Attitash, Black Mountain can be
pulling in the warming rays of the sun. (Of course, that doesn't always
help Black's snow coverage.) And both Black Mountain and Mt.
Cranmore have night skiing, with night racing at Mt. Cranmore a pretty
active scene. If you can't get enough skiing during the daytime at
Attitash or Wildcat, these two areas are tops for stretching day into night.

INSIDE STORY
UNDER THE LIGHTS: NIGHT SKIING

Night skiing is strange, surrealistic stuff. It plays with the senses: Speed is exaggerated, the cold stings the skin, the night air seems to brood with a muffling, unnatural stillness. Other skiers pass through streaks of light on the snow like transient holograms—now you see 'em, now you don't. If you are inclined to believe that spirits inhabit the night, the eerie half-light of fluorescently lit ski slopes is likely to convince you. Strange stuff indeed.

I still regard night skiing as something of a gimmick, as it was when it first came on the scene 30 or so years ago. I actually thought that night skiing would die out in its infancy; it just never struck me as economically viable proposition. Keeping a ski area running under those the energy-consuming lights is expensive, and the skier turn-out at night is usually meager compared to daytime crowds. But what do I know? Several areas continue to offer night skiing, and some, it would seem, do so quite successfully.

North Conway is certainly the hub of night skiing in New England. One reason might be that the North Conway region features several ski areas that are just about the right size—with about 1,000 to 1,200 vertical feet—for stringing up lights economically and efficiently. Of course, there are other places for skiing night owls. Bretton Woods, a little to the north, offers some pretty good night skiing on weekends. You can also go night skiing at Bolton Valley in Vermont. Several small areas in southern Maine, such as Camden Snow Bowl (in Camden), Lost Valley (in Auburn), and Black Mountain (in Rumford) are also on the night-skiing roster.

But if you really think night skiing is your thing, North Conway is the place to be. Mt. Cranmore, King Pine, and Shawnee Peak, about 18 miles east of North Conway in Maine, all allow you to ski under the lights. Of these, Shawnee Peak night skiing gets top billing in New England as far as I'm concerned, followed closely by Mt. Cranmore. Both realized that the appeal of night skiing could considerable for local skiers, more so than out-of-towners who have already put in a full day of skiing. Night skiing gave local 9-to-5ers a chance to put in a few after-work runs.

Still, you can't just turn on the lights and hope skiers will come. You have to offer a little something extra, and that something in the case of Mt. Cranmore and Shawnee has been racing—active citizen-racing programs in the evening. Unfortunately, most of the racing is league oriented, so it's pretty tough for an outsider like you or me to make a one-shot appearance. Still, hanging around on race night is a chance to meet a few locals, experience a little local color, and even tap into the local pipeline of information about the skiing and ski conditions in the region.

What puts Shawnee at the top of New England's night skiing list? For one thing, its lights cover the full 1,300 vertical, while many areas (Mt. Cranmore included) light up only a part of the mountain. In addition, Shawnee's cruising terrain is right for the night. As far as I'm concerned, moguls and steeps don't make it under the lights (although Bolton Valley has tried by lighting up Spillway, its steepest, bumpiest run); moguls are tough enough without having to deal with them in the semi-darkness.

That raises what I think is an important point about night skiing: It's usually a good idea at night to pick on terrain that's a notch below what you're used to. Visibility is reduced, making it harder for skiers to see the trail as well as each other. Conditions are often slick, since night skiing comes at the end of the groom cycle. It's easier to get chilled— there's no sun to warm you while skiing or riding the lift—so your muscles might be less responsive.

All of that contributes to the fact that I am not an avid night skier. But the one time when night skiing can be pure enchantment is during a snowfall, when the lights appear to be draped in amber shrouds of falling snow. That's when I can be inspired to rouse myself from my evening lethargy to hit the slopes. For the novelty, for racing, for the social atmosphere that the night breeds, and for that occasional snowy evening, night skiing is worth a go once in a while.

photo, Linde Waidhofer

PART III
MAINE SKIING

Chapter 7
Southern Maine

SOUTHERN MAINE or eastern New Hampshire? State borders notwith-
standing, southern-Maine skiing might be better defined as an adjunct to
New Hampshire skiing. If you're like me, southern Maine conjures up in
your mind images of a rocky, bay-gouged coastline, and that's not what
we're talking about here. Both Shawnee Peak and Sunday River, the
principal ski areas of the region, are within a few minutes drive of the
New Hampshire border. Both are popular options for skiers based in
North Conway, New Hampshire.

That's not to suggest, however, that the influence of the Maine coast
can be dismissed entirely, at least in a climatic way. The ski areas here
are still near enough the coast to feel the occasional effects of the relatively mild, damp coastal climate (if you know about Maine fog, you can
visualize an exaggeration of the type of weather I'm talking about). In
that respect, the southern-Maine ski areas are different from their coun-
terparts in eastern New Hampshire, where currents swirling around Mt.
Washington wield greater weather influence.

Indeed, southern Maine—at least the part of it I'm describing here—is
something of a land between. The mountains—if they can be called
that—are the last significant highlands as you travel eastward from the
White Mountains toward the lake-mottled midlands of central Maine. At
the same time, this is a land between the settled, civilized coastland and
the true wilds of northern Maine.

It is also, to stretch out this theme as far as I can, a land caught between
old-fashioned grunt work and outright leisure. The grunt work is related
to the timbering business—not so much the logging of wood this far
south as the milling of it. If you want to see a true new England mill
town, drive through Rumford. Smell it, too; one of the unpleasantries
that can beset Sunday River when the breeze is from the east is the pulp

pungency drifting in from Rumford. (A similar effect can set in when the westerlies blow in via the pulp mills of Berlin, New Hampshire.) As for the leisure business, the lakes in the region have long been a popular summer attraction for weekenders from the Portland area as well as Boston. And now that Sunday River is making its presence felt, winter leisure is becoming a part of the regional formula as well.

In all of these land-between respects, it is hard to really put a finger on southern Maine's character. It is neither inherently rustic nor inherently settled. If I had to choose a town that somehow brings out southern Maine's soul, it would probably be Bethel. Bethel has plenty of clapboard, old-New England flavor, but there is an unreconstructed—unpretentious—plainness about it, not a tourist-alluring quaintness that you might find in, say, southern Vermont. Its roots are in the timber business and, with Sunday River just up the road, it's future may be in skiing.

SHAWNEE PEAK

How is it that a ski area half the size of other major New England areas ends up with twice as many names? The answer you might want to hear is that Shawnee Peak, a.k.a. Pleasant Mountain, has been around long enough to earn an extra title. Shawnee Peak—or is that Pleasant Mountain?—has been a lift-serviced ski area since 1938, making it second in age only to Camden Ski Bowl among Maine ski areas.

The real answer, however, is more mundane: "Shawnee Peak" came about as a result of a 1988 ownership change, but before that it was Pleasant Mountain, and the regulars who've been showing up here for years have simply continued calling it that. The Shawnee Group, a Pennsylvania-based company that bought the ski area, wanted to underscore its acquisition by affixing its own name. This struck local skiers as an act of corporate chauvinism, and most continued to call the place Pleasant Mountain. (As part of their nature, life-long Maine residents can be quietly obstinate without much prodding. I sort of feel the way locals do: What was wrong with good, old Pleasant Mountain? After all, Shawnee is the name of an Indian tribe of Pennsylvania and Ohio, and is misplaced in Maine.

I make a point of this name business primarily because it's very possible that you'll be in North Conway (just across the state border in New Hampshire) or Portland and hear both Pleasant Mountain and

Shawnee Peak in conversational circulation. Don't be confused—they're the same place.

Oh well—if the worst thing you can say about a place is that it has too many names, then something must be right. The new owners, despite this word salad they've concocted, have helped to make a good little mountain even better, most importantly by improving snowmaking and grooming. The area now claims 98 percent snowmaking coverage and grooms pretty much everything nightly. There is also a relatively new, well-built cluster of condos across the road—for lakeside visitors in summer as much as skiers in winter.

This doesn't make Shawnee an up-and-coming destination resort; it's still at is essence a family-oriented, day-skier area with just 1,300 vertical feet. But it's got a lot going for it. For one thing, its two main lifts are bottom-to-top numbers, so that every run can cover the full 1,300 vertical. For another thing, you can ski for what seems like forever if you want; Shawnee is open from 8:30 A.M. till 10:00 P.M. Admittedly, an area with just 30 trails—and they had to stretch things to come up with 30—lacks the variety of a larger mountain. But if you go for the full 13-plus hours, you can crank as many vertical feet at Shawnee as you can just about anywhere.

But what's probably best about Shawnee is the intangible—its feel-good atmosphere. It's the kind of unpretentious atmosphere you get when you have a good bunch of people running the place, keeping things down-to-Earth and uncomplicated, and when the principal clientele consists of local families and regulars.

Things can get crowded on weekends or on weekday afternoon when the school kids arrive by the busload. And there's not enough here to keep the average skier interested for more than a day or two at a time. But as a place to escape the madding world of big-resort skiing for a day or two during the middle of the week, Shawnee's worth checking out.

A SHAWNEE STARTERS' KIT. At Shawnee, timing can be everything, and I'm talking as much about the time of season as the time of day. The early-season skiing can be pretty lousy; the rule of thumb is that the skiing doesn't get good until Moose Pond, at the base of the mountain, freezes over. That might sound a little like voodoo meteorology, but there's truth to it. The humidity rising from the unfrozen pond can keep the temperature on the mountain 10 to 15 degrees higher than it is five miles away, according to head ski patrolman Henry Hudson. The phenomenon is misery for early-season snowmaking, and it's not great for natural snowfall either.

When does the pond freeze? That's a little like asking when birds fly south, or when flowers bloom. It varies from year to year, but it's safe to say that, by early January, the Shawnee skiing should be pretty good.

On the other side of the seasonal coin, March can be a prime time to ski Shawnee. While larger resorts in New England generally see crowds swell during spring-break periods, skier numbers actually go down at Shawnee. That's because the local day skiers and weekenders who are Shawnee's bread and butter are doing what other skiers are doing— vacationing at the bigger resorts. If you're looking for a place to escape spring crowds, especially if you're in the North Conway area, Shawnee's not a bad choice.

Now as for the time of day. . .Shawnee is a ticket-checker's worst nightmare; there are seven ticket options (each ticket being a different color) to choose from on a midweek day. It can be something of a ticket *buyer's* nightmare, too. With group rates (for 20 or more), midweek specials, package deals, and so on, you might want to bring along a certified public accountant to help you fish out the best deal.

For my money, the morning ticket (8:30 A.M. to 12:30 P.M.) is the best bargain: You get the most freshly groomed snow, and you beat the afternoon after-school contingent. If you're the sort who counts vertical feet, it's easy to log 20,000 verts on a morning ticket, with generally the best snow on the mountain. Whatever ticket you choose, make sure of your timing; for example, waiting a half hour at mid-day to buy your ticket can save as much as $10.

If you do happen to show up at Shawnee on a busy weekend, drive past the main base lodge unless you need lessons or rental equipment. The East Side Lodge is much less hectic, and starting on this side of the mountain means you start out with the morning sun. (It's also the more wind-protected side of the mountain.) Unfortunately, the lodge is closed on most weekdays.

SHAWNEE FOR NOVICES. Nothing complicated here. The basic Shawnee rule for novices is that the further right you go (right, that is, as you face the mountain) the easier the skiing gets. *Rabbit Run*, the beginners' slope on the far right, is such a beginners' slope that few skiers will spend much time here.

The main lift for lower-level skiers is the Pine Chair. Probably the best of the runs here is *Happiness Is*, looping around to the far right. Unfortunately, the trail is also the main outflow for Haggett's Hurdle, an expert

Shawnee Peak, a reduced view of the trail map

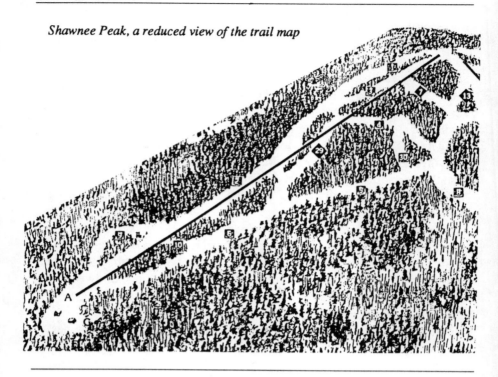

run from the top of the mountain, so that faster skiers often end up trying to share skiing happiness with novices on Happiness Is. For that reason, I'd recommend spending more time on *Pine Slope*, beneath the lift. It's a little steeper (though not much)—enough to rate as an intermediate run—but it sees much less fast-skier traffic.

One Shawnee drawback is that the Pine Chair skiing is pretty much the only lower-level skiing. Ride to the top and you must be able to negotiate solid intermediate terrain.

SHAWNEE FOR CRUISERS. This is the ski area's strength. Despite a few black diamonds that show up on the trail map, Shawnee is almost entirely intermediate and advanced-intermediate skiing. Nothing is going to plunge you into deep trouble as long as you are a competent intermediate. So feel free to roam.

I would start my roaming over at the East Side double chair—assuming that you're beginning your Shawnee day in the morning—because that's where the morning sun is. *Appalachian*, to the left of the lift as you disembark, might be the best intermediate trail on the mountain. It starts

*Shawnee Peak, a reduced view
of the trail map, contd.
(maps overlap in center)*

on a gentle pitch and makes a turn to the left, at which point you should stop to take in the view of Moose Pond. It almost looks as if you're about to ski onto the frozen pond, and the sky reflected on the pond's ice can create an illusion of skiing skyward. After that, there is a short steep section, with better snow usually to be found on the right side, and then a long fast cruise under the lift to the bottom.

The choice route on the front side is the combination of *Jack Spratt*, *The Horn*, and *East Slope*, which sounds like three trails only because of the trail-naming inflation that all New England ski areas indulge in. In my book, it's one trail.

The Jack Spratt section has a couple of neat rolls in it—the kind of landforms that kids jump on purpose (despite efforts of the ski patrol to discourage them) and others jump by mistake, especially when the visibility is poor. Keep your speed in check and your balance centered, or be prepared to take flight.

After the chairlift mid-station, the trail turns pretty much into a straight bolt to the bottom. If there has been a recent snowstorm, stick close to the t-bar on the right (usually not running) if you want to find patches of powder. Just be careful not to take one of the wooden T's in the teeth.

By the way, if you're looking to loop around the steeper section of East Slope, bear right onto *Kancamangus*, where Jack Spratt comes to a flat before the mid-station. Another option is to loop around the left side of the mid-station and connect under the lift with *Main Slope*, about as uncomplicated as the name suggests: It's wide, straight, and fast. In general, try to stay far left of Main Slope; the right side is often used for racing and race training, and even if a racing isn't underway, you can come across race-course ruts and slicks and on the right side.

HALFTIME. On a busy weekend day, the place to go for lunch is the East Side Lodge. The main base lodge is undersized and pretty charm-less; its renovation or replacement is on the owners' list of future projects. If things aren't too busy at the main base, you might want to check out the restaurant upstairs, where the food is much better than the cafeteria stuff and comes at a surprisingly reasonable price. I'm also told by a reliable source that on sunny weekend days, the outdoor barbecue scene is "awesome," but I've never experienced the barbecue myself.

SHAWNEE FOR ADVANCED SKIERS. You're pretty limited here. Unless there is plenty of soft snow from recent storms, the ski area grooms just about everything. The two places you might find some moguls are on *Haggett's Hurdle* on the front side of the mountain and *Tycoon* on the east side. This mogul shortage is a little bit of a surprise for an area that once had one of the top freestyle programs in the East, a program that spawned, among others, Greg Stump, now a successful ski film-maker. Oh well—you should probably figure that if your heart is set on bruising mogul skiing, you should be skiing somewhere else like Wildcat, a half hour's drive away in New Hampshire.

Haggett's is the longer of the two trails, but Tycoon, I think, is more fun in a simple way—a straight, quick, steep blast. If you're looking for funky natural snow conditions, the ski area occasionally opens the East Chair liftline. Even if it isn't open, a few of the local hotshots with brazen disdain for the law occasionally jump the rope, and after a storm you might consider being equally disdainful. On uncrowded weekdays, the ski patrol tends to look the other way or admonishes gently, but on weekends, the rope-jumping guarantees a clipped ticket.

SNOWBOARDING. If you simply like to rip on groomed trails, Shawnee's your kind of place, and it being the kind of family place that it is, you can expect to be joined by plenty of young rippers on weekends. They take particular delight in the rolls at the top of *Jack Spratt*— essentially a series of launching pads—and when last I looked, they were doing a pretty good job of maintaining a half pipe.

THE POST-GAME SHOW. The lakeside condo village is much nicer than you'd expect at such a modest ski area, but these are well-built, comfortable digs. They can also be pricey, although the price shrinks considerably if you buy into a package deal. Other than the lakeside village, there isn't much lodging in the immediate area, although North Conway is about 18 miles away.

As for area dining, the skiers' hangout in Bridgton, the nearest town, is the Black Horse Tavern, a steaks-and-buffalo-wings sort of place. If you're looking for something fancier, head west to Fryeburg and the Oxford House, a Victorian home converted to a mixed-cuisine restaurant. A nice, low-key, by-the-fireplace atmosphere prevails, and you might have it pretty much to yourself; Fryeburg in general and the Oxford House in particular are more visited by summer travelers than skiers in winter.

SHAWNEE DATA
Pluses and Minuses:
Pluses: low-key atmosphere, snowmaking (98% coverage) and grooming, good intermediate skiing. Minuses: small mountain, shortage of novice and expert terrain, limited early-season skiing.
Key Phone Numbers:
Ski Area Information: 207-647-8444
Lodging Information: 207-647-8444
Snow Conditions: 207-647-8444
Location: **6 miles west of Bridgton on Route 302. Mailing address: Rte. 302, Bridgton, ME 04009.**
Mountain Statistics:
Vertical drop: 1,300 feet
Summit elevation: 1,900 feet
Base elevation: 600 feet
Number of trails: 30
Lifts: 1 triple chair, 3 doubles
Snowmaking: 98%
Average annual snowfall: 90-100 inches

SUNDAY RIVER

Les—you're the man!

That, approximately, is the rallying cry at Sunday River, Les being Les Otten, developer of Sunday River. Les is the man as in the Man In Charge, the Sultan of Southern Maine Skiing, the Master Marketeer. *Inc.* magazine named him New England Entrepreneur of the Year in 1989, but I think one of his employees had a better way of describing Les's intense entrepreneurial zeal: "Les is a *driven* guy."

And Sunday River is a ski area driven by Les. When Les decided to buy the place in 1980 from the Sherburne Corporation, the same company that owned Killington, Sunday River hadn't changed a whole lot since its days as a former community rec center. Les looked upon Sunday River and presumably said something more or less Brigham Youngish, something like, "This is the place." And presumably in the way B.Y.'s followers looked out over arid Utah and wondered what the guy was talking about, people must have wondered what Les had in mind for this rather ordinary jumble of ridges and hummocks. That was certainly what the Sherburne people wondered anyway, when they deep-sixed Les's various master plans he had proposed while grunting his way along as a Sherburne management trainee. It wasn't as if Les had suddenly come upon the Jackson Hole of the East.

But topography was a secondary issue in Les's scheme of things. He had studied his marketing tout sheets well and had figured that coming up with a winner in the ski business was less a matter of mountain mass and more a matter of appealing to the human masses. Wide, well-groomed trails, efficient lifts, a convenient place to stay, and, most of all, reliable snow conditions—marketing studies indicated that that was what the majority of skiers wanted. Sunday River was where Les could deliver it all because he wouldn't have a lot of people looking over his shoulder telling him he couldn't do what he wanted to do.

In fact, Sunday River's unprepossessing topography gave Les an edge. As he puts it, "This is not an environmental lightning rod." There was no special flora, fauna, or scenery that cried out for protection. That meant few encounters with environmental groups, whose energies were diverted to protecting other, more scenic parcels of New England land. Les was also working with private land, avoiding the hassles of obtaining public-land-use permits. When Les decided to cut a trail, install a lift, build more lodging, or whatever, he did it, with little legal muss or fuss.

He did a lot of it, too, installing 12 new lifts in 12 years, and when last

I skied Sunday River the trail count had expanded to 93. He built nine trailside condo complexes, a large condo hotel, and a host of base facilities. Along with it came all the snowmaking and grooming hardware, of course—he had to have those reliable snow conditions. And he is the sort of guy who makes my life difficult, because he continues to expand; something new every year is a big part of the Les plan. When you go to Sunday River, you'll come across trails not mentioned in this book, and that's basically because they're so new I haven't skied them. I can't write about what I don't know.

Les dangled the bait, but the Master Marketeer in him told him he had to go further to make the public bite. So he sold Sunday River like crazy—for example, he touted White Heat, his main mogul run as "the steepest, longest, widest lift-serviced trail in the East." ("Les likes -est words," one Sunday River employee said to me.) So what if he was stretching it a bit? So what if there might be trails in the East that are steeper, and/or longer, and/or wider? Skiers apparently like -est words, too. Skier visits increased ten-fold in a decade, to the point where now more than 8,000 show up on an average weekend day. Those reliable snow conditions had a lot to do with it. While other New England ski areas saw skier visits drop by as much as 40 percent through two warm, snow-poor winters ('89-'90 and '90-'91), Sunday River claimed an increase in business.

OK—so Les knows marketing. What about skiing? Well, as one person at Sunday River said to me, "This isn't a classic New England resort, it is a modern New England resort." Modern means wide, fall-line trails. It means high-capacity lifts—five quads among the 11 chairs. It means "pod" skiing, in which each lift services a pod of trails, with pods linked more or less horizontally along Sunday River's ridges. No long, long runs perhaps, but the horizontal layout means that each skiing pod gives you between 1,400 and 1,700 vertical feet. And, of course, it means ultra-groomed snow. In general, Sunday River trails are the skiing equivalent of manicured golf fairways.

Sunday River won't let you down, but it won't surprise you, either. The skiing is fun in an uncomplicated way; the word "cruising" was made for Sunday River, while the word "mogul"—other than on White Heat—is all but deleted from the language. (The area, perhaps sensing a small shift in the wants of its public, was planning to add an intermediate mogul run for the '91-'92 season. I don't, however, take this as indication of an incipient trend.) The base facilities are functionally modern, spic-and-span, and meticulously run.

The combined effect, though, can be a little bit vanilla. In other words, I find it easy to enjoy Sunday River but hard to be exhilarated by the place. I like a little spice, unpredictability, nuance, funkiness—stuff Sunday River might be short on simply due to its newness. But in truth, I think these are things that have been factored out of Les's game plan. In aiming to please most of the people most of the time, Les has been like a smart politician—he's steered deliberately clear of anything that might rub someone the wrong way.

A SUNDAY RIVER STARTERS' KIT. A lot of the way you plan your Sunday River day depends on whether you're there on a weekend or a weekday. On a weekend, 8,000 or more skiers might show up at Sunday River; on a weekday, the number probably won't exceed 2,000.

There are three base areas: White Cap, Barker, and South Ridge. South Ridge is the most complete of the three as far as services—food, ski school, rentals, tickets, etc.—are concerned. Hence, it is the place to avoid on crowded weekends. On busy days, the best base to start from is White Cap, the first base area you come to. If you're not a strong skier, don't be intimated by White Heat, the monster-mogul trail that looms over the White Cap base area. There is some good, easy, uncrowded skiing over on this side of the area, too, and it's possible to work you're way over to all the other Sunday River skiing without going down anything nearly as precipitous as White Heat.

If it is an uncrowded weekday and you don't need lessons or rentals, I'd recommend starting out from the Barker Mountain base. It offers your best bet for getting out on the mountain quickly; this is where the Sunday River Express, the area's one high speed quad, begins from.

Les, of course, has got the entire base area surrounded with condos and sprinkled with restaurants. I'll go into lodging and dining in the "Post-Game Show."

SUNDAY RIVER FOR NOVICES. Look at the trail map, and you'd think that the obvious first-stop for novices would be the South Ridge area. But if you want to avoid crowds on busy weekends, or you want a little skiing pod almost entirely to yourself on weekdays, I'd suggest you check out Lift 11 over at White Cap. Yes, yes—the trails over here are rate intermediate blue. But no, no—don't even think about being intimidated.

I'd guess that all but the most timid first-timers should be able to handle the skiing over here, especially *Moonstruck*, the trail to the far right. This intermediate business, I think, has to do with a little bit of pitch at the trail's beginning—nothing to worry about since the trail is wide, the skiers scarce, and a long, long easy run waiting ahead. The runs on this lift also catch the morning sun and are relatively wind-protected, so that it can be reasonably toasty over here on cold days. The major drawback here is that the lift is something of a slowpoke, but since lift lines are rare, you're not losing too much.

There are, however, a couple of drawbacks to being a novice over at White Cap. The first is a fact that I've already mentioned: The South Ridge base has more complete services in terms of ski school and equipment rentals. The second is that finding an easy route to get from White Cap to South Ridge, home to the other main cluster of novice trails. The way to do it is to ride Lift 9 and cross over on *Overeasy*, but it's no picnic despite the pushover name. The trail itself isn't necessarily too tough, but it does cross over a couple of Sunday River's cruising favorites—Cascade, Monday Morning, and Tightwire—trails that have been known to attract speedball types. All I can say is stick with Overeasy as far as you can take it, and be on the alert for fast skiers as you cross the trails I've mentioned.

Now as for the skiing over at South Ridge, it's pretty straightforward stuff. The ski area has done a nice job here of leaving several tree islands in what is basically a straightforward, fairly long, novice slope. The effect of this, it seems, is to slow down and disperse skiers somewhat, along with adding some diversity to fairly simple terrain.

Assuming it isn't an overly crowded day, here would be my plan of attack for a novice or lower-level skier. I'd spend my morning at the lower South Ridge area, take a lesson there. (There's plenty of morning sun over here, too.) Then I'd ride Lift 1, the high-speed quad, to the Barker Mountain summit and meander over on *Three Mile Trail* to Peak Lodge for lunch. Three Mile Trail is pretty boring skiing, but at least it gets you up on the mountain, and Peak Lodge is the nicest spot at Sunday River to have lunch. After that, I'd work my way over to Lift 11 at White Cap. Because of the minimal skier traffic here, the groomed snow should still be groomed for afternoon skiing. When the day's done, you can ride the shuttle trolley back to South Ridge.

SUNDAY RIVER FOR CRUISERS. This is really a redundancy. Sunday River skiing is cruising by definition. Grooming is what makes it so; at 9:00 A.M. every morning, you'd think a team of 10,000 comb-carrying coolies had been out on the mountain overnight putting every flake in

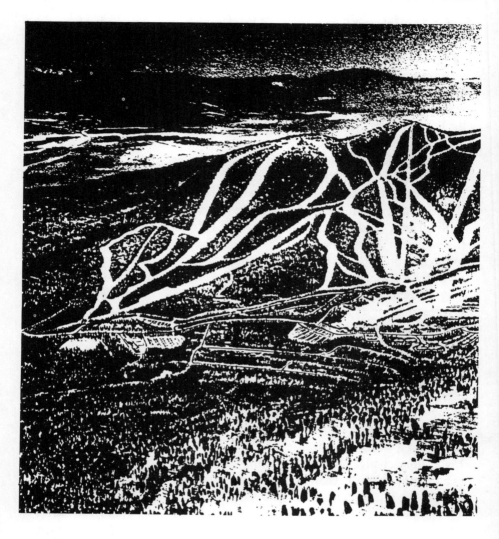

Sunday River, an overview of the mountain and trail layout

place. In fact the job is done by snow cats, but you get the idea: Something like 90 percent of the mountain's terrain is groomed nightly.

The effect can be tricky. When the surface is so uniform, I find that the pitch can deceive. It's hard to tell what's steep and what isn't—it all skis

the same. I say this as a warning: It's easy at Sunday River to get over your head, or perhaps more important, it's easy for someone else to get over his or her head at Sunday River. In other words, as you cruise your heart away be on the alert for skiers going too fast, especially as the pitch steepens.

That caveat out of the way, let's go skiing. The general rule for groomed-snow skiing is to ski the most popular trails first, since these are the trails that tend to be skied off first. So I'd recommend starting your morning at Spruce Peak. (Sunday River, with Killington-style hype, claims "five interconnected peaks." I'll let you decide when a peak is not a peak.) The two prime cruisers here are *Risky Business* and *American Express*, which are certainly at their best before 10:30 A.M.

Risky Business used to be rated as a black expert trail, but only because of one short, steepish pitch just after the trail swings under the chairlift. Check it out on the lift ride up to decide if you can handle it or not, but I'm betting that if you're a confident intermediate, you'll wonder—as I did—how Sunday River could ever consider this an expert trail. In fact, that bit of steepness—the little bit of terrain change—makes Risky Business a somewhat more interesting trail than American Express.

When the skiers begin to appear at Spruce Peak, I'd work my way over to Barker Mountain, home of the Sunday River Express quad chair. The lift line you encounter here might be longer than the one at Spruce Peak, but remember that a) this is a quad as opposed to the triple at Spruce, and b) it's a high-speed number. In other words, the line moves more quickly, and the lift itself moves *much* more quickly. If it is an uncrowded weekday, you can really crank out runs using this lift.

Bear left from the top of the lift onto either *Ecstasy* or *Jungle Road*. Jungle Road starts off flat—you might find yourself poling a bit to get going, but the pitch picks up, and the skiing can be pretty good once the trail runs into *Sunday Punch*. You'll meet up again with the skiers you lost on Ecstasy after the trail crosses under Lift 4. In fact, you'll meet up with a lot of skiers. A lot of trails join together in a knot here, probably the worst spot in Sunday River's trail layout.

I suppose that just about every area has a spot like this, a traffic-circle-like convergence where lots of skiers and lots of trails come together for one, brief and terrifying moment. I'd tell you to avoid it, but the reason this is a problem spot is because it's almost impossible to avoid. Les and the gang have tried to improve matters by taking out a few trees to improve sight lines, putting up "Slow Skiing" banners, and so on. But there is only so much they can do.

The important thing is to make sure you leave this trail knot on the trail you want to be on. *Cascades* is probably the most popular route, a trail that in width and pitch is similar to American Express. But because of

Cascades' popularity, you might prefer bearing right at the upper terminus of Lift 9 onto *Wildfire*, which gets less traffic. Just be sure that if you intend to return to Barker Mountain, you hang a left on the cutback trail near the bottom; otherwise you'll find yourself stuck on a the long flat run over to White Cap.

The Locke Mountain triple chair, incidentally, is something of a redundancy, since it services most of the intermediate terrain serviced by the Sunday River Express. You might want to use it if the lift line is long at the quad, but for my intermediate money, that's about the only reason to do so.

For lunch, you might want to wander over on *Three Mile Trail* from the Barker summit to Peak Lodge. That will give you a chance to take a couple of easy, post-lunch runs from the North Peak triple chair. The terrain here is perfect for legs made lazy by sitting and eating, the sun is here in the early afternoon, and it's an underskied portion of the mountain. I'd go with *Escapade* as the best of the North Peak bunch, but Sunday River instructors have told me that they like *Dream-maker* as teaching trail, an indication of the smoothness of the snow and the easy, evenness of the pitch. An even better option would be to take *Paradigm* and drop into the Aurora Peak basin. Here you'll find one of Sunday River's newest and most enjoyable runs, *Northern Lights*. It's full of drops and rolls and hummocks, and when last I skied Sunday River, I spent a lot of time on Northern Lights, on a powder day, popping off of hummocks and landing in soft snow. What a gas.

Sunday River's lay-out, as I've said, is more horizontal than vertical. Often when a mountain is laid out this way, you find yourself wasting time on roads and cat tracks to get from one side of the area to the other. Not so at Sunday River. I find that it is fairly easy to get in some good skiing as you work your way back and forth. And incidentally, if you do end up all the way over at White Cap and think you're dead meat as an intermediate, *Obsession*, despite its black rating and relative steepness, isn't an exceptionally tough trail to ski, at least in the morning before slick spots begin to appear through the groomed blanket on steeper sections. And if you find Obsession to be more like Persecution, you can always bail out after the first steep on *Heat's Off*, which leads back to Cascades.

HALFTIME. Sunday River bills its Peak Lodge, which opened for the 1990-91 season, as "the largest mountaintop restaurant in the East." (Another selection from Les's -est vocabulary.) It might be the largest, but it certainly isn't mountaintop. I mean, how can a place be mountaintop if you can ski *down* to it? Oh well, maybe that's not the point. The point, really, is that however you chose to describe Peak Lodge, it's a pretty nice place, especially on warm sunny days. It's got a big open deck and nice views, and even if the weather forces you inside, big windows and high ceilings create a nice sense of spaciousness. Should you end up at the base and your appetite won't wait, you'll probably encounter fewer people at the White Cap base rather than the South Ridge base.

Finally, if you're the spring picnic type, there are a couple of nice little clearings off Three Mile Trail near the top of Barker Mountain. You can pick up sandwiches, wine, beer, and other picnic essentials at the Mountain Grocer at the South Ridge base.

SUNDAY RIVER FOR ADVANCED SKIERS. I suppose when an area says that it's got the steepest, longest, widest trail in the East, that's the place start in talking about advanced skiing. So OK—let's talk about *White Heat*. Frankly, when I've been bludgeoned with so much -est bluster, I get a little bit of an attitude. Can't be that great, I figure.

Well, it isn't that great. But when I first skied it, White Heat proved to be much better than I wanted it to be. Probably the best of the -est stuff is the wideness of the trail, which allows the ski area to groom one side and allow the other side to turn to moguls. That's a concept I've always liked; it gives you a choice. And after all the Sunday River cruising you've probably done before arriving at White Heat, you might feel as I do: You'll appreciate having the mogul option.

Only the center third of White Heat, the headwall about a quarter of the way down after the first easy section strikes me as really steep, and it is, indeed, *really* steep. At this point, White Heat is really three trails (or more) in one—the groomed right side, the moguls toward the left, and the moguls of the narrow corridor to the left of the lift. I single out the far left because if you take on the headwall on this side, you're in for some serious skiing. The trail falls of steeply to the left and the moguls drop away jaggedly, as they tend to do when you have a steep double fall line. After that, the moguls I've encountered on White Heat have been large, rounded, and reasonably well-formed, but because the area dumps a ton of snow on White Heat, expect the moguls to be hard as well. You might want to let the morning sun do a little softening of White Heat before you tackle it, or just keep in mind that if the bumps start pound you, rather than the other way around, you can always bail out right.

While you're waiting for the softening to take effect, take a few runs on neighboring *Shock Wave*, so named because of a short but steep drop to a flat at the beginning of the trail, which can indeed give you an unpleasant shock if you aren't ready for it. I know—I executed a world-class face plant here, splitting my goggles in half.

If you're a natural-snow fan as I am, probably the two best places to find it are on *Bim's Whim* and *Locke Line*, the Locke Peak liftline. If you're looking for bumps, *Agony*, the Baker Mountain liftline, is sometimes allowed to to turn to moguls. If there hasn't been much fresh snow and the moguls are getting hard, the groom crew mows 'em down. But let's face it—for advanced skiers as other skiers, Sunday River is basically a temple of groomed-snow, not a place for worshipers of natural snow and moguls.

A groomed, expert triumvirate in Agony, *Top Gun*, and *Right Stuff* can be had at Barker Mountain, although as I've mentioned, Agony and, on rarer occasions, Top Gun are allowed to bump up from time to time. I suggest you do your skiing here early. Top Gun, the steepest of the three, can get skied off quickly, especially toward its steeper right side. As with Right Stuff, your dealing here with a steep double fall line, and there is just no way from keeping loose top snow from working its way to the trail's far left quickly. So if you can keep a tight line left, at least through the steep central sections of both trails, you'll come out of it fine. Once you venture into the middle, especially later in the day, expect a slick and scratchy ride. Should you fall, resign yourself to a long, Gore-tex assisted ride until the pitch of the trail eases off; there are no moguls or loose snow to slow your descent.

For groomed steeps, I think it's hard to beat *Downdraft*, stuck away on the far side of Spruce Peak. It's a little short, but it's got a good even pitch that lies close to the fall line, and it gets less skier traffic than the steep stuff at Barker Mountain. Its drawback is that there really isn't much other expert terrain over here; as I've mentioned, Risky Business is, in my opinion, rated too highly as a black trail.

So in terms of timing, I'd go with this plan: Ski the barker Mountain steeps in the early morning, work over to White Cap to ski White Heat and *Obsession*, and trail that skis much like Right Stuff, during the middle of the day, and hit Downdraft toward day's end. And if there has been a substantial snowfall, narrow Bim's Whim is the place for powder.

In keeping with a recent trend in Eastern skiing, Sunday River recently cleared out a few gladed runs beween trails. I dunno. In general, I have found the trees a little tighter than I like, meaning that it's hard to find a long, consistent line between trees. Too much stopping. And I'm not sure Sunday River attracts enough good natural snow to make these runs enjoyable on anything but a powder day. My experience has been that the snow tends to be hard and/or crusty, and that more often than not there is more fun to be had sticking to the regular trails.

SNOWBOARDING. Head for Aurora Peak as quickly as possible; *Airglow* and *Northern Lights* are made for snowboarding. Both descend the mountain in a series of giant steps, meaning that you can mix big , carved turns with air time and tricks, using the natural contours and drop-offs of the terrain. For fast, flat-out carving, head for *Monday Mourning*. It's wide and has a slight tilt to its fall line, so that you can bank your left turns hard, putting yourself in an an almost full layout position as your board sweeps through its arc.

If you're an expert snowboarder, you might have better luck than I've had on skis on some of these new tree runs. Snowboards obviously can maneuver better in tight trees than skis can, so I'd check out *Last Tango* first—it being the easiest of the tree runs—then, if you're feeling confident, head for White Cap and try the much tougher *Chutzpah* or *Hard Ball*.

THE POST-GAME SHOW. Les did a good job here of blending in almost 4,000 beds worth of condo and lodging facilities with the landscape. Unlike some resorts with that much on-site lodging, Sunday River doesn't feel like a misplaced chunk of suburbia. Condos and lodges are tucked away in the woods.

What you might think of this all depends on your priorities. To move development along as quickly as he has, Les has relied on simple, inexpensively built structures—construction projects that could be started and finished during the short Maine summer. The result: Condo structures that are functional but undistinguished—although moderately priced, I might add. Sunday River also has no real central gathering place or "resort village," and in the evening most people seem to go back to their condos or hotel rooms. For whatever reason, the layout and the architecture simply don't inspire a spirit of night time revelry.

You'll either appreciate this low-key, entertain-yourself character or be bored; the apres-ski scene at Bumps, the bar at the White Cap base, is pretty antiseptic. Again, maybe time is all it will take to infuse Bumps with a little atmosphere.

You'll do better by heading down the road to the Sunday River Brewing Company, a welcome addition to the apres-ski scene. Both locals and non-locals have quickly made this the most popular gathering spot in the area. They come partly to sample the several beer varieties brewed up on site, but they come mostly because there aren't many other choices in the neighborhood. One choice is to head off to downtown Bethel to hoist a few with a *very* local gang at the Sudbury Inn. But Bethel's not exactly your rock-around-the-clock kind of place.

By the way, Sunday River deserves major kudos for its Snow Cap Lodge, a ski-dorm concept. A popular pastime in the ski industry these days is worrying about skiing become an elitist sport. Well, Sunday River is one of the few ski areas to do something about it. At the Snow Cap Lodge (at the resort but not slopeside) you can stay in a dorm room for $20 to $25 a night, get a private room for $40 a night, or share a four-bed room for $80 a night. Like everything else at Sunday River, the lodge is modern and clean; in short, it's been a big hit with the budget-conscious.

SUNDAY RIVER DATA

Pluses and Minuses:

Pluses: good snowmaking and grooming, reliability of skiing conditions, lots of on-site lodging. Minuses: Shortage of challenging, natural-snow skiing, absence of old New England charm, shortage of skiing alternatives (e.g., cross-country skiing, shopping).

Key Phone Numbers:

Ski Area Information: 207-824-3000

Lodging Information: 800-543-2754

Snow Conditions: 207-824-6400

Location: 6 miles north of Bethel off Route 2. Mailing address: P.O. Box 450, Bethel ME 04217.

Mountain Statistics:

Vertical drop: 2,011 feet

Summit elevation: 2,793 feet

Base elevation: 782 feet

Number of trails: 90

Lifts: 2 high-speed quads, 4 regular quads, 5 triples, 1 double

Snowmaking: 95 % (453 acres)

Average annual snowfall: 150 inches

ALSO KEEP IN MIND... *Mt. Abram*

People in the movie business have a term for the positive word-of-mouth that circulates about an upcoming feature: Buzz. In its own small and local way, Mt. Abram has got buzz: It's an area that local skiers often mention as a good, undiscovered place to ski. "A great little mountain," a ski patrolman at another Maine area told me, though I think he was speaking with a fondness inflated by childhood memories. At any rate, I'll be honest with you—Mt. Abram is undiscovered by me, too. I've only been buzzed by it.

Here is what I do know about the area via word-of-mouth: It's basically a cruiser's ski area. I know, however, that there is at least a little bit of steep skiing, since I've come across a couple of pretty hot skiers who've been weened here. There's also a separate little hill for novices and lower-intermediate skiers. What Mt. Abram lacks is size; it stretches the imagination to think that a ski area with just over 1,000 vertical feet can be called a mountain.

Why bother with Mt. Abram when you have Sunday River just to the north and Shawnee Peak just to the south? As much, I suppose, for local color as for the skiing. When you're looking for an antidote to resort sleek, Mt. Abram is probably as good a stopover as any in the eastern New Hampshire/southern Maine area.

INSIDE STORY
NO TIME LIKE THE RIGHT TIME

Every skier-opinion survey I've ever seen from the ski industry tells the same story: Of all the negatives skiers come up with about skiing, the complaint that lift lines are too long comes out on top every time. Give ski areas credit—they've taken all those gripes seriously and responded by building more lifts that are faster and have a greater uphill capacity. Lift-line waits at most areas are nothing like what they were a decade ago.

But that obviously doesn't mean lift lines have disappeared, especially at bottleneck areas at peak times. The solution? Ideally, ski on weekdays in January and February. Ski areas typically earn something like 50% of their season's revenues from three weeks in the season: Christmas-New Years, the week of Presidents' Day, and a week in mid-March when most schools take spring break. If you can avoid those periods, you can avoid lift lines easily. Obviously, though, that's easier for me to say than for most skiers to do.

So on days when you know there will be lift lines, plan your ski day so as to be out-of-sync with everyone else. It isn't hard, and it works. The lift-line flow at most areas on a busy day looks something like this:

8:00-9:00—Few skiers, except die-hards, ski patrol, and skin-flinters taking advantage of a freebie hour offered at some areas— or powderhounds on fresh-snow days.
9:00-9:30—Short lines begin to form at lower lifts.
9:30-10:30—Morning madness; long lines at lifts near the base, especially bottom-to-top and high-speed lifts.
10:30-12:30—Long lines gradually move up to lifts higher on the mountain.
12:30-1:30—Lunch lull at all lifts
1:30-2:30—Post-lunch rush; longest lines of the day at most lifts
2:30-3:00—Lines gradually diminish, especially on lifts nearer the summit
3:00-4:00—Short lines at most lifts

Invariably, the worst lines are at bottom-to-top lifts—e.g., the Loon

Gondola, the Stowe Gondola, the Waterville Quad. At prime-times (morning madness and the post-lunch rush) be prepared to use alternatives, meaning you shouldn't take runs to the bottom at those times. Two other surges to avoid are just after 10:00 A.M. and 1:00 P.M., or whenever an area schedules its ski school classes. It usually takes less than 15 minutes to get all the ski schoolers on their way, but on busy days, those 15 minutes can really stagnate lift lines. (A reasonable alternative, of course, is to take a lesson, which comes not only with an instructor but line-cutting priveleges as well.)

Given the above schedule, how would I plan my skiing for a busy day? First, I'd get to the area well before 9:00 A.M. Yeah, yeah—you say it's hard getting out of a warm bed early on a cold day, and I'll second that. But I'll toss in an added early-bird incentive: At some areas, part or all of the 8-9:00 A.M. period is free skiing, meaning you can test-drive the conditions before buying your ticket. Ideally, I'd get up as early as possible and have my breakfast on the mountain. The Killington Peak Lodge cafeteria, for example, starts serving a light breakfast at 8:00 A.M., and I assure you that it is not heavily attended. Comes with a great view, too.

I'd stay up high on the mountain until well after 10;00 A.M., then work my way toward lower lifts as the crowds work their way upward. I'd ski through the usual lunch hour, then take a break after 1:30 P.M. I'd make sure to save energy for post-3 P.M. skiing, when others are tired and cold. On a nice afternoon, the very last run of the day, when slopes are quiet and deserted, can be a cosmic joy—just ask any ski patroller about trail sweeping. After that, I wouldn't be in a hurry to get home. I'd have a hot chocolate or a beer and let the parking lot empty. The one thing I hate more than a long lift line is a long traffic jam.

Chapter 8
Northern Maine

IF YOU'RE WONDERING just how out-in-the-woods northern Maine is, consider this: When I last was at Saddleback, which is outside of Rangeley, the ski area was having problems with a moose stomping around on its cross-country trails. Ski tracks were being perforated by two-foot-deep moose-prints. When a moose on the loose is a problem you must deal with, you know you're well removed from civilization.

Don't get me wrong—Sugarloaf and Saddleback aren't exactly solitary outposts in an uncharted outback. Both ski areas are in country that, if sparsely populated, is civilized enough. But if you went much further north, you would indeed begin to enter one of the last true wilderness regions of the eastern U.S., a region that winter closes off almost entirely to human visitation.

Remoteness—at least a five-hour drive from Boston, the nearest major metropolitan area (not counting Portland, of course)—is one reason for the sparse settlement around Saddleback and Sugarloaf. A second reason is logging, the current and historical underpinning of the regional economy. Lumber companies that long ago began buying up large tracts of land—tens of thousands of acres at a pop—had timbering, not settlement or industrialization, in mind. Log-laden trucks are a common sight along the roadways, but that doesn't mean the trees are all gone. About two thirds of Maine today remains forested, and as you close in on Saddleback and Sugarloaf, two thirds becomes more like three thirds.

A few things should be coming clear to you by now. One is that this is low-key New England, a world of little nightlife, glitz, or sizzle. Sugarloaf, a self-contained resort large enough to constitute its own township (Carrabassett Valley) might be peppy enough after the sun sets. But when local people go out on the town, it is more likely to be a morning run to the hardware store or doughnut shop than a high-life night of painting the town red. Life ambles through winter, sometimes seeming to fall asleep in its tracks—which for all I know might happen when weekend skiers and snowmobilers aren't around to liven things up and keep the few local lodges and restaurants in business.

Another thing that should be clear is that remoteness brews up a different climate. Sugarloaf and Saddleback are the northernmost ski areas covered in this book (edging out Jay Peak), and their weather has little in common with what goes on along the Maine coast. I say that that *should* be clear, but apparently it isn't to a lot of people. Gregg Sweetser, Saddleback's general manager, tells about the many Boston-area weekenders who show up in their loafers and corduroys and step from their cars into knee-deep, loafer-filling snow. The lesson is implicit: Be ready for snow and cold.

Finally, you can probably figure out that a population shortage implies a shortage of things that tend to go with population-dense areas, things like major highways and supermarkets. Smaller roads, wintry climate, and remoteness should tell you that Sugarloaf and Saddleback aren't areas you can count on getting to in a hurry. And as you near your destination, shopping opportunities fall away. Farmington or Skowhegan are your last shots at a good selection of things like fresh meats and vegetables, should you intend to prepare your own meals.

It's nice to know that if you choose to come this far—and I recommend it highly—you have two legitimately different options. Sugarloaf is a modern, full-service resort backed up by a big mountain; Saddleback is more retreat with a mountain much more substantial than its modest vertical rise might imply. Each is appended by a small town nearby (Rangeley near Saddleback, Kingfield near Sugarloaf) for lodging, dining, and local color.

Most skiers apparently favor the resort concept over the retreat concept. On a typical weekend day, Sugarloaf draws close to 5,000 skiers, while Saddleback's skier total will be nearer 1,200. Neither is especially crowded on most weekdays, since the distance from major population centers limits day-skier traffic. To avoid crowds, ski Sugarloaf on weekdays and Saddleback on weekends.

SADDLEBACK

Saddleback lies where the road ends and wilderness begins. To get there, you drive until you run out of civilized Maine, then take a seven-mile access road that climbs to 2,400 feet and the base of Saddleback—the highest base elevation of any New England ski area.

This is a close to the rugged wilderness as New England lift-serviced skiing gets. In the midst of what once was a 12,000-acre logging plantation, the ski area is surrounded by vast tracts of undeveloped forest and lake land. Look due northward from the summit, and your line of sight carries over only two paved roads for 50 miles or so to the Canadian border.

"The last uncrowded ski area in Maine," is the way Saddleback bills itself, and while tag line is entirely justified, I think John Freeman, a part-time Saddleback ski patrolman, had an even better way of capturing the crowdless essence of the area. Riding the lift one morning after a snowstorm, he saw my eagerness for fresh powder and told me, "Don't worry. Here, you're often not just the first skier down a trail. You're often the second and third skier, too."

Saddleback's crowdlessness is due largely to three reasons: first, it's not easy to get to; second, it has no large population centers nearby for a supply of day skiers; and third, the region is popular among snowmobilers, who have been known to crowd skiers out of the Rangeley area's limited bed base, especially when the "snodeos"— snowmobiling carnivals—come to town.

The lack of skiers has made it hard in recent recession years for Saddleback to make ends meet, but that isn't the only reason the area is underdeveloped. The ski area management and the Appalachian Mountain Club (AMC) locked horns in a lengthy battle concerning the "visual impact" of installing a chairlift to the summit. The AMC folks vehemently resisted the idea of the view of summer hikers on the Appalachian trail, which runs over the Saddleback summit, being impaired by a summit lift station. The Saddleback folks countered that ending the lift just below the summit—as suggested by AMC—would require massive rock-blasting to create a flat terminal area, meaning greater environmental scarring.

Such confrontations between environmentalists and ski areas are not new, and the problem for ski areas—regardless of whether you are for or against development proposals—is the money-draining length of the legal process. Saddleback, lacking the financial reserves to weather years of legal storming, has probably suffered more than other ski areas in the process. Ironically, Saddleback might win the legal battle, but its financial incapacitation has left it unable to install the lift. If you ask me, some mediator, conciliator, or legal genius ought to figure out a far simpler process for resolving these disputes quickly, rather than allowing them to drag on for years and even decades.

But enough of that legal nonsense. Back to skiing: Something about Saddleback's rugged isolation appeals to me. In many ways, I think it's what New England skiing ought to be—narrow trails winding away from a rime-encrusted, windswept summit; stupendous views; lots of natural-snow (rather than manufactured) conditions; the kind of skiing that satisfies by challenging and invigorating more than pampering the ego. But my preferences aside, Saddleback is certainly, to large degree, what New England skiing *used* to be, before the advent of wide supertrails, extensive snowmaking, and fast lifts. When here, you are absolutely in-country, a reality intensified by a jaunt around Saddleback's cross-country trails (see *Free-heeling New England*). When the base-lodge bar shuts down around 6:00 P.M., the nightlife is basically over for the evening. Unless you're willing to drive the eight miles to Rangeley, hardly a hotbed of raucous, late-night revelry, you'd better be ready to entertain yourself with family and friends by your condo fireplace.

Lying at the edge of the wilderness, Saddleback can also attract wilder-ness weather, a phenomenon that can be both nasty and nice. On the nasty side is the wind; when I was last at Saddleback and scrambled to the summit, the steady 40-mile-an-hour bluster was literally hard to stand up to. However, all lifts (for reasons mentioned in the previous para-graph) terminate below the summit, where the wind tends to be *substan-tially* less fierce.

Don't think of Sugarloaf as a windy-day alternative. Sugarloaf is exposed to most of the winds that whistle around Saddleback—often more so, being a higher mountain. In fact, Saddleback is probably the better windy-day choice, its t-bars being lower to the ground, more shielded by trees, and less susceptible to wind holds than its own chairlifts or those at Sugarloaf. By riding the Pony t-bar and skiing "the Pass," a narrow connector trail, to the Fargo t-bar, it is possible to access all of Saddleback's skiing without having to dangle on a cold chair in a cold wind.

The nice side of the wilderness-weather conditions shows itself in two ways. First is a generally reliable cover of natural snow. Second is the natural beauty it creates: When the sky clears and the sun glistens from the rime-caked trees near the summit, Saddleback is a work of rugged mountain art.

SADDLEBACK FOR NOVICES. A shortage of extended novice and

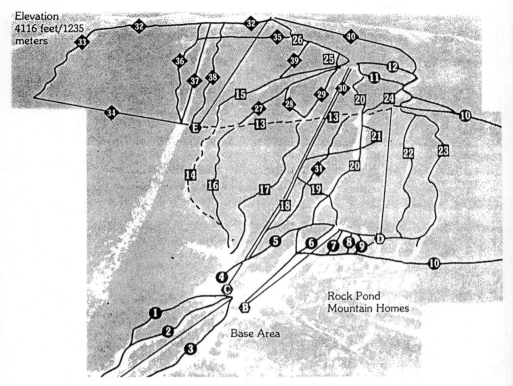

Elevation
4116 feet/1235
meters

Rock Pond
Mountain Homes

Base Area

Saddleback, a reduced view of the trail map

lower-intermediate terrain is Saddleback's principal weakness, especially on weekdays, when the lower Buggy t-bar is usually not running. What's more, Saddleback's three t-bars, which provide great line-avoiding—and, when such conditions apply, wind-avoiding—alternatives to the chairlifts, often make for hard uphill going for less experienced skiers.

On the plus side, the simplicity of Saddleback's layout makes it far less intimidating for novices than larger, more complex resorts. The small base lodge and the usual crowdlessness means that getting set up with lift tickets, rentals, and lessons is basically a one-stop-shopping process—go to the desk right inside the front door and your on your way. Another nice thing about the simple layout is that parents can let kids off the leash; the single base lodge with one big wide slope, *Goldrush*, in front of it is a back-to-basics, hard-to-go-wrong playground for the younger set.

The principal novice terrain is right out the front door of the base lodge: Goldrush and the narrower *Panhandler*. Both are serviced by the Surrey Double Chair, short but slow for the sake of novice skiers and kids. Goldrush, especially early in the morning and after lunch, is the better choice, since better skiers tend to use Panhandler to access the Stagecoach chair, the main lift to the upper mountain.

The early-morning and post-lunch rushes are good times to spend on the Buggy t-bar (if it's running), which features three nice variations in *Whispering Pines, Jolly Jamboree,* and *Cowpoke's Cruise.* Because the t-bar serves exclusively novice terrain, you needn't be concerned about being blitzed by better skiers. The terrain belongs exclusively to you and other skiers of similar ability.

As your ability and confidence grow, the next step up is *Lazy River*, which can be reached either from the top of the Stagecoach chair or the Pony Express t-bar. Lazy River is a pretty, narrow wander through the woods, its challenge come less from its pitch than from the variable quality of its snow. The trail has no snowmaking, and its narrowness makes it difficult to groom. For that reason, make sure Lazy River is open before leaving the base; it is more likely than other trails on the lower mountain to be closed.

The next step up for novices and lower intermediates is *White Stallion*, which circles around to the left of the Stagecoach chair. It has but one steepish pitch as it turns into the fall line before making an ambling run back to the chairlift base. One warning: If the wind is out of the north/ northwest—the predominant high-pressure, arctic direction—it will be in your face for that last stretch, making for a slow, cold run to the bottom. That makes White Stallion a better choice for periods when the wind is low or from a warm-weather direction.

SADDLEBACK FOR CRUISERS. The most popular intermediate trail is *Haymaker*, for good reason: it's wide, well-groomed, and has a nice variety in its pitch and fall line. I've found a good quality test for an intermediate run to be its adaptability to being a giant slalom course. Most GS skiers are looking for what most good intermediates are looking for: length, changes in pitch, no extended flats, and room to ride an edge through big turns—in other words, room to cruise.

Sure enough, Haymaker is the trail of choice for Saddleback's race programs, which can be something of an annoyance at times when race training is in progress. Races or training sessions don't necessarily close

Haymaker down, but they do restrict the amount if terrain available for recreational skiing. The area usually tries to restrict race activities on the trail to the beginning and/or end of the skiing day. So the best time for Haymaker is prime time, from 11:00 A.M. to 2:00 P.M. At a busier area, the snow on the most popular intermediate trail might be scraped off by noon, but minimal skier traffic at Saddleback usually keeps Haymaker's snow fresh through most of the day.

Where to go for Haymaker alternatives? *Wildfire* and *Desperado*, side-by-side trails from the Pony t-bar, are good choices. Both are slightly narrower than Haymaker, but their overall pitch profile is very similar. If you use the Pony t-bar rather than the Stagecoach chair as your main access lift, you sacrifice vertical footage (650 vertical feet from the t-bar compared with 1,150 from the chair), but you avoid flat runouts and any lift lines that might develop.

The big difference between the two trails is that Wildlife is groomed regularly while Desperado is not, an option I think more areas should offer. After your confidence is high from skiing Wildfire's groomed snow, Desperado's small moguls and variable snow are an ideal next step for putting your basic skiing skills and balance to the test.

On a clear day, *Cliffhanger*, one of the most inappropriately named trails in New England, is a must from the top of the Fargo t-bar. Cliffhanger, despite its fearsome name, is a lower-intermediate-level cruise to the top of the Stagecoach chair. (In fact the ride up the t-bar, especially when the lift line crosses wind-scoured crust and rock patches, is more challenging than the ski down.) The low ridgetop trees along the trail permit expansive views of Maine's mountain and lake country, and when the air is clear and blue, you should be able to make out Sunday River's trails to the south and New Hampshire's White Mountains to the southwest, with Rangeley Lake in the foreground. Conversely, Cliffhanger isn't much of a run on a raw, overcast day, the skiing itself not being what sells the trail.

At the high end of Saddleback's intermediate skiing is *Gunslinger*, to the left from the Stagecoach chair, a trail ideal for stronger intermediates who want to test their mogul mettle. The pitch isn't steep, the trail is wide, and the moguls aren't huge, and its exposure—a slight tilt eastward—allows parts of the trail to catch softening morning sun. (Gunslinger can also be a good powder day choice because of its exposure, being somewhat less exposed to predominant storm winds.) The trail's one tricky spot is at the *Sidewinder* juncture, where ice, as hard as blue quartz, forms on the left side of the trail. Take it slow and stick as far right as possible; after that entire trail again becomes skiable.

One other note: Only the top half of Gunslinger is allowed to turn to moguls. After crossing over the intersection with the Pass, you'll find yourself—perhaps thankfully—on groomed snow again.

HALFTIME. We're not talking many choices here. The base-lodge cafeteria's food is adequate—no more, no less—but it is priced accordingly. Picnicking near the summit is a better way to go, especially on warm spring days. Pack a lunch, check in with the ski patrol at the top of the Fargo t-bar, and make the five-minute scramble to the broad, above-treeline summit ridge. At that point, find your favorite rock (there are plenty of good flat ones to spread out on). If it's a nice warm day, other picnickers will be doing the same, seeking that hallowed spring mix of food, sun, and view.

If the weather is less-than-perfect, you can take your picnic lunch to the warming hut at the Stagecoach chair summit. With wood benches, a woodburning stove, stacks of magazines, and a big window looking out toward Rangeley Lake, the hut has a cozy, true-grit feel. A homey feel, too; don't be surprised to find someone—perhaps yourself—grilling a sandwich or warming soup on the stove.

SADDLEBACK FOR ADVANCED SKIERS. Cruddy, bumpy, stumpy, powdery, wind-blown, narrow, and gnarly—Saddleback has everything to challenge the best, including a classic, hike-out back bowl that sets up well for spring-season corn skiing. Saddleback's expert trails aren't demanding just because they're steep—which they can be—but because of their constant variation in pitch, width, and snow conditions. It's the kind of skiing that can be as much an intellectual exercise as it is physical. You must think your way down the mountain, pick your routes intelligently, and earn from that a satisfaction that by my measure is far richer than what comes from skiing the groomed, wide steeps proliferating at other New England areas.

On to the trails. *Gunslinger* is good place to start, a moderate bump trail described above in "Saddleback for Intermediates." The next rung on the challenge ladder is *Rough Rider*, reached by cutting right from the top of Haymaker. The trail's pitch is no steeper than Gunslinger's, but its narrowness makes it seem so.

In places, Rough Rider is no more than 20 feet wide, and because of the trail's big S turn, the sense of being surrounded by trees is total. It's a far cry from those straight shots where you can scope the entire length of the trail from the top. Despite the winding across the fall line, I've encountered fairly uniform and skiable bumps on Rough Rider; lack of skier traffic keeps them from getting large and choppy. When the snow is soft, the trail is a corridor of old-fashioned New England pleasure; in marginal conditions, the narrowness can make it tough to ride out or slide through turns.

El Hombre, the Stagecoach chair lift line, is a more modern type of trail—a straight cut on the fall line, covered with artificial snow. This combination, I think, robs El Hombre of character, but a more significant shortcoming is that the wind tends to sweep the trail's top knoll, so that trying to ski it can be like trying to ski along the fuselage of a 747. Too bad—because the trail's two steep pitches offer good mogul skiing, especially on the left side, underneath the lift, where fresh snow tends to collect (be blown) more abundantly.

What's a skier to do? The Saddleback regulars have an answer in a local tradition call "enduro runs." These runs link the best sections of various runs, and you have attained true enduro status when you can ski them top-to-bottom, non-stop. Not an easy task, since as I've said, Saddleback's expert skiing requires that you be mentally and physically on your toes with every turn.

A favorite enduro is to ski the top of *Silver Bullet*, your first left off of the Stagecoach lift, that begins benignly enough on a narrow easy pitch. Then the bottom drops out with a short fall-away punctuated with a big rock in the middle that can provide big, unscheduled air time if you're not alert. After the steep, cut left on *Sidewinder*, on which you should stay high and keep up your speed to avoid hoffing up a slight upturn at the trail's end. That lands you at the top of the best and steepest section of El Hombre. Favor the left side and be on the lookout toward the bottom of the pitch for an unmarked, path-like opening in the woods that leads to the Rough Rider mogul fields. If you make all the right turns and pull it off non-stop, report to the ski patrol for enduro club induction.

There's an even longer enduro run from the top of the Fargo t-bar, and when the snow's soft and deep, it's certainly the preferred option. Bear right off Cliffhanger onto *Nightmare Glades*, a glade trail neither as steep nor tight as its name suggests. When you exit the glades onto White Stallion, keep going straight through the woods to connect with Sidewinder, then on to El Hombre and Rough Rider, as above. One alternative to consider, in order to avoid the bottom flats that lead to the Stagecoach chair base: Cut left on *Wrangler's Run* after the last mogul chute on Rough Rider and ride up the Pony t-bar, connecting with the

Fargo t-bar by way of the Pass.

From the summit, *Bronco Buster*, the never-to-be gondola's lift line, is the most popular expert run. For my tastes, Bronco Buster's width, coupled with the lowness of the trees near the summit, give it a barren feel, although it can be a good steep cruiser in spring.

A far more interesting trail, one with a gnarly, backcountry character, is *Muleskinner*, reached via a 5- to 10-minute traverse/hike that runs beneath the summit ridge. Actually, Muleskinner is the only official name; unofficially, it is referred to by locals, especially those who participated in cutting the trail, as "HFC." The H stands for hard, the C stands for climb, and if you can imagine the chainsaw-toting trail-cutters slogging their way up through the mud, stumps, and sawdust, then you can probably imagine what the F stands for.

I'm sure the descent on skis is more enjoyable than the ascent with chainsaws. Three steep pitches seem to hoard snow, especially on the trail's left side, narrowness and a slight turn in exposure shielding Muleskinner from the wind. It's a place to find powder, but it is a trail to negotiate with backcountry-style caution. Beneath the snow lurks a rough surface of rocks, stumps, and other treacheries, and if you hurt yourself or lose a ski here, it may be a while before help arrives. You're a long way from the core of the ski area, as evidenced by the half-mile road at the end of the trail, just to get back to the Fargo t-bar base.

Finally, I can't omit mention of that back bowl. I've never skied it, but I've scoped it and am impressed. When the prevailing wind blows over the summit, it deposits snowdrifts on the back side, that bury 10-foot trees in a good season. When all that snow softens in spring and you've checked in with patrol (you might be required to enlist a patrolman, although you'll find many eager takers if conditions are right), the skiing, I've been convincingly told, is sensational.

The bowl's pitch is an even 30 degrees or so, contoured along a classic, convex bowl shape. Its shortcoming is literally that—there are only about 400 to 500 skiable vertical feet. Also, once skied, the bowl offers no logging roads or other escape hatches. You've got to climb back up, but if the skiing's good, who cares about a half-hour huff-and-puff?

SNOWBOARDING. I wouldn't put Saddleback high on the snowboarder's list of preferred Eastern ski areas. For one thing, Saddleback's t-bars can be a pain—not impossible to negotiate, but difficult. For another thing, some of the trails for getting back and forth across the mountain—some of the narrow tracks that connect those wonderful enduro runs—are flat in places, while some of Saddleback's best runs are well-moguled, and I've never thought of a snowboard as a device well-suited to take on moguls. And finally, there is just a weird, gut feeling I have that Saddleback and snowboarding are somehow an uncomfortable match—the wrong terrian, the wrong lifts, the wrong atmosphere, the wrong crowd. If you want snowboarding in northern Maine, I'd say Sugarloaf is the place to go.

THE POST-GAME SHOW. If your the main ingredients of your apres-ski stew are a good meal, a fireplace, and a cluster of friends or family, Saddleback's for you. If you want much more, you'll be chewing your toes in boredom after a night or two. What nightlife and dining there is is in Rangeley, the night-on-the-town favorite of most local folks being the Rangeley Inn, with sit-down, New-England-inn character and menu to match. For lower budgets, there's Mike's. And if you're up much past 10:00 P.M., you're more imaginative about your night activities than I am.

SADDLEBACK DATA

Pluses and Minuses:

Pluses: Good, old-style expert terrain; good spring skiing; quiet, wilderness character, especially on touring-center trails; uncrowded. Minuses: Hard to get to; antiquated lift system; lack of novice terrain; lack of nightlife.

Key Phone Numbers:

Ski Area Information: 207-864-5671

Lodging Information: 207-864-5671 (resort lodging), 800-685-2537 (area lodging)

Snow Conditions: 207-864-3380

*Location***: 7-mile access road begins one mile southeast of Rangeley on Route 4. Mailing address: P.O. Box 490, Rangeley, ME 04970.**

Mountain Statistics:

Vertical drop: 1,830 feet

Summit elevation: 4,116 feet

Base elevation: 2,286 feet (at Buggy t-bar base)

Number of trails: 40

Lifts: 2 double chairs, 3 t-bars

Snowmaking: 55%

Average annual snowfall: 200 inches

SUGARLOAF

What a surprise Sugarloaf is. There you are, cruising around northern Maine, with nothing around you but trees, a building every 10 miles or so, and logging trucks spraying road slop on your windshield as they rumble south towards mills in Rumford and Berlin, New Hampshire. Then up jumps Sugarloaf, looking like a pre-fabbed section of Downtown USA that got shipped to the wrong mailing address. Sugarloaf, in other words, is anomalously modern for outback Maine. The immediate area around the base has almost a city-center, high-rise feel to it. In this neck of the woods, the seven-story Sugarloaf Mountain Hotel qualifies as a skyscraper.

Sugarloaf might have roots reaching back more than 40 years, but you wouldn't know it by looking at it. There is such a newness of design and concept here; Sugarloaf vies with Stratton for the title of Vail of the East in the sense of being a self-contained, according-to-the-blueprint, condo-heavy destination resort. Sugarloaf is thoroughly modern Maine, right down to automatic-teller machines, fax machines, airport shuttle buses, and haute-cuisine restaurants. You can travel for hours in this part of Maine before coming across someone who's even *heard* of that sort of stuff. Sugarloaf has it all.

In a way, of course, it has it all *because of* Sugarloaf's remoteness, not in spite of it. The resort's developers figured that if skiers were willing to make the substantial effort to get to Sugarloaf—I'll remind you that it's at least a five-hour drive from Boston—then the resort ought to offer something substantial as a reward. And substantial it is—more than 5,000 beds at the base of the mountain as part of a full-service community that is, as I've said, large enough to be its own township.

But the most substantial thing about Sugarloaf is the skiing. The ski area certainly belongs in the upper echelon of "skiers' mountains" in New England, with a truly unusual feather in its historical cap to prove it. This is the only ski area in America that can claim to have hosted the famed Arlberg Kandahar downhill race. No kidding—in 1971, when snow was lacking in Europe, the Kandahar people shopped around for a big mountain with sufficient snow, and Sugarloaf fit the bill. Since then, Sugarloaf has hosted several World Cup races and the World Junior Alpine Championships (in 1984), and racer types seem to hang around Sugarloaf in abundance.

A racing tradition, though, isn't Sugarloaf's chief credential as a class-A skiers' mountain. Variety's the thing; this is one of those rare areas that has plenty of good skiing for all levels of skier. A case could be made that the resort base has been overdeveloped (in fact, a case has been made by local environmentalists), but I can find little argument with the skiing here. It is a superb mix.

Admittedly, the full mix isn't always available. The above-treeline snowfields that Sugarloaf hypes with great gusto are often closed, due either to lousy snow or the high winds that rake Sugarloaf from time to time. If you're like me, you don't have much taste for battling the chill winds of mid-winter, so skiing below the summit is just fine. I can't say I throw enthusiastic support to Sugarloaf's idea to make snow at the summit; in my book there are certain types of terrain that are simply ill-suited for the manufactured stuff, and the Sugarloaf snowfields are terrain that belong in that category. That aside, spring is snowfields prime time for; the local hardcore, spring skiing on the snowfields and front face is the crown jewel of Sugarloaf skiing.

Back for a moment to the overdevelopment issue. For the most part, a sense of good taste has gone into the resort's development, although the angular modern design of base facilities, from an aesthetic perspective, might clash a bit with the surroundings. As for those 5,000 beds, the fact is that if Sugarloaf were forced to rely on lodging in nearby communities such as Kingfield, or to rely on day skiers, it simply couldn't afford to be the caliber of ski area it has come to be. Now you can get into an argument as to whether or not there should be a ski area here at all, but that's another issue entirely.

The bottom line is that Sugarloaf is a fully developed, fully serviced resort with lots of amenities. If you like that kind of complete package, you'll like Sugarloaf. If you find it overbearing, then you can take the escape hatch to Saddleback, the retreat-like area down the road. It boils down to a matter of personal preference. My preference tends to flip-flop; I'm someone who simply likes having choices.

A SUGARLOAF STARTERS' KIT. Sugarloaf's distance from civilization centers makes it somewhat less of a weekend-intensive resort than areas further south. The average crowd of about 4,000 skiers that shows up on a weekend day is about half the typical weekend crowd at Sunday River, for example. By the same token, weekdays at Sugarloaf, especially during the school-break weeks in February and March, can still draw healthy numbers. In short, you might not encounter weekend masses at Sugarloaf, but by the same token you might not have the mountain to yourself on weekdays.

If you aren't staying in or close to the village, I'd suggest two options for minimizing hassles. Option 1 is to pull in at the Snubber chair parking lots; they're the first lots on your left after you pass the check-in center. You can ride the lift for free and then buy your lift ticket at the village. I'll admit that the Snubber ride is long and flat, but the parking lots are flatter and closer to the lifts than those up at the village. And if you have to park in the lower lots at the village, you'll have to deal with a shuttle bus to the base—something that's never been to my liking.

Option 2 is to turn right on West Mountain and head up to the West Mountain base. You can buy tickets here only on weekends and during vacation weeks, but this is truly a way to get away from the morning base-area knots. The main drawback to starting out at West Mountain is that, on a sunny day, it starts you out on the wrong side of the mountain. Sugarloaf is one of those areas at which the best strategy is to follow the sun—east side in the morning, west side in the afternoon.

Having given you the alternatives first, I should note that on days that aren't especially busy, starting out from the Village is probably the best way to go. It's where all the services—ski school, rentals, day care, etc.—are located and it also avoids the extra lift ride that are a part of options 1 and 2. Just try to park in the uppermost lot possible, and be prepared for a bit of an uphill scramble to get to the base of the lifts.

SUGARLOAF FOR NOVICES. "Skiers' mountain"—a term often applied to Sugarloaf—tends to connote difficult skiing. Yes, Sugarloaf has plenty of the tough stuff. But what really makes it a skiers mountain is the quality terrain it has for all skiers, and lower level skiers don't get cut out of the deal. In fact, Sugarloaf's expanse of novice and lower-intermediate terrain is as good as it gets in New England, with four lifts, from the very short to the very long, devoted almost entirely to easy skiing. (I'm not including here three chairs—Snubber, West Mountain, and Sawduster—which are primarily access lifts for mountainside condo-dwellers.)

The shortest of the four, Skidway, is basically a beginners' chair, one to move on from quickly. Next up is Double Chair East, which services superwide *Boardwalk*. (Be careful not to get on Double Chair West, which runs parallel and carries you to higher, more challenging terrain. It will probably have the longer lift line anyway.) Boardwalk's main drawback is that it is a thoroughfare for skiers coming down from the upper mountain, so you want to avoid it during typical down-mountain rush periods—e.g., lunchtime and late afternoon.

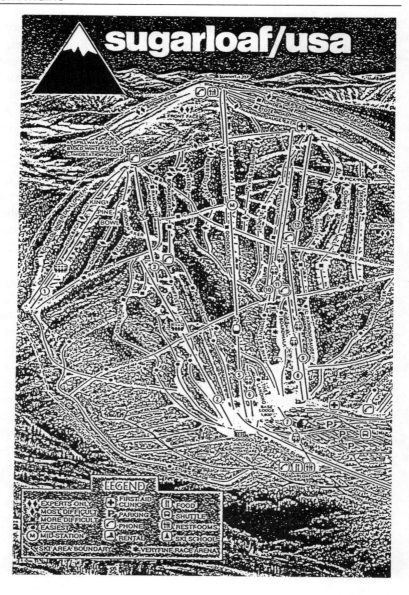

After a few confidence-building morning runs on Boardwalk, the place I'd go for late-morning skiing is the Whiffletree Quad Chair, to the far left of the lift layout. There is terrific skiing here for novices and lower

Sugarloaf, a reduced view of the trail map

intermediates: four trails that increase in difficulty as you move left to right (facing down the mountain). *Whiffletree*, the trail furthest left is long, gentle, and wide. If you want a little more challenge, cut right from

Whiffletree to the lift line. Later you can work your way over to *Cruiser* and *Buckboard*, slightly narrower and with slightly more pitch than Whiffletree, but finishing with long and gentle outruns.

The last of the easy four lifts is Bucksaw, the double chair to the far right of the Village base. Yes, the top couple of hundred yards of the trails here—*Windrow*, the liftline, is the best choice—have a solid intermediate pitch. But after that, it's long, easy skiing on underpopulated trails; the lift is out of Sugarloaf's skiing mainstream.

SUGARLOAF FOR CRUISERS. Let me make one general comment about Sugarloaf skiing before delving into the trail details. This can be a windy mountain, as I've mentioned, and when the wind blows hard, it usually comes from the northwest. As a result, as one local who skis the mountain almost daily told me, "9 out of 10 times, the snow is better on the right side coming down." That said, let's move on to the skiing.

If Sugarloaf skiing has a weakness, it is a shortage of long, solid-intermediate cruisers. For example, *Sluice* is a wonderful, wide, let-em-fly type of trail from its midsection down, but the top few hundred yards are steep, a steepness complicated by a double fall line, and the grooming gets trashed here very early. I've fallen on this section and have schussed the entire top section on my back, and I'm not the only person who can make the claim; I've seen other skiers go for the same ride. All I can say about Sluice is that you should ski that top section as early as possible and work the left side, where softer snow tends to accumulate. Thereafter, ride the Spillway West chair (of the two parallel chairlifts, it's the one on the right), which terminates before that steeper top section, and ski the wider, more moderate mid-section of Sluice as the day wears on.

A better—and very popular—trail from the summit of the Spillway East chair is *Narrow Gauge*. This is a classic giant-slalom-type trail and in fact is often used for race training by students at Carrabassett Valley Academy, the ski-oriented school at Sugarloaf. It winds around flats, drops steeply into little pockets, has a tree island in its center (left of the island is the lesser-skied route), and is never boring. Just watch out for the racer jocks who like to ski it fast.

Sluice and Narrow Gauge get a lot of skier traffic, and lift lines for the Spillway chairs tend to be longer than lines elsewhere on the mountain. A better cruiser than Sluice, especially in the morning when the sun's on it and the crowds haven't arrived yet, is *Ramdown*, off the King Pine chair. King Pine is a relatively new addition to the Sugarloaf network, and it gets surprisingly little skier traffic. I don't mean to suggest that it never gets crowded, but given the quality of terrain here, there ought to be as many skiers at King Pine as at Spillway. Perhaps longtime Sugarloafers still aren't used to the idea that King Pine is around.

At any rate, the one unpleasant section of Ramdown is right at the top, where the trail crossed a road and passes the t-bar summit. Apparently it is difficult getting grooming machines into this little slot, but regardless of the reason, it's narrow and slick. And short—after that, you'll find the best cruising on the mountain.

Haulback, the King Pine liftline, rates as an expert trail, and a couple of sections are steep enough to merit its black-diamond badge. But it's wide enough so that solid intermediates shouldn't have a problem handling it. One thing I like about it is that the groom crew usually leaves a patch of moguls on the far right side. That makes Haulback a place to go to try out your mogul skills without feeling committed to a long, grueling bump run. Incidentally, the other expert trails at King Pine tend to be groomed, too, although they are steeper than Haulback. If you feel you've met your match in Haulback, I wouldn't recommend your trying *Choker* or *Flume*.

If you're looking for some easier cruising, you can head over to the Bucksaw chair, on the area's western extreme. (Actually, the West Mountain chair is further west, but unless you're looking to max out on your tan on a sunny afternoon, the skiing here is pretty dull.) *Windrow*, the Bucksaw liftline, is the way to go, especially if you like skiing fast; the trail is wide and easy and gets little skier traffic.

One Sugarloaf's biggest drawbacks is the nuisance involved in getting from one side of the mountain to the other. If you're skiing at King Pine, for example, and you want to get over to Bucksaw, probably the best method is to take *Old Winter's Way*, a road, to the Spillway lifts, ride the Spillway East chair, then ski *Tote Road* over to the Bucksaw summit. Two road runs hyphenated by a lift ride (and possibly a lift line— Spillway West is Sugarloaf's most popular chair) is not my idea of great skiing fun. Your alternative is to ski Ramdown to *Pole Line* to the base, working your way across the bottom flats to the Bucksaw base. During rush hours (10-11:30 A.M. and 1-2:30 P.M.), when you'll want to avoid the Spillway chairs, this is probably the better way to go, even if it requires poling or walking at the bottom.

HALFTIME. If you like those sundeck/amplified-music/barbecue scenes that seem to gain momentum and rowdiness late in the season, you might want to check out the action at Gladstone's. At the Village base, it's certainly a better hangout than the Narrow Gauge cafeteria, inside the main base lodge, which has all the atmosphere of a cross between a shopping mall and an airport terminal (although the cafeteria food is well above average).

For considerably more atmosphere, I'd suggest you drop in at Bullwinkle's, at the summit of the Bucksaw chair. A neat little hangout, really: a sugarshack kind of place surrounded by birch saplings. Rustic intimacy is its drawing card, but it can also be its drawback; during prime lunch hours, it doesn't take much of a crowd to make Bullwinkle's seem crowded. For a different kind of atmosphere, you might want to pack a picnic lunch to tote up to the summit snowfields if it's a totally sunny, totally windless day (not a common occurrence at Sugarloaf, at least before mid-March). D'Ellie's in the Village produces excellent sand-wiches and picnic lunches, though they aren't produced at bargain prices.

SUGARLOAF FOR ADVANCED SKIERS. You can't keep the number of hot skiers the hang around Sugarloaf happy without giving them plenty of hot skiing. Groomed steeps, natural snow steeps, moguls: Sugarloaf has it all, to go along with its above-treeline snowfield-skiing, unique to the East.

I've already mentioned some of the steep, groomed runs in "Sugarloaf for Cruisers"—runs like Narrow Gauge, Haulback, Choker, and Flume. I'll throw in one more, *Competition Hill*, although it's often closed for race training. If it isn't closed, it's a great trail and a great variation alongside neighboring Narrow Gauge. While Narrow Gauge is a wind-ing, pitch-changing, rollercoaster, Competition Hill is straight and on the fall line, and I recommend it as a trail to ski top to bottom to test your turn-shaping abilities. Try maintaining a rhythmic, mid-radius turn pattern throughout, and see how crisp your turns are as your legs tire toward the bottom. That, at least, is what I like doing on Competition Hill, since it is the trail with the most consistent steep pitch on the mountain.

Now if you don't care for turning at all, you might want to do what a few loony locals like to do—that is, "zoom the Flume." Flume is the steep, groomed trail over at King Pine, and it has a pretty good knoll on its top right side as it falls right off of *Widowmaker*. Local racer types tell me that if they hit the knoll with enough speed, they can get as much as 150 feet worth of air time—your basic turn-free zoom of the Flume. Not recommended without a spotter below the jump or without a screw or two loose in your head.

I'm not a zoomer. I do like moguls, though, at least when they're soft, and Sugarloaf has three natural-snow classics to satisfy that desire: *Winter's Way*, *Bubblecuffer*, and *Wedge*, in the order that you come to them as you bear left on the Spillway Cross-cut from the top of the Spillway West chair.

If there has been a recent snowfall, I'd suggest going straight to Wedge, bypassing the other two for the first few runs. Don't be put off by slick spots at the very top of the trail as it falls away steeply from the Cross-cut—blame it on the wind and the manufactured snow the area uses to cover the exposed top section. Once you're a turn or three into the trail, the snow should soften considerably, and the trail has a couple of pockets, especially toward the left side, that tend to gather in soft snow. In short, Wedge is the place to find some of the best powder skiing on the mountain.

As the powder begins to get skied out on Wedge, go for the moguls on Bubblecuffer or Winter's Way. I personally prefer Bubblecuffer because it has a little more character in that it's windier and has more changes in pitch. Winter's Way is a little straighter, but I'm really splitting hairs here in choosing one over the other. A couple of things to keep in mind, though: Stay right (especially if there has been a post-storm wind) for better snow, and be wary of these trails if there is little fresh snow (especially early in the season). The sub-surface is rough with roots, rocks, and other grim stuff, and the trails require a good snow cover to bring out their best. If it has been a long time since a fresh dump, you'll probably want to stick with the groomed steeps.

Incidentally, a mogul run I don't particularly like is *Spillway*, beneath the Spillway lifts. It's moguls tend to be hard and cruel (as moguls of manufactured snow tend to get), even if the young hotshots who migrate to the trail make the skiing look easy. If you want to ski a fall-line mogul run from the Spillway chair (when natural snow is short on the three classics mentioned above), *Skidder*, on the left flank of Competition Hill, is a better deal. As for groomed cruising, I don't care much for *Gondola Line*, which has all the trail character of a fire-cut, with hard, manufactured snow. Local skiers tell me it can be a great high-speed cruisers, but I remain unconvinced; for that purpose, I much prefer Haulback, Competition Hill, and Narrow Gauge.

Summit skiing at Sugarloaf is uncommon; conditions have to be just right to make it worthwhile. "Just right" means lots of snow and little wind, conditions you're most likely to encounter in spring. Whatever the conditions might be, you should check in with the ski patrol at the

Spillway lift terminal to find out if the summit is open to skiing and if the skiing is good enough to make the hike up worthwhile.

I say spring is the most likely time for good summit skiing, because Tom Bird, a Sugarloaf instructor, tells me that spring storms tend to track in from the south, filling in the rock-and-tree stubble surface with denser, wetter snow. But the skiing can be good in mid-winter, too, if there has been a rare, wind-free storm. (Relatively wind-free, anyway.)

To be honest I can't tell one "trail"—as designated on the Sugarloaf trail map—from another on the snowfields. *White Nitro* stands out to some degree because it is the swath that is usually groomed, but if you ask me, skiing groomed on the snowfields is missing the whole point of skiing the snowfields.

The point is to seek out lines, and I've usually had better luck the further right I've gone, depending on where the wind has been blowing from. Be ready for some short by funky chutes between rocks and stubby trees, and every so often you'll find pockets of soft, fantastically deep snow. On deep-powder days (which, for whatever reason, I've lucked into often at Sugarloaf) skiing the snowfields and connecting with Wedge, Bubblecuffer, or Winter's Way, you can get a 2,000-plus-vertical soft-snow run as good as it gets in New England—or anywhere else in the world, for that matter.

SNOWBOARDING. I've probably had more fun skiing with snowboarders at Sugarloaf than anywhere else in New England, a fact I attribute to two reasons: the snowboarders themselves and the terrain. The snowboarders I've spent time with here have been hotshots in the first-rate competitive snowboard program at nearby Carrabassett Valley Academy, and they have been able to open my eyes to some of the amazing things possible on a board. As for the terrain. . .no question, about as good as it gets in New England.

It barely needs saying that all of the things that make the snowfields unique—the deep, wind-rippled snow, the rocks, the stunted trees, the contours of the land, the choice of lines—are the stuff of dreams for experienced and imaginative snowboarders. Another great snowboarding trail is *Ripsaw* from the King Pine chair. Exposed stumps, stream beds, and other terrain oddities make this a natural snowboarding playground. And if you like exploring, check out the trees on either side of *Upper Gondola Line*. When last I looked, this was technically illegal, but since I've seen so many snowboarders and skiers—including myself—poking around in these trees from time to time, I assume the rules are lax. But if you do get reprimanded, just don't say I didn't warn you.

THE POST-GAME SHOW. The lodging choice basically boils down to staying at the mountain or staying in Kingfield, about 15 miles away. Kingfield, of course, has more New England charm, but it's just far enough removed from the mountain to make the drive an inconvenience, especially if you've already spent more than five hours in a car getting here. The on-mountain lodging isn't cheap, but I'd say that considering the quality of accommodations—in its modern, urban-hotel way, the Sugarloaf Hotel is a pretty nice place—you get a fair deal. You're not paying through the nose here just to be near the mountain.

There is also a fair choice of dining and night activities. If you're seeking out the locals scene, the $10 Sunday night buffet at Gladstone's is a happening scene, as is Blues Night at the Bag. If you're looking for tonier continental fare, Truffle Hound more than adequately fills the bill. What the mountain village lacks is a substantial grocery/supermarket; what's there is a bare step above 7-11, which isn't quite adequate if you've got a condo full of family and friends to feed. The thing to do is to make sure you stock up in Farmington on the drive up if you plan to be doing much of your own cooking.

SUGARLOAF DATA
Pluses and Minuses:
Pluses: Great terrain variety, lots of resort lodging and amenities, good spring skiing. Minuses: Remote location, occasional high winds, little old New England character.
Key Phone Numbers:
Ski Area Information: 207-237-2000
Lodging Information: 800-843-5623 (on-mountain), 800-843-2732
Snow Conditions: 207-237-2000
Location: **12 miles north of Kingfield on Route 27. Mailing address: RR #1 Box 5000, Kingfield, ME 04947**
Mountain Statistic:
Vertical drop: 2,820 feet
Summit elevation: 4,237 feet
Base elevation: 1,417 feet
Number of trails: 92
Lifts: 1 gondola, 2 quad chairs, 1 triple, 8 doubles, 2 surface lifts
Snowmaking: 90%
Average annual snowfall: 170 inches

INSIDE STORY
COTTAGE CRAFTSMEN

Rodney Richard of Rangeley, Maine, likes to call himself the Mad Whittler. Actually, that is a moniker created from half truths. The only madness I can detect in the man is a streak of eccentricity that runs through an otherwise kindly and good-humored spirit. And while Richard might do a little pocket-knife whittling—one of his favorite pastimes is handing out hand-crafted, pearl-sized bunnies to young women that catch his eye—he is, primarily, a chainsaw carver. If you're interested in dropping by Richard's home and workshop in Rangeley, look for the wooden bear chasing a wooden woodsman up the tree at the end of his driveway. Both bear and woodsman are samples of the chainsaw art of the Mad Whittler.

Richard, who spent most of his working life in the timber business, began chainsaw carving in 1975, and the wooden Indian at Fitzy's Donut Shop in downtown Rangeley is the first piece of his work to go on display. Since then, his chainsawed Indians have shown up in places as far-flung as the lobby of the Saddleback base lodge and the stadium in which the Atlanta Braves baseball team plays. Richard has built some-thing of a national reputation for himself, having shown his stuff at the Smithsonian Festival of American Folklife.

You can pick up a Richard original for as little as $25 by making an appointment to meet him at the small shop near his home (207-864-5595). Or you can look for him on the Saddleback slopes—he works there as a part-time host. But chainsaw carving is more than a business for Richard; it is his way of contributing to the preservation of a woodsman's culture. Logging, after all, has played a major role in the life of northern Maine, and Richard doesn't want people to forget it.

Richard isn't, of course, the only one using his craft to preserve ves-tiges of New England's heritage. Cottage craftsmen are numerous throughout Maine, New Hampshire, and Vermont, producing (depending on your definition of crafts) everything from home-made jams to Richard's life-sized, chainsawed bears and Indians.

Another, like Richard, who caught my attention, is Treffle ("Baldy") Bolduc, who makes snowshoes by hand at the Kancamagus Snowshoe Shop (603-447-5287) in Conway, New Hampshire. Bolduc, who learned the snowshoe craft from Cree Indians in Quebec, makes snowshoes the old-fashioned way, with wood, sinew, and leather.

There are Conway locals who insist that Bolduc is among the finest snowshoe makers in the world, which must certainly be true—there can't be a whole lot of them around. Although snowshoes come in many different shapes and sizes, Bolduc favors three styles: the bearpaw, a basic, ovate pad for plodders in all types of terrain; the beavertail, a larger, more stream-lined pad for easier walking; and the smaller Yukon, best for the open country and racing.

So poke around on a lousy-weather day. For some reason, northern Vermont seems to have attracted a goodly share of craftspeople; look, for example, for hand-made quilts in Jefersonville or hand-pulled rugs in Johnson. Wherever you're skiing in New England, I can guarantee that somewhere close by there is someone plying an interesting and/or traditional craft by hand. If you want to sample a broad range of regional arts and crafts—there are a few places to check out. In Vermont, a variety of arts and crafts are on display (and on sale) at two state-backed, not-for-profit centers: Frog Hollow Craft Center in Middlebury (802-388-4964) and Windsor House in Windsor (802-674-6729). The place to go in New Hampshire is the League of New Hampshire Craftsmen on Main Street in North Conway (603-356-2441).

Chapter 9
Free-heeling New England

LIFE WAS ONCE MUCH SIMPLER. I remember, for example, when there used to be just two kinds of athletic footwear—regular and high-top sneakers. I also remember when there used to be just two kinds of skiing—downhill and cross-country. But just as the sneaker has become an archaeological relic of another time in America, so the simple, bifurcated world of skiing—alpine and cross-country skiing—seems now to be a fading memory.

I knew things had changed big-time a few years ago when I first heard a guy in Telluride, Colorado use the word "quiver" to describe his ski-rig collection. No archer carries just one arrow in his quiver, and presumably the complete skier carries more than one pair of skis in his. I figure that the complete skier's starter quiver now includes five types of ski: equipment for diagonal (i.e., straight-track) cross-country skiing, for cross-country skating, for backcountry touring, for telemark turning, and for good old downhill skiing. (I suppose the complete skier should own a snowboard, too.) I am not, I confess, a complete skier, but then I don't know many skiers that are—or who can afford to be.

Now if you are strictly a downhill skier—or "alpine" skier to be more correct, since you can go downhill on any kind of equipment—a case could be made that you're missing out on four fifths of the fun. But I can understand why most skiers don't switch-hit. For one thing, there is the expense of extra gear. In addition, you might be like many confirmed alpine skiers I know—people who have a hard time clearing their heads of the image of cross-country skiing as an exercise in aerobic ennui, a process of slogging around snow-covered golf courses.

I also know that a lot of skiers don't cross over because of the strange socio-political barrier that separates the cross-country and alpine worlds. Whenever I walk into a cross-country touring center decked out in alpine gear, I feel I might as well be a big-game hunter crashing a Sierra Club fund-raiser. "Free the heel and you free the mind," someone is apt to say—whether as bit of wit or advice, or as some ethical declaration, it's often hard to tell. Alpine skiers aren't a whole lot more understanding. If I show up at the base lodge of a ski area geared out for the backcountry, skiers look at me as if I were an infiltrator from the caste of the unclean.

My response is simple: The hell with all that stuff. Go out and give cross-country skiing, with its many variations, a shot. It's certainly not expensive to get started: For track skiing, the combined expense of trail fees, equipment rentals, and lessons probably won't cost you more than $30; you can come in even cheaper for backcountry skiing since you usually don't have to slap down up to $10 for the trail fee.

Before I move on to recommending specific places in New England for free-heel skiing, I should establish a few loose definitions. Free-heel skiing, that catch-all term, can break down first into two basic categories: track skiing and backcountry skiing, and each of those can be divided further into two sub-categories. Track skiing includes the diagonal (also called "traditional" or "classical") method and skating, a relatively recent invention that boomed in the 80's. Backcountry skiing includes touring—cruising around on rolling terrain—and telemarking, the old-fashioned method of turning (going downhill) by splitting the feet and raising the uphill heel during the turn.

These distinctions are worth making because each type of skiing calls for—or at least is best executed with—equipment specifically designed for the purpose. The design of the skis, the stiffness of the boots, and the length of the poles are different in a diagonal set-up as opposed to a skating set-up. It's possible to skate on diagonal gear, but it's a whole lot easier if you're geared up with the right stuff.

Touring and telemark skis, both of which are much wider and heavier than track skis, are similarly differentiated by their flex and shape. Touring skis are designed primarily to float through deep snow on more-or-less flat terrain, so they often have what is called a double camber. Camber is the amount of bowing a ski has between its tip and its tail; the extra bow of a double-camber ski gives it a little more bounce, which gives you a little extra kick and rebound when you're skiing along flat terrain.

Telemark skis, on the other hand, are designed for turning, and single camber usually works better for that purpose. Telemark bindings often come with a cable attachment that reaches around the boot heel to provide extra leverage in turning, while touring skis are usually attached just at the toe, for unencumbered heel lift while kicking and gliding. Telemark boots are usually higher and stiffer than touring boots—in some cases very similar to alpine boots. In fact, telemark equipment, since the rebirth of telemarking about 15 years ago, seems to come closer and closer each year to alpine gear, to the point where it's possible now on a good telemark set up to make smooth, parallel turns, alpine-style.

So when renting or buying gear, have in mind the principal type of skiing you plan to engage in—straight-track skiing, skating, touring, or telemarking. Again, you don't have to have the proper equipment (although backcountry skis are usually too wide to fit into set tracks). But if you do a good job of matching the equipment to the type of skiing you'll be doing, you'll have more fun, simple as that.

And what type of skiing are you most likely to encounter in New England? Let's start with the *least* likely, that being backcountry telemarking. In the open country of the West, climbing into backcountry areas and skiing down on telemark gear is a much more common activity than in the tree-blanketed mountains of the East. Yes, there are places in the East for backcountry telemarking—I'll mention a few later in this chapter—but they generally call for a high level of turning proficiency, since tight trees are likely to be involved.

So if you head into the New England backcountry, more often than not a touring set-up will work best. When you add up the ski trails, hiking trails, old logging roads, etc., backcountry touring options abound.

If you do head out for an extended backcountry jaunt, I strongly recommend that you go with a guide or skier very familiar with the area you're skiing. And whether you go guided or unguided, spend the extra buck or two to get a good map. I find the little trail sketches at touring centers often to be out-of-scale or inaccurate. They aren't, to be fair, the creations of certified cartographers, and they're perfectly adequate if you stick to marked trails. But don't rely on them beyond that. When you're surrounded by trees—obviously a common state of being in the New England backcountry—establishing your location by visual references to mountains, lakes, and other land features can be difficult. Getting lost in the cold winter woods is obviously nobody's idea of grand fun.

As for track skiing in New England, most cross-country centers now set parallel tracks for straight-track skiing and skating on at least half of their groomed trails. Don't, however, expect that necessarily to be the case, and definitely don't expect it to be the case for all of an area's listed groomed mileage. Skating is the faster, and, in my opinion, the more fun of the two skiing methods, but it also requires a little more technical proficiency right off the bat. So if you've never been on cross-country skis, I wouldn't recommend jumping right into skating. On the other hand, anyone without prior cross-country experience should have little problem negotiating straight tracks from the start. To be really *good* at straight track skiing requires just as much—if not more—skill than skating, but simply sliding one foot in front of the other is obviously not difficult at all.

A couple of New England cross-country centers do make some snow on some tracks, but my experience has generally been that if the natural-snow conditions aren't good, the cross-country skiing isn't very good, either. I wouldn't be scared off by a little rain or ice, however. Groomers and track-setters at the larger areas do a pretty good job of chopping things up and restoring good skiing conditions. In fact, lots of fresh snow can be an impediment; the tracks can get soft and rutted—not to mention sticky if the sun hits the fresh snow. But if you're like me, those fresh-snow days are when I want to be out on my alpine gear going downhill anyway.

On then to the skiing. I've been very selective here—there are many, many more places for cross-country/free-heel skiing in New England than I've included in this chapter. In Vermont alone, there are something like 50 touring centers that set tracks.

The one standard that I have used is that I've chosen places affiliated with or relatively near alpine ski areas, and as a result have left out a few good touring centers like Blueberry Hill in Goshen, Vermont and Mountain Top in Chittenden, Vermont. This being essentially an alpine skier's book, I'm figuring that free-heel skiing is to you approximately what it is to me: An occasional alternative to the lift-serviced stuff or something for friends who aren't alpine skiers to do. Other than that, I've made no effort to use any objective standards to compile the list of areas here; I'm simply singling out those areas that, in my judgment, represent the best non-alpine skiing in New England.

One reason not to use objective standards is that the type of skiing can vary so dramatically from one area to the next. What common standards could you possibly use, for example, to compare the relative merits of backcountry skiing on Mt. Washington and track skiing in Wilmington, Vermont? Totally different ballgames, obviously.

FREE-HEELING VERMONT

BOLTON VALLEY. Bolton would be a nightmare for flatland aerobophiles. In fact, Bolton's cross-country terrain is appealing primarily because it is the very antithesis of flatness—full of ups and downs, twists and rolls. I mean *big* ups and downs; a few of the 100 kilometers of trails (about 30 of which are groomed regularly) are relatively easy going, but when 1,800 vertical feet are packed into the trail system laid out on a mountainside, flats are hard to come by. In other words, Bolton is better suited to backcountry skiing than rhythmic track skiing.

There are a few unique things about the Bolton trail system that I really like. For one thing, the touring center is at 2,000 feet, the highest touring base in New England. When snow conditions are marginal elsewhere, especially later in the season when the valley flats are turning green, they are often very good at Bolton. Don't be fooled by the snow levels at the beginning of the Bolton access road from Route 2: The road climbs 1,400 feet in four miles to the ski area, which sits in something of a natural snow pocket. When it's snowless on Route 2, there can be three feet of snow or more at Bolton.

Another thing I like about Bolton is its telemarking potential. The cross-country layout lies just to the left of the lift-serviced ski area, so that you can ski up the cross-country trails to the summit and telemark down on the alpine trails. Or you can ride up Lift 1 and ski *down* the cross-country trails. The interconnection of cross-country and alpine terrain at Bolton is the best in New England.

A third Bolton bonus is that you don't have to stick around Bolton. It's possible to ski from Bolton and connect with the considerable Stowe and Mt. Mansfield trail networks. It's about 20 kilometers from Bolton to the Trapp Family Lodge, a pretty rugged, backcountry workout, and not one you'll have to yourself on weekends. For good reasons, this is one of Vermont's more popular tours.

If you go this route, a) get a good map or a guide who knows the way, b) pick a fair-weather day, and c) arrange for someone to pick you up at the Trapp Family Lodge. The drive back to Bolton is about 25 miles; the ski back is cruel and unusual aerobic masochism unless your a fitness monster who can ski through the woods in the dark—I can't conceive of completing 40 up-and-down backcountry kilometers before nightfall, unless you're committed to a heads-down, ignore-the-scenery push.

THE CATAMOUNT TRAIL. The Catamount Trail is more a concept than a true trail, conceived in the early 80's as a winter equivalent of the Long Trail, the great hiking trail that runs the north-south length of Vermont. The Catamount creators realized that the Long Trail, passing over all heights of land, from one mountain summit to another, was simply too rugged a route for regular winter travel. So they came up with an idea to string together a route by making use of existing cross-country trail networks, backcountry trails, roads, hiking trails, and so on.

In short the idea was largely to piece together a 280-mile, north-south trail rather than to cut one. Thus the work of the Catamount Trail Association (CTA) has involved a lot more persuasion than chainsawing to bring about the cooperation of the National Forest Service, touring centers, and (most importantly) private landowners. It is still a work in progress—a little over 200 miles of trail are now under the Catamount aegis.

The result so far, as might be expected, is a kind of mish-mash: a combination of backcountry touring terrain and groomed tracks. And there obviously aren't a whole lot of skiers who ski the complete route. Perhaps the best way to bite off a chunk of the Catamount Trail is the inn-to-inn method; the trail passes by or near numerous country inns and bed-&-breakfasts.

What part of the trail is best? I certainly haven't skied the full length of the trail, so I couldn't possibly tell you. If the trail intrigues you, I'd suggest you contact the Catamount Trail Association (P.O. Box 897, Burlington, VT 05402). CTA publishes the comprehensive *Catamount Trail Guidebook*, although other, more selective, tour books are also available.

MAD RIVER GLEN. There is really no cross-country terrain at Mad River, unless you count the Tucker Hill Touring Center, a few miles down the road. So what's Mad River doing in this chapter?

The answer is that this is really the mecca of telemarking in the East, the place where telemarking really took hold when it was reborn as a legitimate skiing sport in the mid-70's. Mad River is also home of an increasingly popular telemark festival run every March by the local National Telemark Organization.

In many ways, Mad River is anything but the ideal place to telemark. Steep, firm moguls—a Mad River specialty—aren't the sort of snow conditions that are to my liking when I snap into three-pins. If I can't have powder, I'd just as soon go for groomed snow. But Mad River lays out the welcome mat to telemarkers more as a matter of attitude than a matter of terrain. As a telemarker, you come to Mad River because there are other pinheads hanging around that you can pal around with. And even alpine skiers at Mad River have always had a kind of backcountry spirit about them, so when you show up on tele-gear, you aren't ostracized—in fact, you're treated sort of special, like someone with the right stuff. Kinda nice.

STOWE. Stowe is in many ways the Vermont equivalent of Jackson, New Hampshire: A complete free-heel package that comes with the biggest mountain in the state. What Stowe's got that Jackson doesn't is an extra little bit of history. The Trapp Family Lodge claims to have opened the first touring center in the U.S., which is probably true. What is certainly true is that, yes, the Trapp family here is the same Trapp (actually (*von* Trapp) family that sung its way through the Alps with Hitler on its heels in "The Sound of Music."

History and music aside, the skiing at Trapp's is superb—a 100-kilometer mix of groomed and backcountry trails, from the easiest to the most difficult. And that's really just the beginning. The Trapp network is just one segment of a vast, interconnected trail system that links together four touring centers—Trapp's, the Mt. Mansfield Touring Center, Topnotch Touring Center, and Edson Hill Nordic Center. Add 'em all up, and you've got more than 200 trail kilometers, and we're not even talking yet about the huge backcountry network that ribbons around Mt. Mansfield, leading to Bolton Valley to the southwest and Smugglers Notch to the north.

Nor are we talking about the Mt. Mansfield alpine skiing. Locals like to use the lifts to access the backcountry—economically sensible if you've got a season's pass, but who wants to spend close to 40 bucks for a day ticket just for one lift ride? For day-trippers, it makes more sense to ski up a backcountry trail to the top of Mt. Mansfield and finish the day by putting in some turns on the groomed alpine runs. Of course, you can avoid the alpine trail network entirely. A favorite descent of locals is Teardrop, which falls, quite steeply for its first half, off the backside of The Nose, Mansfield's southern sub-summit.

Keep in mind, of course, that the backcountry skiing on Mansfield is a pretty serious undertaking. You have to know where you're going and you might need logistical support; for example, if you ski Teardrop, skiing back to Trapp's (especially if you've made the climb up Mansfield) is a pretty long haul. Locals who do it generally arrange to have a car in Underhill for the drive home. You should be getting the picture: Get a guide or knowledge local before planning this kind of outing.

Back to Trapp's briefly. It's got one of the best cross-country ski school's around, and, by reputation, it serves some of the best food in Stowe. I say "by reputation" because I've never eaten there, but I've never heard anyone say anything bad about the place. There's also a neat little cabin/tea house about five kilometers from the lodge—a good destination for a relaxed day's ski. However, this is popular touring country; people come here, just as they do to Jackson, for nothing-but-cross-country-skiing vacations. Unless you venture way off into the Mt. Mansfield wilds, expect to share the trails with other skiers—lots of other skiers on weekends. My choice—albeit it expensive—would be to stay and do most of my skiing at Edson Hill Manor, a beautiful little place tucked away in the woods, with perhaps the best restaurant in the Stowe area. One great thing about cross-country skiing—you earn your eats.

WILMINGTON. I'll give you four good reasons why Wilmington makes my cross-country cut. Reason #1: While there is no mega-touring center here, four mid-sized centers combine for over 120 trail kilometers. Reason #2: There's some decent and relatively easy backcountry skiing possibilities here, such as a ski around Somerset Reservoir. Reason #3: There are some terrific country inns in the area, and for whatever reason, I have it in my mind that country inns and cross-country skiing are creations of the same muse. Reason #4: Mt. Snow, the region's principal alpine ski area, just doesn't have enough variety to keep me interested for more than a couple of days of skiing at a time. I need skiing alternatives.

Actually, Reasons 1 and 3 are somewhat connected. Two of the four touring centers are hooked up with two of the nicer inns in Vermont—or anywhere in New England, for that matter—the White House and the Hermitage. The idea that you could build a popular success with a combination of wine cellar, wild game birds, and cross-country skiing seems a little bizarre, but that's what the Hermitage has managed to do.

You might appreciate the ski-terrain variation at the Hermitage, which is the best of Wilmington's four touring centers. Personally, I go for the idea of celebrating with a bottle of Chateau Just-About-Anything after a good day's ski, although the dining room is a little formal for my tastes. The White House is a little on the formal side, too, but then old-style elegance is often a big part of the romance in this country-inn thing. If you don't like it, you can do your skiing at the touring center at the Sitzmark Lodge. There isn't a whole lot of skiing—just 30 kilometers of track—but then there isn't a whole lot of formality, either. How could there be at any place named Sitzmark?

The Somerset Reservoir skiing is of the lowland, brooks-and-beaver-ponds variety. If you want more of a highland style of skiing, there's the Haystack Ridge trail, which eventually climbs Mt. Snow. You can get your backcountry touring going up and your telemarking going down on the Mt. Snow trails. If you really like that X-C/downhill combo, you might also want to check out Prospect Mountain, about 10 miles west on Route 9. They've got a few alpine trails intertwined with 40 kilometers of the cross-country stuff. Whatever you your preference, you can get more trail information by contacting the Green Mountain Club or by asking a lot of questions at any of the area's touring centers.

FREE-HEELING NEW HAMPSHIRE

BALSAMS WILDERNESS. To me, half the fun of the Balsams is the drive north to get there. You hit the road heading north on Route 3, passing through towns Lancaster, Groveton, Stradford, and Colebrook and every trace of New England gloss peels away. It's the kind of world where flannel overshirts and felt hats with those flip-down earflaps are still in vogue, and where a man's a man when he puts in an honest day's work for an honest wage at the lumberyard. It's hick in a way that I'm sure makes all the local teenagers want to split town as soon as they get their driver's licenses and the nerve, but it's also hick in a way that reminds me that they just don't make America the way they used to. Want a night on the town? Wait for the church social.

Then you arrive at the Balsams, a big old hotel assembled gradually since 1873 as if 40 different architects had their hand in things. It's a 232-room rambling collision of styles surrounded by 15,000 private, undeveloped acres. They do things the old-fashioned way here and are stalwartly proud of it—a patrician New England style which is all fine with me except for the business about requiring men to wear coats and ties for dinner.

The Balsams gives you a lot to do, as it had better—I mean, you didn't come such a long cold way (and the Balsams is a long way from just about anywhere) to hang around the Saturday bake sale in Colebrook. So there's a small alpine ski area (3 lifts, 1,200 vertical feet), guided snowshoe tours, an ice-skating rink, movies and parlor games at night, and cross-country skiing, which is the best part of the package.

There are more than 50 kilometers of trails, 40 of which are tracked, but the appeal here is more the style of the terrain than the amount of it; you could call it backcountry track skiing. A few trails might be on the golf course, but for the most part the wilderness feel is authentic. Regulars have told me about wildlife sightings—moose and snowshoe hare in particular—but I'm willing to be impressed simply with the variety of trees along the trail: maple, cherry, birch, spruce, hemlock, and (of course) balsam fir.

The skiing tends to be on the easy side, although there are a few steep ups and downs, with the highlight run a ski-cum-picnic to Mud Pond, a round trip of from 15 to 40 kilometers, depending on your choice of trails. Yes—Mud Pond. I'm told it was once called Lake of the Floating Islands, which sounds better to me, but it's a moot point: whether floating islands or mud, it's all snow in winter.

JACKSON TOURING CENTER/MT. WASHINGTON. The king of X-C in New England. If you want the full cross-country gamut, you've got it here, from flat, perfectly groomed tracks to some of most challenging backcountry action you'll find anywhere in the world. Yes, anywhere in the world. If you have ideas of skiing Mt. Washington in winter—and brave souls do it—you'd better be ready for everything from avalanches (not just a Western phenomenon) to utter frigidity. The summit weather station at Mt. Washington can claim the highest wind ever recorded— 231 m.p.h.—and when the January temperature on the summit tops 0 degrees F, it's a positive heat wave.

But back to the touring center, which was conceived as a "destination" cross-country resort. The folks in charge of the Jackson Ski Touring Foundation, have told me that they consider Jackson, as a cross-country resort, to be on a par with Vail or Aspen as alpine resorts. Well, I don't know, but you get the point. This is the big-time.

The numbers are pretty staggering. The Jackson Touring Center maintains 150-plus kilometers of trail of which 80 kilometers are groomed; in addition, the Appalachian Mountain Club maintains another 44 trail kilometers in the vicinity. The elevation difference between the center's lowest and highest points is 3,245 feet, greater than the vertical rise of any *alpine* area in New England. And I'm not even talking yet about what's just up the road at Mt. Washington.

When you've got that much terrain, there's obviously a lot you can do with it. Inn-to-inn touring on groomed tracks is possible; there are 13 country inns on or very near the trail system. You can be competitive, because the local club always seems to have some kind of race action working. And you can hit the backcountry by skiing from the touring center to the summit of Wildcat, about a 10-mile, very uphill jaunt. Or you can take the easier reverse route: Ride the lift to Wildcat's summit and ski down to Jackson.

One drawback I've encountered at Jackson is the weather; most of the tracks are at a low elevation (the touring center is at 755 feet), so that the snow conditions can be pretty crummy. The grooming here, like everything else, is big-time, but when the snow is especially mushy, the groomers can't do much with it. For spring skiing, you'll want to be at higher elevations.

Which brings us to Mt. Washington. Mt. Washington is best known for the late-spring skiing at Tuckerman Ravine. It is perhaps *the* rite of spring in New England skiing; put another way, it can attract a crowd. On weekend days when the snow's right and the weather's right, as many as 3,000 skiers make the climb up to Tuckerman's, leaving cars parked as far as a half mile down the road on Route 16.

So if it's early May and you're sitting around the house with nothing better to do that watch baseball on the tube, toss the alpine boards or the tele gear in the back of the car and join the Tuckerman's gang. (The Tuckerman season begins picking up steam in late March, but late April and May, after the ski areas close, is when the real action happens.) Yes, it's steep, but it's only *really* steep, as in hellaciously steep, if you take it all the way from the top of the headwall. Go ahead—you can hack it.

I say all of that as a preface to the fact that, despite all you might have heard, late-spring Tuckerman skiing isn't the only skiing on Mt. Washington. The hub of Mt. Washington skiing activities is the Appalachian Mountain Club hang-out at Pinkham Notch, just across the Route 16 from Wildcat. There is a hostel for those who like crashing super-cheap, as the backcountry hardcore seem to enjoy doing. But whether you stay at Pinkham Notch or not, it's absolutely essential that you check in here. It's the place to find out about snow and weather conditions, avalanche danger (yes!) and so on.

If you want to stick to the trails (hiking trails in the summer) within a couple of miles of Pinkham Notch, you'll find it hard to get into too much trouble. You can try a few turns on sections of the Shelburne Trail, which leads down from Tuckerman's. But if you want to get well up into Mt. Washington's bowls and ravines, I strongly urge you to check in at a shop in North Conway (e.g., Eastern Mountain Sports), to hook up with a guide. You don't want to take a mountain with places that go by such fear-inspiring names as the Gulf of Slides lightly.

WATERVILLE VALLEY. Waterville is one of the few alpine-oriented
resorts in New England to take cross-country skiing seriously. *Very*
seriously, as in competitively. The 70 kilometers of groomed tracks are
honed for racing and race training, and unconscionably fit, rainbow lycra
bodies are constantly flying by. Waterville is arguably *the* center of
competitive cross-country skiing in New England.

Now, I'm not saying that to suggest that only competition-hardened
skiers are welcome. There's obviously plenty of skiing here for everybody. One thing it should tell you, though, is that Waterville, to earn its
reputation as a major New England racing hotbed, sets a very high
standard for track maintenance.

What it also ought to tell you is that Waterville cross-country is very
track-oriented, which is to say that many other places in New England
are better if you're more interested in backcountry touring. But if you're
into the pure aerobic rush of track skiing (skating or diagonal), Waterville
is hard to beat. The German word for cross-country skiing is
"schilaufen," which literally means ski running. Waterville is the kind of
place where you can really uncork the ski-runner in you.

There are a couple of things I don't like about Waterville's cross-
country network. One is that you never get the feeling of ever being very
far from the village and outlying condos. (Maybe there *are* trails that
reach deeply into the woods; I just haven't found them.) The other is that
the resort claims to have a total of 105 kilometers of groomed and
ungroomed tracks, but when I add up what's on the trail map, I don't
come up with anywhere near that total.

On the plus side, this is a great place to take lessons. There's a good
instructional staff and the quality of the tracks makes the learning easier.
Just when you're getting the hang of kicking and gliding, you're not
likely here to have your rhythm wrecked by crust, ice-balls, or potholes.
And there also is something to be said for being close to the village if the
weather socks in; you're never too far from a warm fireplace.

FREE-HEELING MAINE

SADDLEBACK. Cross-country skiing at Saddleback is much like alpine
skiing at Saddleback—an understated combination of rough-hewn and
homespun. What I like about the skiing here is the immediacy of the
wilderness. Within a kilometer or two of the base lodge, you feel as if

you are in the middle of nowhere—which, in a sense, you are. Your odds of spotting a moose or some other creature of the wild are pretty good; I've seen enough moose tracks on the ski tracks to know that the Bullwinkle gang is around.

Something else I like about the Saddleback scene is that base of touring operations (for rentals, maps, lessons, route recommendations) is the alpine base lodge. That makes switching from an alpine mode to a touring mode and back on the same day is easy, and I've done it. When the weather gets cold on the mountain, I've found that thrashing around in the woods on touring gear for an hour or so is a good way to get the blood flowing again.

The skiing is not, for the most part, especially difficult. It mostly involves short or long loops around lakes and ponds. Although some tracks are groomed and set, most of the work is done with snowmobiles, so don't expect anything fast or fancy. But then that's not really the point at Saddleback. When an ski area measures its cross-country terrain by square miles—18 in this case—rather than groomed trail kilometers, you know that it's heart is more in backcountry touring than track skiing. Head for the woods, enjoy the solitude and scenery, maybe meet a moose—that's what Saddleback cross-country is all about.